MARKETING HANDBOOK

MARKETING HANDBOOK

Second edition

Edited by Michael Rines

Gower
in association with **marketing** magazine

© Gower Publishing Company Limited 1981

Published by
Gower Publishing Company Limited,
Gower House, Croft Road, Aldershot
Hampshire GU11 3HR, England

Reprinted 1983

British Library Cataloguing in Publication Data

Marketing handbook. – 2nd ed.
  1. Marketing
  I. Rines, Michael
  658.8   HF5415

  ISBN 0-566-02200-1

Typeset by Inforum Ltd, Portsmouth
Printed and bound in Great Britain at
The Pitman Press, Bath

Contents

Foreword

by Ron Halstead, CBE
Chairman of Beecham Products

In the 19th century Britain was the leading trading nation in the world with 40% of world trade. We now have less than a 10% share. Import penetration of the UK market is increasing rapidly and our industrial base is shrinking.

We have great scientific and technological resources and skills, but too often have been unable to translate them into successful products in the world markets. This is in striking contrast to the major countries with whom we compete – the USA, Germany and Japan. These countries not only have good products, but have been extremely successful in the market place, making maximum use of all the available marketing tools in a highly professional way.

If the UK is to survive and succeed as an industrial nation, we must at least match this marketing expertise across the broad range of British industry. This will require changes in attitudes of many companies towards the marketing concept and more education and training of management to be better at the total marketing process – designing for the market, producing efficiently, delivering on time, and selling and advertising aggressively at home and overseas.

The new edition of the *Marketing Handbook* is very timely and I am pleased to see that the contributors have such a wide range of professional backgrounds and practical experience of marketing. The Handbook is a very practical exposition of the different marketing functions necessary for a successful business and I am sure it will prove invaluable to management at all levels across the broad spectrum of British industry.

Preface

This second edition of *Marketing Handbook* has been revised almost completely, and the material in it has been restructured in three logical parts.

Part I, 'The Nature of Marketing', analyses marketing in its many different forms, examining how and why purchasing decisions are made in the various types of market in which selling has to take place. An understanding of these aspects of marketing is the essential first step in obtaining an eventual profitable sale.

The second stage, which forms the subject of the second part of the book, is the development of the marketing strategy, from the method of acquiring the necessary market information through to the creation of the marketing plan, including the development and launch strategy for new products.

The third part covers the implementation of the marketing plan – 'Marketing in Action'. It describes the weapons in the marketer's armoury from packaging and pricing, through promotion, to selling and distribution and the method of controlling the whole process in financial terms.

The authors are all acknowledged authorities on their subjects. They were selected on the basis of my ten years of commissioning features for *Marketing* magazine. In that time I have come to know not only who the leading experts are on each aspect of marketing, but, equally important, which of them have the quite rare ability to transmit their ideas clearly, logically and readably.

But the best business writing in the world is useless unless it can be turned to action by the reader. So even though some of the authors who have contributed to this book are eminent academics, all of them have had their thinking tempered by practical experience in marketing.

The practical approach has throughout been considered essential. This is not only because the book is aimed at executives who want to achieve better profits through better marketing thinking and action, but also because it was believed from the start that this was the right way to make it interesting, attractive, instructive and readable for students too.

The Handbook is no run-of-the-mill text book, because every chapter is contributed by an expert on his subject who, in many cases, throws instructive new light on it. As an introduction to the subject and as a text-book it therefore has a significant advantage over other single-author books on marketing, since no single author can be an expert on every aspect of such a wide subject. And by the same token it is of value to the experienced marketer because he cannot be *au fait* with the latest thinking on every marketing topic.

Finally, I am grateful to all my authors and proud to be associated with them. That so many of those I have come to respect agreed to appear between the covers of one book has given me great pleasure and should provide corresponding benefit to readers.

Michael Rines
January 1981

Notes on Contributors

Michael Baker (Developing and launching a new industrial product) is Professor and Head of the Department of Marketing at the University of Strathclyde. Before embarking on a distinguished academic and consulting career he started work in the steel industry. He has taught at the Harvard Business School and is the author of eight books on marketing, including two on new industrial products, on which he is a recognised authority.

Gordon Brand (How industrial purchasing decisions are made) is Principal Lecturer and Activity Manager for marketing at the South West Regional Management Centre, Bristol Polytechnic. His experience has included sales, market research and general marketing posts with Standard Telephone and Cables (IT & T), in both consumer products and electronic components. He was at one time Head of Research at Industrial Market Research Ltd and is the author of *The Industrial Buying Decision* and co-author of *How British Industry Sells*.

Malcolm Carlisle (The legal framework) is a legal adviser at Colgate Palmolive. He started his career with ICI's Pharmaceuticals Division marketing ethical drugs in Europe. Whilst at ICI he studied for the bar and qualified as a barrister in 1976. He is a regular speaker at legal conferences and has contributed to professional journals on subjects of marketing law. He is legal correspondent to *Marketing* magazine.

Evert Gummesson (How professional services are bought) is a senior management consultant at Ekonomisk Företagsledning (EF) AB, the Swedish subsidiary of the large British management consultancy PA International. Before he joined PA in 1968 he worked for several years for the *Reader's Digest* in Sweden in close cooperation with its European headquarters in London. He has paid particular attention to the service sector and its marketing problems. In 1975–77 he carried out a major research project on the marketing and purchase of professional services

Norman Hart (Public relations) is Director of the Communication Advertising and Marketing Education Foundation. Previously he was Chief Marketing Executive of Industrial Advisers to the Blind Marketing, a government-sponsored management consultancy. A former Group Chief Executive of industrial advertising agency Roles & Parker, he left to join a Unilever Company, Thames Board Mills, as Publicity Manager. He subsequently became Marketing Manager, and finally went into publishing with Morgan-Grampian, where he was Divisional General Manager. A frequent speaker both in the UK and overseas on advertising, public relations and marketing, Mr Hart is author of a number of books, including *Industrial Advertising and Publicity.*

John Hobson, CBE (Advertising) Honorary President of advertising agency Hobson, Bates & Partners, is a former President of the Institute of Practitioners in Advertising and a former Chairman of the Advertising Association. He formed his own agency, John Hobson & Partners, in 1955 and merged it in 1959 with Ted Bates New York to form Hobson, Bates & Partners.

Peter Kraushar (Developing and launching a new consumer product) is recognised as a leading authority on new product development and has worked personally on more than 1,000 major projects covering new products, acquisitions and joint ventures. In 1971 he helped to set up Pricing Research and in 1972 started the monthly marketing journal, *Mintel,* with Richard Eassie. He has regularly contributed articles to the *Financial Times* and other business publications and wrote *New Products and Diversification* (Business Books).

John Lidstone (The art of negotiation) is deputy managing director of Marketing Improvements Limited. He is internationally recognised for his consultancy, lecturing and writing, on sales, marketing and management. His first book, *Training Salesmen on the Job* (Gower, 1975) is regarded as the standard reference on this subject. His *Negotiating Profitable Sales* (Gower, 1977) was made into a two-part film by Video Arts in 1979 with John Lidstone acting as technical adviser.

Frank Livesey (Pricing as a marketing tool) is currently Professor and Head of the School of Economics and Business Studies at Preston Polytechnic and has taught at the Universities of Aberdeen, St Andrews and Manchester. He has written nine books, including *Pricing* in the Macmillan Studies in Marketing Management, and a large number of articles on various aspects of economics and marketing. He has acted as a consultant to organisations both in the private and public sectors.

Bill Livingstone (Direct marketing) has been Senior Writer at Primary Contact Ltd since 1971. Before that, he worked for Bertram Pulford, and before that at Dexion Ltd. He has spent most of twenty years cajoling response from apathetic markets through words. Recent awards include campaigns for Bonusbonds and Redirack.

Harry McDermott (Exhibitions) is currently Director of Surveys with the research-consultancy Exhibition Surveys, which he founded in 1970. The consultancy is devoted to improving the cost-effectiveness of exhibiting, particularly at trade and technical events. He lectures on this subject in both the UK and Europe. He has held a wide variety of posts in research, general management, and marketing communications, with such companies as the UK Atomic Energy Authority, the International Publishing Corporation, and Unilever.

Ian Maclean (Marketing data) formed IMAC Research in 1971 to carry out surveys in industrial markets and to conduct marketing and research training courses. He is a former Chairman of the Industrial Market Research Association. He is currently Chairman of the Organisation of Professional Users of Statistics, Editor of the *Marketing Year Book* and Chief Editor of the *Handbook of Industrial Marketing and Research*.

Simon Majaro (Product planning – a new perspective) is one of Britain's leading thinkers on marketing subjects. He has had extensive business experience in the plastics, chemicals and packaging industries as Managing Director of an EEC-based Unilever company. For a number of years he was the Head of the Marketing Department at the Centre d'Études Industrielles, Geneva, followed by experience as a senior partner with Urwick Orr & Partners. A Director of Strategic Management Learning and also the Managing Partner of a firm of International Management Consultants that bears his name, Majaro is author of *International Marketing — A Strategic Approach to World Markets* (George Allen & Unwin).

Alan Melkman (The computer as a marketing tool) is Managing Director of Marketing Dynamics Ltd, the consultancy and training organisation. His experience includes working with Fine Fare and then with a subsidiary of W.R. Grace, the US multinational, holding sales brand management and marketing positions. He has been a consultant since 1970 dealing with a wide range of marketing, distribution personnel and sales problems. One area in which his organisation specialises is the application of computer concepts to the marketing function. Mr. Melkman is the author of *How to Handle Major Customers Profitably* (Gower, 1979).

Eric Morgan (Marketing to retailers) is Managing Director of British American Cosmetics Ltd, which combines the cosmetics and perfumery interests of B.A.T. Industries – including Yardley, Lentheric, Morny, Cyclax, Germaine Monteil and Juvena. The business operates in over 140 countries with manufacturing facilities in 38 of them.

Morgan spent 8 years in Sterling Drug (he was Chairman of the Phillips Scott and Turner division in the U.K. and Europe) and 10 years with the Overseas Division of Procter and Gamble. He is the author of 'How to do business in branded goods' and 'Choosing and Using Advertising Agencies'.

Leslie Rodger (The marketing concept) is Professor of Business Organisation at Heriot-Watt University, Edinburgh. Before this he had a successful career of twenty-five years in business. This included membership of the board of advertising agency McCann Erikson. He was also at one time General Manager of the Central Marketing Services Division of Mullard Limited in 1969.

David Senton (Sales management) is General Manager of the Marketing Improvements consulting group. After experience in heavy industry in sales and marketing posts, he studied human relations and industrial psychology and began a career in management development. He has been a consultant for over twelve years. He was responsible for Marketing Improvement's Continental European operation before his present appointment.

J.E. Smith (Financial Control) is a senior lecturer in financial management at the Aston Management Centre. Formerly Secretary and Chief Accountant to Beans Industries Ltd, he is also a director of J.H. Lavender & Co. Ltd. He writes on financial management, management accounting and control procedures.

John Stapleton (Making a marketing plan) is a senior lecturer in the Department of Marketing and Advertising at the College for the Distributive Trades in London. He is an active business adviser to both Ayala Sales Limited and Abbott and Butters Limited. He was the author of the winning submission for the Lord Mayor of London's marketing award commemorating UK entry into the European Economic Community. His publications include *How to Prepare a Marketing Plan, Marketing,* the first edition of the *Marketing Hand-*

book, and (with Norman Hart) the *Glossary of Marketing Terms*. In 1980 he established the Marketing Tuition Centre for Businessmen and Executives.

R.N. Theodore (Packaging as a marketing tool) is an economist and consultant at Peat, Marwick, Mitchell. He was formerly Marketing Information Officer of the Packaging Industry Research Association – the research body for the paper and board, printing and packaging industries.

Michael Thomas (The organisation of the marketing function) is an International Marketing teacher and consultant. His home base is now the School of Management Sciences at the University of Lancaster, but he holds visiting professorships at Temple University, Philadelphia; at the University of Gdansk, Poland; and at the University of Nigeria, Enugu. His interests in marketing organisation stem from his work on strategic marketing planning, and on product management systems. He is a Fellow and National Council member of the Institute of Marketing and Vice-Chairman of the Marketing Educator's Group.

Alan Toop (Sales promotion) is Chairman of the sales promotion consultancy, The Sales Machine, co-principal of The School of Sales Promotion and author of *Choosing the Right Sales Promotion* and *Only £3.95?!*, as well as a large number of articles in business publications.

Edward Walker (Marketing to the middle man) runs his own marketing consultancy company based in Guildford. After twenty years' experience of marketing and marketing research in the industrial products' fields, he now provides specialised consultancy services to companies throughout Western Europe and other parts of the world. He is particularly interested in distribution problems and has helped many companies to establish and maintain effective distribution of their products at all levels.

Leslie Walsh (International aspects of marketing, Market research) is currently Director of Marketing Studies at Sundridge Park Management Centre, Bromley, Kent. He began his business career with a steel and engineering works, of which he eventually became Export Marketing Manager. In 1961 he joined PA International Management Consultants Limited as a marketing consultant, holding various positions, including the number two position in the Industrial Market Research Division, Divisional Director International Marketing Division, and Regional Director (Latin America). He has written a number of marketing and market research case studies and is the author of one of the few available UK textbooks on the subject of international marketing.

Don Weller (How consumer purchasing decisions are made) is Principal Lecturer in Marketing at North Staffordshire Polytechnic. He entered the academic world after a varied career in industry. His experience includes posts as a salesman, sales manager, merchandising manager and managing director of a market research agency. His teaching activities have taken him across Europe from the Helsinki School of Economics to Malta University, and he has also contributed to the educational work of UNCTAD in developing countries.

Jack Wheatley (Distribution channels) is Sales Director at continuous stationery company Moore's Modern Methods. He started his career with the James Keiller subsidiary of Crosse & Blackwell, but has since specialised in the paper and stationery business where he has earned a reputation as a company 'doctor'. He is currently (1980) Honorary Treasurer of the Institute of Marketing.

Philip Winrow (Physical distribution) is principal of his own consultancy specialising in problems of logistics, applied economics, productivity and corporate planning. Originally trained as an accountant, he switched to the management services field, but has also worked in marketing. As a corporate planner with National Carriers he was probably one of the first to apply corporate planning principles in nationalised industry.

PART I

THE NATURE OF
MARKETING

1

The marketing concept

Leslie Rodger, Professor of Business Administration, Heriot-Watt University

PAST AND PRESENT

Ends and means

Marketing in the United Kingdom, viewed as a separate and scientifically-based activity within the firm, is a phenomenon of the second half of this century. Even in the 1960s the practical application of marketing as a management concept based on the belief that a firm's competitive effectiveness, measured in terms of profitable sales and a satisfactory return on investment, could be best achieved by the planned identification, anticipation, and satisfaction of customers' requirements, was very much the exception. At the present time, firms paying more than lip service to the marketing concept are, perhaps, still in the minority.

Many definitions of marketing exist but it is not proposed to argue their relative merits. There is now, probably, a measure of general agreement that marketing's principal concerns are the identification, creation and delivery of optimum customer values, i.e. maximum values at minimum costs, and the organisation of a firm's total resources and skills to achieve this at a profit. The words 'at a profit' are crucial. On the one hand it is no part of marketing's job to seek to get the firm to satisfy customers' requirements at *any* cost irrespective of what the customer is able and willing to pay. On the other hand marketing should not be seen by a firm's general management as a means of exploiting the customer for short-run profit gain at the expense of the customer's short-term and long-term interests.

Although many top managements may profess belief in the marketing concept, in practice, line marketing executives are judged and rewarded on their short-term sales and profit performance. While paying lip-service to high sounding ends, general management has too often gullibly or deliberately, allowed or required its executives to employ means which carry no firm commitment to the customers' longer term interests and welfare. This is the real shame of the marketing concept as applied in practice.

However, taking the long-term view, it should be self evident that in order to survive and grow, a business *must* earn a satisfactory planned rate of profit. Only in this way can it continue to serve its customers on a long-term basis and fulfil its obligations to its own managers and employees, its shareholders, its suppliers, the local community and society at large.

Everyone in the firm from the shopfloor to the boardroom is involved to some degree in creating value for the customer or in minimising the delivered cost of the product or service. Being marketing-oriented means encouraging everyone to consider his or her individual tasks and responsibilities with the interest of the customer in mind; it means making everyone aware of the impact of his or her decisions and actions on the customer. It also means abandoning the idea that there are some people in the firm who serve the customer and others who do not or think that it does not matter.

In theory, the marketing function is essentially a matching process. It is concerned with the profitable matching of the firm's resources and capabilities with the requirements of the customer, and it was the recognition and acceptance of the need to plan ahead to achieve the *best* match that resulted in the formalisation of marketing as a specific function and in the establishment of marketing departments within firms.

The past twenty years have seen the development and refinement of sophisticated techniques in marketing research, market and sales forecasting, product planning, advertising and sales promotion, distribution and after-sales service. Even more important has been the development of skills in the management of these specialised marketing activities not only in their separate effects but also in their interactive effects.

Marketing has never been and is never likely to be without its critics. It could hardly be otherwise. Marketing is primarily concerned with the creation, presentation and communication of the firm's offerings. It is, of necessity, that part of a firm's activity which is most exposed to public scrutiny. Businessmen, in their corporate clothes, are neither philanthropists nor angels any more than are politicians or churchmen or customers. But this is something quite different from claiming that businessmen, more than others, act from ulterior motives. It must also be said that the market mechanism, as a means whereby customers' needs can be properly expressed and efficiently met, is not without its imperfections either.

With all its operational shortcomings, the marketing concept has survived, through progressive adaptation, as a valid business philosophy and is capable of providing a means of commitment to the customers' short- and long- term interests in a free society, consonant with the achievement of management's business objectives.

The marketing channel of commitment

Marketing's future efficacy as a channel of commitment to the consumer will be in proportion to the degree that it succeeds in enhancing the quality of customers' judgements and in maintaining fair, competitive market conditions that permit customers to make free and informed choices between alternatives.

This means providing customers with much more *relevant* product and service information, e.g. performance and safety in use, unit pricing, open dating, ease of access to complaint procedures and efficient redress of grievances, easily understood terms and conditions of contracts and guarantees free of exception and exclusion clauses. It also means that businessmen must accept that the maintenance of fair, competitive market conditions and the safeguarding of consumer rights cannot be left entirely to their own self-regulatory codes. Legislation, however, should be kept to a minimum and only enacted as a last resort.

> Long-term consumer education, self-regulating codes of practice, adverse publicity for those who transgress such codes, combined with a determined effort to ensure that consumers understand their rights under existing law, are likely to prove more successful in providing real consumer protection. For the

quality of consumers' judgements in the market place will not be enhanced by removing from consumers the necessity to make their own decisions or by imposing on the market conditions which limit the freedom of a consumers' choice or the means of developing their powers of judgement.[1]

THE FUTURE

Society and technology

Marketing is an entrepreneurial and innovating activity. Like any creative activity it both pioneers new forms and pathways and reflects social and technological change.

Marketing has borrowed and adapted methods and tools from other scientific disciplines – the behavioural sciences, operational research, mathematics and statistics, as well as from technologies such as electronic communication and data processing. Marketing, by definition, has to satisfy the ever-changing requirements of customers. Changes in social attitudes affect products, markets and marketing strategies and marketing personnel must develop a high degree of sensitivity to such changes if they are to respond and provide satisfactory solutions to customers' problems.

Marketing-oriented computer systems

In the years immediately ahead computers will make a dramatic impact on marketing practice. Computers have been around for quite a long time and their ability to generate high speed data has intimidated rather than helped the marketing manager. What marketing managers need and what computer technology is now able to deliver is a reliable desk-top interactive computer-based system that will provide executives with specific decision-oriented information. An 'ideal' system will allow the marketing manager 'to retrieve, display and manipulate any data he wishes . . . to expand his conscious train of thought when trying to solve a problem by screening various

---

1 Jeremy Mitchell (ed.), *Marketing and the Consumer Movement,* McGraw Hill Book Company (UK) Ltd, 1978, p.133. See also Chapter 15, 'The legal framework'.

assumptions or alternative solutions . . . and to adjust his or her requirements or thought processes as the system is being operated'.[2]

Tomorrow's marketing information systems will be capable of providing data in ways which will help marketing managers 'to solve problems that are highly subjective, difficult to analyse, imperfectly understood and continually evolving'. Computer applications will become much more marketing problem-oriented. More than at any time in the past, marketing success will depend on the linking of enhanced computer power to imaginative planning.

Distributed data processing

Another development which will have a major impact on the marketing scene is the capability to capture data at the precise locations of origin – at the sales checkout, on the factory floor, in the warehouse or distribution depot. Data captured at these points can be sent to a central computer where instant adjustments will be made to sales and stock records, orders generated to replenish inventories and routed automatically to suppliers' computers.

The development of laser-scanning electronic checkouts in the retailing sector is only part of a new computerised electronic technology which is likely to create as much of a revolution in retail marketing as the introduction of self-service marketing techniques has done over the last thirty years or so. The new technology can be expected in time to change completely the face of retail management information and control systems. This will, in turn, have major repercussions on manufacturers' marketing policies and strategies.

Of major concern to manufacturers will be the opportunities that the new technology will provide to retail management as the holders and users of key marketing information. A significant shift in the strategic balance of 'information power' in favour of distributors – acting singly or in concert – could intensify the conflict of interest between distributors and manufacturers. The speed of access to key marketing data and cost advantages that the new technology will confer on the distribution channel will require manufacturers to rethink their marketing negotiating and bargaining strategies. Dis-

---

2   'Information systems for marketing in F. Graf, *Marketing Trends* no. 2, A.C. Nielsen Co., 1979.

tributors will also have to rethink their own strategies including whether or not to provide the information to manufacturers on a straight commercial or cooperative exchange basis or whether to exploit their information advantage vis-à-vis manufacturers.

Chips with everything

The microprocessor – the so-called 'computer on a chip' – represents a new wave of technological change which will not only have fundamental implications for marketing procedures, practices and organisation but will also open up a whole gamut of new market opportunities, particularly in the consumer sector. Quite apart from telephonic and visual display communication and storage facilities in the home, microelectronics will invade households in a variety of forms without the owner necessarily being aware of the fact, e.g. domestic appliances, environmental monitoring and control systems. The home may become an extension of the office to an ever-increasing degree with the aid of data display units linked to head office. The ubiquitous chip will certainly have profound social effects which at the moment can only be guessed at. A social impact study of microelectronics should receive top priority if the 'future shock' effect is to be contained.

Agricultural marketing

Agricultural technology has outpaced the industry's marketing capacity and capability. Indeed, agriculture remains the one major area within the economy where scientific marketing has yet to make a major impact. UK producers and distributors of agricultural products, principally vegetables, fruit and meat are still primarily product- or sales-oriented, giving scant attention to consumer wants and preferences. Farmers and breeders and meat producers will have to adopt much better marketing techniques if they are to compete effectively in home and overseas markets, particularly against EEC producers. A rationalisation of the whole marketing cycle from farmer or breeder through slaughtering and/or processing to the retail outlet and final consumer is long overdue.

Relationship with other management functions

Marketing has been an integrating force within the business firm in so far as it has been responsible for pulling together and coordinating a number of interdependent activities, viz. product planning, personal selling, advertising and sales promotion, and distribution – the so-called 'marketing mix'. It has also sought to integrate marketing research, market estimation and sales forecasting into the firm's total marketing planning operation. It has been much less successful in integrating itself into the total business system as a subsystem along-side research and development, design, engineering, manufacture and finance.

There has been a growing recognition in recent years that what is really needed is to provide a marketing-orientation to the overall business plan. To be more effective in the future, marketing must be prepared to cross functional boundaries freely and to lubricate the system as a whole, identifying sources of friction and where possible removing them and developing balanced cooperative solutions to problems. This will inevitably involve trade-offs of various kinds between the different functions in the business. The computer can help here to the extent that the screening of assumptions and alternative solutions and the application of optimising procedures on an interactive real-time basis, is a mutual learning and appreciation exercise from which all participating functional managers can benefit and perhaps draw objective and, therefore, more acceptable conclusions.

In the past, general management has tended to look to marketing management for the answers to the more intractable problems of the business as though the latter had some god-given gift denied to others. This was an erroneous approach. Marketing management's most important future role will be to ensure that the right questions are put at the right time, to the right people and to get general management and the operational or line managers to come up with their own and, one would hope, better answers. The chief executive of the firm will have the primary responsibility to establish and encourage a climate in which the key marketing questions get asked at the critical decision points in the research, development, design engineering, production, sales, distribution stream of activity and planning so that the answers provided by the functional and line executives actually involved are reflected in the overall business plan.

The end objective remains the creation and delivery of optimum customer values at a profit.

2

How consumer purchasing decisions are made

Don Weller, Principal Lecturer in Marketing, North Staffordshire Polytechnic

There are a number of common misconceptions, particularly among economists, about the way consumers' purchasing decisions are made. These misconceptions are based on a belief in rational economic man whose purchasing behaviour is governed by a desire to maximise utility. The misconceptions are:

1 Products are bought because of their material usefulness.
2 The usefulness of a product can be determined by objective criteria which will be commonly applied by everyone.
3 When a consumer sets out to spend a sum of money, he calculates the combination of available goods which will provide the maximum usefulness in exchange for that sum.

Such views do not relate to real life. Where do yoga classes, romantic novels and household pets fit in? Why do some choose cars for their lively performance, others for their low fuel consumption, and yet others for their colour? How can the woman loading the week's shopping into the trolley as she scurries through the supermarket make complex calculations to maximise the utility of her purchases?

MARKETING APPROACH TO PURCHASING BEHAVIOUR

Though modern economists take more sophisticated lines, most of them persist in trying to describe purchasing behaviour in the idiom of obsolete systems of thought, and it is not surprising that those lines often snap under the strain of practical application. To avoid being cast helplessly adrift marketers have developed their own approach. In doing so they have found ample scope for argument, and the ideas presented here should in consequence not be seen as part of a marketing gospel, but as helpful rules of thumb.

The marketing approach to purchasing behaviour begins with acceptance of the findings of psychologists like Lund, that there is a low correlation between belief and evidence, and in contrast a high correlation between belief and need. In other words we tend to believe whatever we need to believe. Translated into action this tendency might lead a youngster determined to prove his manhood to turn to the drink 'which separates the men from the boys'. Equally the girl who cannot find boy friends might try to make life cosier by buying the latest magical deodorant.

The assumption can then be made that the rationality of purchasing behaviour is subjective rather than objective, or put another way:

1　People buy goods because at the time of purchase they believe they need them.
2　People's needs vary, and so their choices of brands and their purchasing priorities also vary.

To most this seems a sensible starting point and to move forward it helps to envisage the process of need satisfaction as

NEED ⟶ RESPONSE or ⟶ GOAL ⟶ RELIEF OF NEED
　　　　　PURCHASE

Keep in mind that a need is not an independent entity but a feeling experienced by a person. Add the facts that the same need does not evoke the same response from everyone, nor even a standard response from the same individual, and it becomes clear that something is missing. Notions about conditioned reflexes derived from rat watching do not seem to tell the whole story. But what can be put in their place?

Here the theory of intervening variables can help. Essentially it does no more than give form and definition to the commonsense supposition that people behave in accordance with their psychological make-up, and their mental set at the time: 'Dad's always been a bit strait-laced, so I knew he wouldn't like it when I told him Fred had put me in the club. But he'd never have thumped Fred if he hadn't been in a nasty mood because Liverpool lost at home.'

It does, however, provide a foundation on which further other useful ideas can be built, by representing the make-up as a complex of variables, through which each need must filter before it is translated into a response.

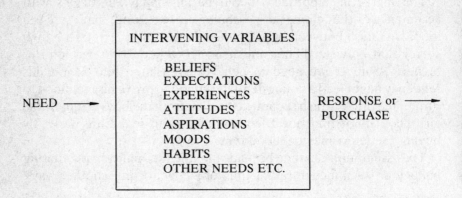

INTERVENING VARIABLES

NEED ⟶

BELIEFS
EXPECTATIONS
EXPERIENCES
ATTITUDES
ASPIRATIONS
MOODS
HABITS
OTHER NEEDS ETC.

RESPONSE or ⟶
PURCHASE

It is easy to appreciate the broad effect on purchasing decisions of some of the list of variables.

Moods can cut across normal behaviour. In a fit of elation a careful housewife might squander a week's housekeeping money on a new dress and a bikini she would be scared to wear. On holiday some buy all manner of bric-a-brac which will be tucked discreetly out of sight within a few weeks of their return home.

Habits of buying a favoured brand through thick and thin are a delight to the lucky brand manager. More frustrating might be the habit of shopping at a particular store.

Experiences. On hearing of the plight of a fatherless family, a husband might well take out heavier life insurance. If he had thrown his wife's last grotesque attempt at sponge making into the dustbin she might well change her brand of sponge mix.

Aspirations. Having set his heart on becoming a famous cricketer, a lad might well buy a new pair of cricket boots on receiving an invitation to a trial at the county ground.

Beliefs, however, are difficult to analyse and are varied in their nature and their influence on buying decisions. Perhaps the only valuable commonsense observation on them is that people tend to cling to their existing beliefs, and are disturbed by ideas which run counter to them. They do not want the worry and upset of remoulding their views on life, and in self-protection often shun or mock evidence which threatens a quiet mental life. 'That fellow Columbus is just a lying rogue. Everyone knows that the earth is as flat as a pancake. He's probably been keeping out of sight in Grand Canary for a couple of years while he worked out the details of his stupid confidence trick.'

ROKEACH'S BELIEF THEORY

Milton Rokeach's belief theory based on years of careful research goes deeper and is of more practical value. He suggests that people's belief systems are like onions. The central core is surrounded by interfolded layers. To remove the core is to destroy the entire onion, and for this reason core beliefs are not given up, except under the pressures of a calculated brainwashing process.

He calls them *primitive beliefs*. These are axioms commonly taken for granted and mainly consist of beliefs about self and social and physical reality. For example:

> Day follows night.
> Water is wet.
> My name is Horatio.

The next layer is of more direct interest to marketers. It is composed of *beliefs derived from deep personal experience*. Most of our deepest experiences are about ourselves and might include:

> I have a quick mind.
> I am a good listener.
> I never worry.

More easily exploited by marketers, however, are negative beliefs such as:

> I lose my temper easily.
> I never know what to say.
> I put boys off.

13

Often such a belief triggers a need to scotch the shortcoming. Provided their advertising promises that they will turn boys on, hair shampoos, hair removers, diet charts, pimple removers, jeans and foundation garments can all be sold to yearning womanhood.

Authority beliefs form the third layer. It is hard to form a view about many parts of social and physical reality. They are controversial and cannot be personally verified:

> Did Christ really live?
> Is permissiveness good or bad?
> What is the best bet for the Derby?

For answers to these types of question we develop beliefs about the veracity of different types of authority. The Pope may become our authority on religious thought, and at a more mundane level a pop idol may become our guide on the way to dress and the wisdom of sexual adventures before the age of consent. To marketers the usefulness of sponsorship has long been apparent, and to varying degrees sponsorships exploit authority beliefs.

Peripheral beliefs depend on the authority beliefs which their layers surround in the system. Accepting the Pope as his authority on religion, a Roman Catholic may in consequence regard contraceptives as beyond the pale since that is where the Pope has put them.

The key fact of high importance to marketers is that though such beliefs form the penultimate layer they are very different to shift. Staying fleetingly with birth control, remember that most Indian and Indonesian women in the face of years of propaganda costing much more than could be afforded by a commercial concern, have clung to peripheral beliefs fostered by their religious authorities, and shunned interference with nature.

Nor do people always accept high or credible authorities. Not so long ago a plastic fountain pen was launched in the USA with a powerful advertising campaign. It claimed that the pen was so strong that it would remain undamaged if a bus ran over it. The launch failed. An investigation showed that few believed the claim. Its truth was demonstrated many times. Sales did not grow, and indeed did not pick up until the campaign was withdrawn and replaced by a less astounding message. For astounding it was to many people, who accepted the myth generated by their mas and pas and big sisters and other notable scientific inexperts that all plastics are fragile. Maybe it could not happen today, but tales of similar misjudgements of the beliefs of advertising audiences accumulate year by year.

Inconsequential beliefs form the outside layer of the onion. To remove one therefore scarcely disturbs the rest of the system. Only beliefs of this type can be easily shifted by commercial persuasion. Among them might be found:

Italian food is stodgy.
Switzerland is the best place for a holiday.
Cutless are the best razor blades.

What does all this add up to? Rokeach's work underpins some ideas gained by many through workaday experiences. Perhaps the most important are:

1 Never advertise without assessing the audience's probable response to the message.
2 Never risk insulting or disturbing an audience by projecting a message running counter to their deeply held beliefs.
3 Look for opportunities to shift lightly held beliefs, such as those in favour of a competitor's product, by reinforcing more deeply held beliefs.
4 Remember that many beliefs stem from local culture, and that a persuasive message in one country may be offensive in another.
5 When marketing an innovation which differs widely from the product which it would outdate, do not assume, however great the improvement it represents, that it will be ecstatically welcomed. Its performance may seem incredible, its method of achieving it beyond belief, its appearance outlandish.

This leads to two well recognised ideas. Big innovations are less easy to accept than minor changes. The reaction of an individual to an innovation depends on the way his beliefs have been marshalled into attitudes, which can be thought of as predispositions to react in a particular manner. The consequences have been examined and organised in the theory of the diffusions of innovations, parts of which are now sketched.

MARKET ACCEPTANCE OF INNOVATIONS

Innovations are divided into three types. A *continuous innovation* does not disrupt existing purchasing behaviour and can gain market acceptance with little resistance. Simple modifications to existing products, such as a new range of colours for telephones, fall into this category.

A *dynamically continuous innovation* tends to be more disturbing and will be accepted less readily. A telephone with the dial replaced by push buttons might be a good example.

A *discontinuous innovation* involves both the creation of a new product concept and the establishment by the consumer of new forms of purchasing or user behaviour. A telephone with video facilities would qualify for this category. Such products are difficult to launch because old habits and attitudes must first be eroded by consumer re-education.

Whatever the product people will show varying degrees of willingness to purchase it and research has identified six categories of adopter.

The venturesome. Defined as the first $2\frac{1}{2}$ per cent of a market to adopt a new product, they are people or companies to whom newness is almost an obsession. Willing sometimes to put themselves at risk to satisfy a desire to be first, they tend to be regarded as off-beat or quirky, and for this reason their purchases do not much influence the rest of the market.

The early adopters in contrast are respected as opinion leaders in taste, fashion or technical and commercial matters. Only when this $13\frac{1}{2}$ per cent of the market begins to adopt a product are there genuine prospects of success.

The early majority are the next 34 per cent of the market to adopt. They take up products with a deliberate willingness to follow the lead of the early adopters, and it is when they begin to buy that market acceptance begins to become widespread.

The late majority are the 34 per cent of the market which follows, often sceptically, in the wake of the earlier comers. The weight of market opinion must clearly favour the product before they take it up, and even then they may purchase it only from economic necessity, or under pressure to conform.

The laggards are the last reluctant adopters. Often traditionalists, they begin to buy the product when it is far from new, and possibly beginning to be superseded by something else.

The non-adopters never buy the product.

It is easy to recognise that a graph of the percentages is reminiscent of the product life cycle. The shallow curve after launch is mirrored by the small percentage of the venturesome, and the steep climb at the growth stage is triggered by the early adopters, and sustained by an early majority. Fairly even sales volume in maturity is obtainable by winning over late adopters to replace forerunners who take up new products.

MASLOW'S THEORY OF NEEDS

Into the complex of intervening variables flows a steady stream of needs. To grasp how to sell products a clear view of their nature must be formed. Many find the heirarchy proposed by Abraham Maslow of great help. Unlike the majority of his fellow psychologists, Maslow was mainly interested in the minds of normal people – the masses to whom marketers seek to sell. His theory distinguishes several types of need and arranges them in an order of potency.

Physiological needs are satisfied before all else. In developed countries, however, most people earn enough to expect to be able to eat well, keep the house warm and pay the rent. Unlike the less fortunate in poor countries, their lives are not built round survival, and they would therefore, for example, feel little interest in this advertising message: 'Give the kids Swell for breakfast. Watch their eyes shine, their little tummies swell, and feel sure they won't ask for more till bedtime'.

Safety needs. As anxieties over day-to-day survival fade, they are replaced by concern about the future. Pressure grows to guard against deprivation caused by calamities or loss of earning power. Mass expression of such needs by social underdogs often takes the form of demands for state pension schemes, medical care and unemployment benefits. Once people feel cushioned against their future, they feel an increasing urge to satisfy social needs.

Needs for love and affection should not be equated with the need for sex which is arguably physiological. While some needs of this type find expression in sexual behaviour, the entire array is wider and more complex. They can, for example, be felt in terms of despon-

17

dency at the absence of children or friends, or as a desire to belong to a club, or a neighbourhood group. Though their exact nature and boundaries are hard to define, the drive to gratify them is powerful and much exploited by marketers: 'Our kids' best friend is our dog, Chuffles. They get such a lot of fun out of him, he deserves only the best. That's why we always give him Bounce'.

Needs for esteem begin to be keenly felt only after needs for love and affection have been largely assuaged, and fall into two distinct groups. One contains the cluster of needs surrounding a general desire for self-respect, like needs for achievement, strength, adequacy and self-confidence. The other consists of needs centreing round a desire for the respect of others, like needs for status, recognition, attention and appreciation: 'Your red setter is the pride of the neighbourhood, Lucy. I always say a top-hole dog is the sign of a top-hole owner. Goodness, he's really tucking into that Bounce!'

Needs for self-actualisation. As needs for esteem are satisfied, desires to become, or at least to appear to become, the self of one's dreams are paramount. A would-be member of the landed gentry, might, for example, buy a country estate, two or three dozen tweed suits, and a couple of horses to race at point-to-point meetings: 'Pedigree is always important, Jenkins. In people, in dogs, and in dog food. Time for Archduke's Bounce, Jenkins'.

Beyond this point Maslow suggests more controversially that people become motivated by aesthetic needs and desires to know and understand. Here, however, only the broader implications of his hierarchy can be considered.

1 Satisfaction of keenly felt needs shapes purchasing behaviour.
2 Levels of need satisfaction are closely linked to levels of discretionary income.
3 Income brackets are therefore useful clues to the level of need in the hierarchy which a sales prospect, or an advertising audience, is mainly concerned to satisfy.
4 Persuasive appeals should stem from insight into the dominating needs of a target audience.

It is helpful to know something about need formation and the individual strands of intervening variables. But how is interaction between need and the variables converted into a choice, and how could such a choice be predicted through market research?

FISHBEIN'S THEORY OF CHOICE

Perhaps the most cogent ideas are those of Fishbein. He suggests that interaction among the variables crystallises into two key determinants of choice.

1 *Attitude towards the behaviour in question.* It is crucial to understand the distinction between 'behaviour' and 'object of behaviour'. People may, for example, have quite different views on immigrants (objects of behaviour), and preventing immigration (behaviour). The latter group of attitudes, Fishbein believes, are uninfluenced by other people's views.
2 *The subjective norm* consisting of beliefs about the way those who are of importance to the decision taker would react to his choice.

Clearly the comparative influence of the determinants varies from situation to situation. In a choice between turning right and crashing into a wall, for example, it is unlikely that the subjective norm will exert much influence. But in selecting a new carpet it may be very important. Each situation must therefore be researched to arrive at realistic weightings for the two determinants.

Beyond the evidence which is accumulating to support it, Fishbein's proposition is attractive because it gives a simple outline within which to design many forms of market research, and a useful formula for analysing research findings. With Fishbein's aid the original model of need satisfaction can be developed thus:

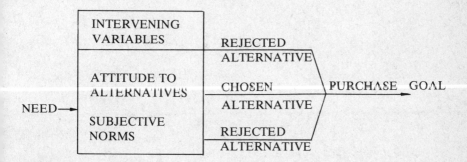

CONCLUSION

Anyone trying to depict human nature is like a sculptor chipping away at marble with inadequate tools. The raw material is fascinating but the likeness can be crude. Here, also, the space is too cramped to allow us to stand back and take a proper look at each man's work. In fact the contributions of many worthwhile thinkers cannot be included, but the ideas presented should whet the appetite for wider inquiry and a number of suggestions are shown below.

READING LIST

J.G. Meyer & W.H. Reynold, *Consumer Behaviour & Marketing Management*, Houghton Mifflin, 1967.

M. Fishbein & F.S. Coombes, 'Basis for decision: an attitudinal analysis of voting behaviour', in *Journal of Applied Social Psychology*, 4 February 1974.

Don Weller, *Who buys: A Study of the Consumer*, Pitman, 1974.

Gordon R. Foxall, *Consumer Behaviour*, Croom Helm, 1980.

A.H. Maslow, 'A Theory of Human Motivation' in *Psychological Review*, no. 50, 1943.

Engel, Kollat & Blackwell, *Consumer Behaviour*, Holt, 1979.

3

How industrial purchasing decisions are made

Gordon Brand, B.Sc(Econ). M.Sc., M.Inst.M.

Industrial purchasing decision behaviour can hardly be described as a neglected subject. Journals abound with numerous articles on some aspect or other of industrial purchasing. Industrial marketing research surveys also frequently include a study of purchasing decision processes along with the more traditional aspects of market size, structure and specifications required, but these facts remain confidential to clients. There is a wealth, therefore, of individual studies, many specific to certain aspects of industrial purchasing behaviour, but limited either by confidentiality or the resources of academic researchers.

This is not the fault of the researchers or their sponsors because for their work to be viable they need to concentrate on particular products or particular aspects of the decision process. The apparent abundance of uncoordinated research results, however, does not really help a marketing manager who requires a good flow of information which he can use either to apply to his own market situation or to spark off ideas and applications suited to his own circumstances.

It is the purpose of this chapter to bring together the main ideas circulating around the topic of industrial purchasing behaviour and to suggest ways in which these ideas can be of practical use to an industrial marketing manager.

PURCHASING AS A PROCESS

Are you getting in at the right stage?

First and foremost it is as well to recognise that industrial or organisational purchasing is a process taking place over periods of time. It has a beginning, a middle and an end together with important stages in between. This process may involve many months of detailed and protracted contact between supplier and purchaser or it may be concluded in minutes by a simple clerical act, but the concept of buying stages of itself provides a valuable framework to assess where you are and what to do next.

Various descriptions have been given to these stages but one of the most popular is the series of events suggested by Robinson and Farris at the American Institute of Marketing Science in the late 1960s (see Figure 3.1).

There have been attempts from time to time to discredit this approach by researchers wishing to prove that the framework is too rigid and not applicable in all cases. This may be so, but most practitioners will recognise that stages do exist whatever the titles given to them. You can test this by setting out the stages you recognise as being important in your own customer industries. If you disagree over the wording, it does not matter. The value of the exercise is to be found in the thought it provokes.

One observation is very important from the marketing point of view. If you have a sequence of stages then decisions taken at one stage are bound to influence the scope of the decisions to be taken at the next, and so on. The implications of this are that the sooner you become involved at the early formative stages, the more likely you are to be successful at the final supplier selection stages. This may seem obvious when written down, but use this idea to test out how much business is lost because the first you heard of it was during the middle stages when buyers were asking for quotations to supply. The suppliers who are involved at the early problem stages and who assist the purchasing organisations' technical staff in making up their minds can provide a far more persuasive quotation.

A common cry of purchasing managers is that there can be no industrial marketing in the United Kingdom because whenever they want to buy something they have to do all the running in finding out

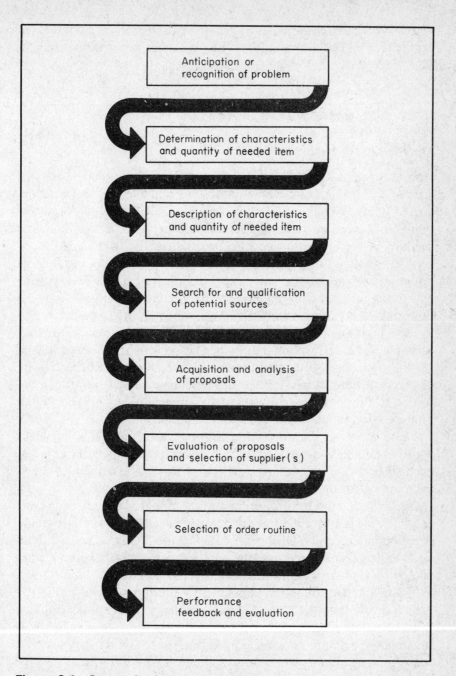

Figure 3.1 Stages in the process of purchasing industrial goods

where to buy. We could all find cases to disprove this claim, but when it is true it is because suppliers are not using their knowledge of buying stages.

THE DECISION-MAKING UNIT

Are you talking to the right people?

Another aspect worth discussing in your own particular industry or area of interest is that, at different stages of the buying decision, different types of decision makers are present. In the early formative stages the decision makers are technical in their background and thinking process. Within certain broad price limits they are concerned mainly with specifications and performance. As the field of potential suppliers is narrowed the technical decision makers give way to the more commercially minded purchasing staff who look for their buying advantage through negotiations on price, delivery, credit, stockholding procedures etc. A manager or production director responsible for scheduling output may be present at this stage having been absent from the earlier discussions. Once he is satisfied that the products offered by competing suppliers have passed the criteria set by his technical staff, his only interest may be delivery or price and the final decision is made on these aspects alone.

There are many variations on this theme and it would be misleading to prescribe a set pattern of behaviour that occurs without fail at each stage of the purchasing decision process. The principles, however, apply throughout. Industrial goods and services are rarely purchased by one man but rather by a group of people interacting over considerable periods of time. For convenience these groups are called decision-making units (DMUs), but jargon apart, the presence of these units calls very strongly on one of the main characteristics of the successful industrial marketing approach, namely adaptability.

Managers with industrial experience are fully aware of the DMU principle, but does the newest recruit understand the implications, or does he have to learn the hard way? The use of such a principle is invaluable for training especially during in-company courses with senior management present to discuss customer situations and promotional investment with complete security.

Take, for example, a group of sales representatives of a company supplying packaging materials working in syndicates preparing a list of job functions likely to decide or influence the decision to purchase their product. In reporting back, the junior staff benefit from the broader views of the more experienced. Included in the list, along with 'internal' decision makers, are personnel in advertising agencies. Many of the managers present will be aware of the role of advertising agencies in the industry, but raising the topic in general discussions may lead, for example, to important questions as to the amount of sales effort directed to that sector.

FLEXIBILITY AND ADAPTABILITY

Are you saying the right things to the right people?

Buying and selling can be seen as one transaction which may appear to have two opposing sides, but is in reality one single process through which buyer and seller engage to their mutual advantage. Both 'sides' will have their objectives so the transaction has the ingredients of opposition and conflict, but to be successful with a continuing relationship both interests must become enmeshed or engaged like cogs in a wheel.

The prospective supplier must adapt his offering, either the product or the service itself, but more simply his method of engaging interest, to suit the buyer's needs. The ability to do this is normally described as 'empathy' or the ability to 'put oneself in another's shoes', but it goes further than just seeing the buyer's point of view. The supplier must be flexible enough to present what he wants in such a way that the buyer or buying team see the offering as a solution to their problems. The DMU concept indicates that within the buying team there are a number of different problems to solve, some technical, some commercial. The seller too has a great number of different features or 'benefits' to talk about. The true engagement of interests, and thereby the fullest rapport, will flow when the sales representative has the ability to interpret the messages he receives from the buyer and adapt his presentation to the needs of his audience. This adaptability may extend from the presentation of complicated technical information to one member of the DMU, a detailed financial appraisal for another, to an adroit change in the direction half-way through a sentence when the listener's eyes betray that the discussion is going down the wrong path.

FIRST TIME PURCHASE OR REPEAT

Another aspect of the DMU concept is that not only does the composition of the DMU change with the different buying stages, but it also changes when a product or service is completely new to the purchasing organisation in contrast to a repeat purchase. Table 3.1 shows the buying stages mentioned above with typical DMU members for a new item of industrial equipment and for the repeat purchase of an electronic component. Between these two extremes is to be found another buying pattern when the decision is taken to change the supplier of a standard repeat purchase item to an alternative competitor. This table refers to real buying situations, but it is up to each marketing manager to work out the DMU for each major customer organisation and for typical products supplied.

The industrial purchasing decision, therefore, can be viewed as a pattern of activities changing in structure, people and time dimension as the buying organisation adapts itself to the many varied reasons for the need to buy in from outside suppliers.

These variations in buying patterns can present a daunting prospect to the industrial marketing manager planning his promotional strategy, but the complications in fact offer many prospects for adaptable approaches in sales, advertising support, price, delivery, maintenance and general service back-up. The variations in the way goods are supplied help the buying organisations to choose from a number of competitor suppliers the one that is best suited to their needs.

Underpinning these apparently complicated structures are two basic concepts which should always be borne in mind when planning both strategy and tactics, but in particular, tactics. The first is that people, and groups of managers, only buy products or services to solve a problem that could not be solved without a purchase. Also associated with the problem-solving concept is the additional fact that products (as well as services) are purchased not for what they *are* but for what they *do* – a very important factor when deciding how to describe or refer to your offering.

Table 3.1 DMU members involved by type of purchase

Purchasing stages	New purchase	Change in supplier	Repeat purchase
Recognition of need to purchase	Board, general management	Buyer	Stock control system
Determination of product characteristics	Technical personnel	As specified when new purchase	As specified
Description of product characteristics	Technical personnel	As specified	As specified
Search for suppliers	Technical personnel	Buyer	Approved suppliers
Assessing qualifications of suppliers	Technical personnel	Technical personnel and buyer	Approved suppliers
Acquisition of proposals	Buyer and technical personnel	Buyer	Purchasing staff
Evaluation of proposals	Technical personnel	Buyer	Purchasing staff
Selection of supplier	Technical personnel general management buyer	Buyer	Purchasing staff
Selection of order routine	Buyer	Buyer	Purchasing staff
Performance feedback and evaluation	Technical personnel and buyer (informal)	Buyer (informal) System (formal)	Buyer (informal) System (formal)

A second key concept is that when solving problems by buying, those taking or influencing the decisions to buy perceive certain risks in their actions. They may not get good value; their technical knowledge may be lacking; new cheaper substitutes may be just around the corner; the supplier may not keep his promises. These risks are only perceived and may not be real, but real or not they have to be taken into account and reduced in some way by the prospective supplier, if he is to be successful.

THE APPLICATION OF BUYING KNOWLEDGE TO THE SALES APPROACH

The most important aspect of the growing awareness of industrial purchasing behaviour and decision making is not the knowledge itself but the use to which it can be put. Each item of research knowledge should be tested by such questions as: What does it mean to our marketing operations? What have we got to do or change to make the most use of this knowledge?

This should be possible for every piece of information collected but as an example a suggested use of the finding by Scandanavian researcher Hakansson and colleagues on risk perception is given in Table 3.2. The researchers categorised three types of perceived risk described here as the uncertainties of (product) need, market (buyer's knowledge of the supply situation) and transaction (commercial aspects). On the left hand side, these research classifications

Table 3.2 Interpretation of buyer/seller relationship score

Buyer's perceived risk areas: uncertainty of buying unit	Selection of sales approach to reduce uncertainty
Need uncertainty	Uncertainty rating
1 To what extent can the buyer or buying group state the specification required?	*High*: problem solving, knowledge of customer manufacturing methods and markets; information provision. *Low*: stress commercial factors; non-price advantages; delivery service.
2 How critical is the product/service offered to the customer company's production process?	*High*: strategic decision; wide DMU, stress technical competence; provide independent references; locate key decision makers/influencers. *Low*: price advantages; commercial terms; note change in customer cooperation; seek product differentiation.

(*Table 3.2 continued*)

Market uncertainty	Uncertainty rating
3 To what extent is your product/service different from others on the market?	*High*: stress contribution to customer's own market performance; innovative advantage. *Low*: stress commercial terms; call regularly on user and buying departments.
4 Are buyers aware of range of competitor products/services available?	*High*: note change in customer manufacturing procedures providing opportunity for the 'out' supplier; increase own knowledge of competitor product performance.
5 Are differences in product performance: (a) occuring rapidly, or (b) static for some years?	(a) supply information to reduce risk of change to new supplier; (b) Call regularly; anticipate change in customer requirements; supply regular information on delivery, prices; provide information emphasising uniformity in the market.

Transaction uncertainty	Uncertainty rating
6 Are delivery dates for the supply of your product crucial?	*High*: refer to other customers dependent on regular supply; offer buffer stocks; joint transport/stock systems. *Low*: stress technical advantages, cost saving.
7 Are trading procedures in your industry: (a) standardised, (b) complex (tailored for each customer)?	(a) stress product differentiation; facilitate repeat ordering; supply reasons for deficiency in service. (b) depending on marketing strategy, reduce buyer's perception of need for complexity *or* exploit perceived needs of individual key customers.

are listed. On the right of the table are my suggestions for the tactics to be used in selling to help reduce these uncertainties in the buyer's mind. They are offered in response to high or low ratings which can be determined and agreed by a group of practitioners familiar with the customer, industry or organisation in question. For example in question 1: if, in the opinion of supplier personnel, the buying team have limited technical knowledge, or are undecided on the specifications required to do the job, the uncertainty rating is high. The suggestion then is for the supplier to reduce that uncertainty through problem solving, by application of his knowledge of the customer firm and by providing a good deal of information. To the skilled buying team with low uncertainty, such a presentation would be wasted. To them it is better to stress commercial factors which differentiate you from equally technically proficient suppliers.

Research into the buying structures of customer organisations must continue to supply information which provides, at the very minimum, a discussion topic to concentrate the minds of managers responsible for industrial marketing strategies. Dig it out and see if the findings can be used to probe your own methods of operation. If it does have some bearing, discuss how the information could be applied to the practice of one aspect or another of your marketing. If it does not apply, give it a healthy kick to one side – better that than ignoring it.

It would be inappropriate here to name specific articles but a number of major journals which regularly publish important research findings are listed below.

READING LIST

Industrial Marketing Management, Elsevier, New York.

Harvard Business Review.

European Journal of Marketing, MCB Ltd, Bradford, Yorks.

Industrial Marketing Digest, Haywards Heath, Sussex.

Marketing, 2 Lancaster Gate, London W2.

Quarterly Review of Marketing, Moor Hall, Cookham, Berks.

4

How professional services are bought

Evert Gummesson, Senior Management Consultant, Ekonomisk Före-tagsledning (EF)AB

WHO IS SELLING PROFESSIONAL SERVICES?

This chapter is concerned with professional services offered to industry and other organisations and is limited to producer services, as opposed to consumer services. The terms 'professional' and 'consultant' are used differently in different countries. To some readers the use of professional and professional service may seem strange, but those terms have been adopted rather than the more familiar 'consultant' and 'consulting service' because their use seems to prevail generally in marketing literature. A physician renders consumer services – he helps individuals – but a lawyer may restrict himself to providing either consumer or producer services, or he may do both. The groups of professionals which have been studied in particular are advertising agencies, public relations consultants, market research institutes, management consultants, consultants in the computer field, auditors, lawyers, architects and other consultants in the building and construction field and other areas of technology.

The conclusions presented here may also be of use and interest to other types of professionals. Among them, *public organisations,* for example, weather forecasting institutes, export and trade promotion authorities, central statistical bureaux and institutes that provide testing facilities of various kinds. Such bodies often have the capacity to undertake more work but do not market their services (some indeed put off potential customers by their rigid and unhelpful responses to inquiries). Similarly *trade associations* may offer a set of services to their members (often within the yearly fee) but could also provide tailor-made extras (even for non-members) at special fees.

Systems selling is becoming an important strategy for many firms who traditionally worked with single commodities. A system is a package composed of commodity products and related services. The services may to some extent be consultancy services concerning construction, management, training etc. Thus today, the *manufacturing firm* could also profit from a knowledge of professional service marketing.

IS PROFESSIONAL SERVICE MARKETING DIFFERENT FROM OTHER KINDS OF MARKETING?

Some people hold the view that marketing techniques are the same whatever the product may be: toothpaste, ocean tankers, cars, films . . . This, however, is a delusion that derives from the inability to distinguish between the general and the particular. The marketing philosophy – that all business should start from needs in the market – is general. Many ideas, concepts, models and theories are useful in all businesses. Market research models, segmentation, the meaning of brand image, buyer behaviour models etc. are all of value. However, each industry, each firm, each market has certain unique features which must be considered in the practical application of those concepts. Professional services have specific characteristics which influence their marketing:

1   A professional service is qualified, it is advisory and problem-solving, even though it may also encompass some routine work for clients.
2   The professionals involved have a common identity, as, for example, management consultants or lawyers, and such professionals are regulated by traditions and codes of ethics.
3   The service on offer, if accepted, involves the professional in taking on assignments for the client and those assingments are themselves the limit of the professional's involvement. Such assignments are not undertaken merely as overtures to

the generation of other business, as they are, for example, by banks.

In contrast to tangible products a service *cannot be stored, it cannot usually be standardised* and it is *often produced in interaction with the customer.*

IS MARKETING NECESSARY FOR PROFESSIONALS?

Professional service firms have, as compared to other types of firms, an obstacle to efficient marketing: in some professional groups, marketing is actively resisted; it is looked down upon and considered below the dignity of the professional man. The following three quotations illustrate how differently the marketing of consultancy can be interpreted and viewed:

1   The essence of the professional approach to acquiring business is that it should be allowed to come without being actively sought by the practitioner. (F.A.R. Bennion, *Professional Ethics*, London, 1969, p.132.)

2   A common belief is that the various codes of ethics in the professions are so restrictive in regard to marketing that marketing isn't done. On the contrary. *What the code means is that a different type of marketing is done.* Instead of giving explicit recognition to the marketing function, these practitioners have resorted to various obtuse devices, some of which show extreme sensitivity to the marketing problem. (Philip Kotler, *Marketing Management*, New Jersey, 1972, p.871.)

3   As professionals, possessing professional skills, we still have not only the requirement but the obligation of actively and energetically selling these skills. *They won't sell themselves!* We *have* to sell them. And if we have to sell them, it is better that we do so on a conscious, explicit basis rather than on an unconscious, implicit, hit or miss basis. (Warren J.Wittreich, *Selling – A Prerequisite to Success as a Professional,* Philadelphia, 1969, p.4.)

To the modern marketing man who has worked with both consumer and producer goods and also with the active marketing of management consultancy, the negative attitude to marketing is difficult to accept. Marketing orientation in the professional field is based on the following principles:

1　You do not automatically become known because you are skilled in your profession. A superior product does not sell itself – its advantages must be communicated to the market.
2　The client has imperfect information. It cannot be assumed that he will find what he needs without assistance.
3　It is not unethical or unworthy to express the advantages of a service of a professional man as long as the truth is told.

A professional firm which has a full workload today may not feel spontaneously the need for marketing; there is no direct need to go out and acquire new clients. However, marketing strategy considerations are always significant: which services should we offer the market ('our service line'), which types of clients shall we aim at ('segmentation'), what should our price level be, shall we prepare for growth, the establishment of new local offices, start up international operations, join another professional firm? These questions are a part of marketing as are analyses of the market, marketing planning and organisation. All these problems need constant or at least periodical consideration – when the professional firm is in trouble it is often too late to begin, the options within the available time scale are too few.

WHO SHOULD DO THE MARKETING?

Everybody in a firm who has contacts with a client performs marketing tasks. This is especially evident in service firms because services, as opposed to tangible products, are often produced together with the client. At one time the marketing of professional services was often handled exclusively by the directors of the firm. In times when competition is tougher another organisation model has to be used: everybody takes responsibility for attracting business. Why is this more efficient? The reasons are these:

1　The client prefers to negotiate the assignment with someone who is going to carry out the job.

2   Every professional, in the operation of the assignment, is in contact with clients and can then see new needs for assistance.
3   Social contact between the individual professional and the client is important: mutual understanding and trust, which are crucial for the long-term development of the firm, are fostered by the interaction of work and social relationships.
4   Every professional has contacts who can give him information on what is going on in the market. From his friends or from fellow members of associations he may learn of potential clients. This multitude of contacts cannot be achieved by a marketing director or some salesmen.

HOW DO CLIENTS ASSESS THE QUALITY OF THE SERVICE?

Quality is an elusive concept. *It can be concluded that the quality of a professional service is a subjective measure.* Assignments are assessed as producing only indirect, although positive effects and they are only one of several factors that influenced the situation of the client. In four cases that have been studied, the goals/results of the professionals' work were the following:

Case 1: Advertising agency. The client believed he would obtain more effective advertising and consequently increased revenue and/or decreased costs, thus improving his profitability.

Case 2: Management consultant. The client wished to remove a conflict that delayed work. The result was fewer disturbances in the organisation and increased motivation among its personnel.

Case 3 and 4: Construction engineers. Plans for new plants had to be made before they could be built. New plant was a prerequisite for more rational production which in turn would lead to increased return on investment.

Occasionally it is possible to specify the effects on profitability by assessing revenue increase, cost reduction or capital reduction or some combination of these that gives a net result which, compared with the initial state, shows an improvement. One such case is a cost reduction campaign organised by a management consultant. Another is a business lawyer helping his client to a favourable solution of a contract dispute. A consulting engineer may recommend a layout of a new plant that is economical both to build and to operate. However, the client will never know what he would have got using another professional.

What is assessed, by the use of intuition and rule of thumb, is the credibility of the professional, scrutinising his time plan, looking at reference assignments, judging his personality. It becomes a matter of a subjectively perceived quality. This is also influenced by the professional's ability to sell himself and to sell his results. *The customer of the professional service enterprise is buying confidence.*

DO NOT SELL – HELP THE CLIENT BUY!

Because it is difficult to assess the quality of the service, both beforehand and afterwards, the client feels uncertain and may react to *reduce his risk* in the following ways:

- (a) by remaining loyal to his existing suppliers of professional services, i.e. the stability of relations becomes important.
- (b) by making sure that others in the organisation are involved in the choice (large buying centre) so that he can feel secure and not be criticised.
- (c) by putting in extensive resources in time, people and costs in order to make sure he is buying the right professional.
- (d) by treating the problem as a gambler would and taking a chance.
- (e) by lowering his demands on the professional to well within a realistic level, thus increasing the chance of reaching expected results.

Buying can be classified according to the client's familiarity with the service he is buying. It could be a *new task,* a *straight rebuy* or a *modified rebuy.* If it is a new task his uncertainty may be great. It may also be less than it should be – in some cases the client does not understand the difficulties of buying professional services. In most cases the buying of professional services is a new task or a modified rebuy.

Thus it is important to find out if the prospect feels insecure about making his decision, what makes him insecure and how he attempts to reduce his insecurity. Help him to reduce his insecurity – that is an important need of the client.

In order to help a prospect buy the professional must be a skilled salesman. The *first* task for the salesman is to *find out the actual needs* of the client (which are not necessarily those he states initially). The *second* task is to *assess whether his firm is able to help*. The *third* task, then, is to *convince the prospect* that his firm should be given the job and to agree on the terms.

WHO MAKES THE BUYING DECISION?

The *buying centre* is the group of people who contribute in different roles to the final decision of selecting a professional. Five roles can be identified and one individual can play more than one of these roles.

The decider has the formal authority or informal power to make the final decision in selecting the professional. *Influencers* are those who influence the decision in some way, e.g. by special know-how on the subject. A product manager may influence the selection of an advertising agency while the marketing director is the decider. *The buyer* is the one who administers the purchase. Professional services are not usually bought by a purchasing department or a specialised buyer (an exception is often found in building and construction which affects consulting engineers). *The user* of the service may have important views on the selection, e.g. a management consultant may be working with the personnel in a certain department to reorganise for better efficiency. *The gate-keeper* may be a secretary who lets some professionals but not others get through to her boss, it may be a buyer who prefers to recommend some firms for the job whilst others are excluded at an initial stage.

The members in the buying centre interact. They are likely to have differences in the perception of reality and therefore conflicts may exist.These conflicts may be solved by different methods:

1   Local rationality: the decision is delegated to the unit most affected by it and its goal and evaluation is accepted.
2   Finding a satisfying solution rather than the optimal solution.
3   Different values or goals may be given priority on different occasions.
4   More information about the professionals is collected.

5   Persuasion: getting the others to accept your own view.
6   Politicking, i.e. various tricks, more or less unethical.

The individual members' predispositions, preferences and methods of making decisions affect the final outcome. The individuals have different personalities, experience of their role, motivation, cognition of the problem, expectations etc.

The professional should attempt to identify the members of the buying centre, the interaction between them, their strengths and weaknesses, their ways of resolving conflicts and the individual members' behaviour and attitudes. This may be difficult in practice but is worth working for.

HOW RATIONAL IS THE PROSPECT?

When the client feels a need for professional services he will start some kind of search process. This process can have a number of characteristics:

1   He turns to colleagues and friends and asks for advice.
2   He contacts one or several professional firms which he has heard of or read about in advertisements.
3   He interviews a number of professionals. He may pay a lot of attention to fees (which are easy to compare) rather than quality (which is difficult to assess).
4   He has attitudes which may or may not be based on fact: large professional firm is reliable, large firm has big overheads, local firm is cheaper etc.
5   He may try to get a picture of the total market of available professionals and rank them according to specific criteria. This, however, is usually both difficult and time-consuming.

What is clearly important, therefore, is to find out how the buyer obtains his information and what information may affect his decision-making.

Task variables are those directly associated with the selection of the right professional firm: its fees, time plans, resources etc. *Non-task variables* are the other factors that influence the purchase: the client likes an individual professional because they interrelate well, both play golf or come from the same part of the country. It may be the personality of the client or the professional: dynamic behaviour, calm, hard-working, his age etc.

Formerly one used to talk about rational and irrational (or emotional) variables. But what is rational and who is rational? Life consists of both logic and emotions and so does the purchase of professional services. There are some professionals who are extremely well aware of the existence of non-task variables and their significance, and others who seem to believe that task variables are the only ones that count (this is not uncommon among engineers). It is, however, a judicious balance: the professional can become socially too flexible and forget about his responsibility to solve the client's actual problem.

It follows from this that it is necessary to find out which variables are important to the buying centre. Remember that non-task variables are always there and are sometimes more important than task variables.

HOW TO DEVELOP MARKETING SKILLS – SOME FINAL ADVICE

If a professional service firm decides to improve marketing there are many roads open, depending of course on the resources the professionals want to use.

One way is for one person, the marketing manager (if there is one), or a professional who is temporarily assigned to the task, to make an inventory of existing ideas and suggest areas for improvement and action. His memo, marketing plan or presentation can then be discussed with the management team or a group of professionals. Another way is to analyse the firm's marketing in a series of small groups, at a marketing conference or seminar, and come up with lists of ideas and recommendations. This second method has advantages over the first: more ideas are likely to be generated and everybody gets involved from the beginning, thus facilitating decision making and implementation.

A marketing consultant may also be engaged to assist. It is then important that he works closely together with the professionals so that his recommendations become practical and accepted.

It is important for practitioners to understand some basic theory of marketing in order to become skilled marketers. This can be done through reading, attending marketing courses, arranging conferences etc.

To learn *sales techniques* properly it is necessary to combine various methods: training courses where film and TV are used, on-the-job training visiting clients together with professionals who are good salesmen, and practising on one's own. Reading books can be useful in order to understand the basic attitudes and techniques of good salesmanship.

Little has been written directly on professional service marketing, but ideas could be derived from several other areas of marketing such as general marketing management, industrial marketing, systems selling, organisational buying behaviour, sales techniques and marketing audit. From these areas one can select models and advice which one finds pertinent to one's own situation.

Finally, here is a selection of modern articles and books on service marketing which could inspire the professional to develop his marketing ability.

READING LIST

P. Eiglier, et al, *Marketing Consumer Services: New Insights,* Marketing Science Institute (MSI), Cambridge, USA, 1977.

C. Grönroos, 'A Service Orientated Approach for Marketing of Services', *European Journal of Marketing,* no. 8, 1978.

C. Grönroos, 'An applied Theory for Marketing Industrial Services', *Industrial Marketing Management,* No. 1, 1979.

E. Gummesson, 'Toward a Theory of Professional Service Marketing', *Industrial Marketing Management,* vol. 7, no. 2, April 1978.

E. Gummesson, *Models of Professional Service Marketing,* Marknadstekniskt Centrum (MTC)/Liber, Box 6501, S-113 83 Stockholm, Sweden, 1979.

E. Gummesson, 'The Marketing of Professional Services – An organisational Dilemma', *European Journal of Marketing,* vol. 13, no. 5, 1979.

L. Shostack, 'Breaking Free from Product Marketing', *Journal of Marketing,* April 1977.

A. Wilson, *The Marketing of Professional Services,* McGraw-Hill, London, 1972.

A. Wilson, *Professional services and the marketplace,* Marknadstekniskt Centrum (MTC), Box 6501, S-113 83 Stockholm, Sweden, 1975.

5

International aspects of marketing

Leslie Walsh, Sundridge Park Management Centre, Bromley, Kent

Marketing is marketing the world over. The concepts and techniques discussed throughout this book will hold good whether you are in Cleethorpes, Cape Town or Katmandu. Those techniques, however, are necessarily adapted to particular markets, particular industries and particular geographical regions. Typically, the differences *between* nations – differences in economic and technological development, in culture and social structure, in political and legal systems, and in business customs and practices – are much more significant than regional differences *within* any one country. It is these fundamental differences, and their effect on marketing policy, that justify a separate treatment of the international aspects of marketing. It is with these special international aspects, and in particular with considerations of international marketing strategy, that this chapter is concerned.

When a company contemplates marketing abroad, or expanding its existing international activities, it is faced with five major decisions:

(a) the international marketing decision, the fundamental decision on whether or not to market abroad, or whether to expand (or contract) its international operations;

(b) the market-selection decision, determination of the markets to enter (or withdraw from);

(c) the market-entry decision, determination of the most appropriate method of access to new markets (e.g. direct export, licensing, local manufacture);

(d) the marketing-mix decision, planning a marketing mix

appropriate to the selected markets;
(e)   the organisation decision, determining the appropriate organisation structures and staffing levels.

These are not, of course, once-and-for-all decisions. They should be regularly reviewed, perhaps annually at the time of preparation of the company marketing plans.

THE INTERNATIONAL MARKETING DECISION

Some companies begin, or extend, their international operations almost accidentally, perhaps as a result of an approach from potential customers or would-be agents. A marketing policy and organisation then gradually develop, often in haphazard fashion. The results in profit terms are often not at all unsatisfactory, but they will usually be sub-optimal, while sometimes mistakes in the early stages can give rise to expensive complications in the longer term.

The international marketer must plan logically, step by step, with one eye on the current situation and the other on the possible future implications of his actions. Very many reasons can be, and are, adduced for marketing abroad, such as the national interest, the need for growth, or possibly prestige, but logically the only valid justification for any international activity is that profit opportunities, at least in the reasonably foreseeable future, are greater than those at home, either because they are in themselves especially attractive or because there is a general lack of profit opportunity in the home market.

That, of course, is a statement of the obvious; yet, paradoxically, it cannot be stated too often, particularly in relation to abandonment of markets once profitable but now no longer holding out any hope of long-term or short-term profit. Cutting one's losses is always a painful process, but particularly so, it seems, in international marketing.

THE MARKET-SELECTION DECISION

There are companies which can successfully market their products in most countries of the world. Those products are more or less standardised and, apart from necessary changes to allow for differences of language or available distribution facilities, marketing programmes can also be standardised. Such products might include jeans, pop records or, in the industrial field, high-technology items. A homogeneous market exists and undifferentiated marketing is possible.

Such markets, however, are open to very few companies. For most, either product or marketing programmes or both need to be adapted to suit the particular country, or group of countries, at which the company is directing its efforts. There are companies that can sustain a differentiated marketing approach in perhaps thirty, forty, fifty or more countries. But they will usually be the large multinationals.

For many other companies, an attempt to cover so many markets will usually mean that any attempt at a genuine marketing operation will quickly degenerate into haphazard selling, into the old-style export bagman selling to, but not through, distributors, with little knowledge of what happens to his product when it leaves their hands and even less time to find out. There is evidence that a very large number of UK companies are still falling into this fundamental error. The Barclays Bank report [1] for instance, came to the conclusion that:

> The most frequent danger in market policy is a dispersal of effort. A distinguishing feature of French companies is their tendency to sell to fewer markets than the British. This applies even more to German companies. There can be little doubt that the wisdom of this policy has a lot to do with their success. The concept of concentration, whilst not a panacea for solving the problems of exporting companies, can be a valuable principle.

If we are to concentrate our marketing effort, we must, of course, concentrate on those markets offering the greatest profit opportunity. How, among all the markets of the world, can we be sure that we have selected those that are the most profitable? Will not the research task ahead of us be hopelessly uneconomic?

---

1 'The Barclays Bank Report on Export Development in France, Germany and the United Kingdom: Factors for International Success', prepared by ITI Research for the BOTB, London Chamber of Commerce & Industry and Barclays Bank International, January 1979.

The answer is, not really. Some significant research expenditure will be required, of course, but much can be achieved by relatively inexpensive desk research, much of it quite satisfactorily undertaken in the UK. Initially all markets likely to offer potential should be considered; the less suitable markets can be eliminated in successive stages; the remaining few markets can then probably be ranked in some reasonable order of priority for the more expensive field research in the market country. Some systematic desk research process will be required, (see Chapter 9), while the starting point for all inquiries will, of course, be the Statistics and Market Intelligence Library.[2] Export market research may be funded in part by government grants under the Export Market Research Scheme.[3]

THE MARKET-ENTRY DECISION

For market entry the choice lies between indirect or direct export (see Figure 5.1)[4] and manufacture abroad on either a joint-venture or an independent basis (see Figure 5.2).[4] That choice is often critical to the success of an operation and demands the most detailed evaluation of all alternative routes in every specific case.

Indirect export

As a long-term operation, indirect export is perhaps more suited to the small exporter or to the less important markets. Nevertheless, most companies would do well to investigate the services offered by the seven or eight hundred UK export houses, which are believed to handle perhaps 20 per cent of the nation's export trade. These export houses have developed not only close market contacts in specific countries but also expertise in specialist fields such as barter trading. A list of export houses and their specialisms is given in the *Directory*

---

2   Statistics and Market Intelligence Library, Export House, Ludgate Hill, London

3   BOTB Export Market Research Scheme, Export House, Ludgate Hill, London.

4   Adapted, with permission, from *International Marketing* by L.S. Walsh. © Macdonald & Evans Ltd, Plymouth, 1978.

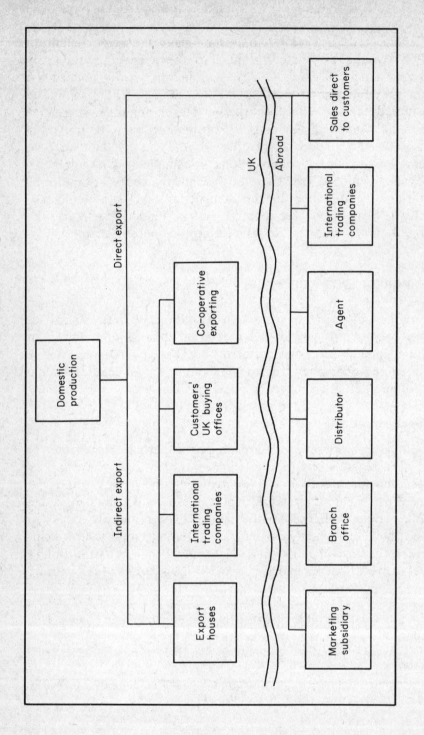

Figure 5.1 Distribution channels between nations (direct and indirect export): principal alternatives

of British Export Houses. [5]There are also other methods of indirect exporting.

International trading companies are highly diversified and large-scale manufacturers and merchants whose origins lie in the early days of colonial expansion. They are of particular importance in South-east Asia and the former African colonial territories, where their influence makes them particularly attractive as potential distributors. Trading companies are also to be found in several other countries, notably France and, of course, Japan.

Some overseas governments, and many of the world's major department stores and mail-order houses, maintain their own buying offices or purchase agents in London. A complete list can be obtained from the BOTB.[6]

Cooperative export marketing is perhaps better known as 'piggy-back exporting': under such an arrangement a major exporting company uses its established overseas marketing and distribution network to carry another manufacturer's complementary, but not competing, lines. The BOTB has organised an exporter's register for UK manufacturers interested in this approach.

Direct export

Using an agent is the easy way to export: the exporter obtains the services of an experienced local national, often with invaluable local contacts, at negligible investment cost. Results in terms of a few initial sales may well be immediate and congratulations all round seem in order. But is an agency the right way to exploit the market in the long term? Is it the right channel through which to conduct a marketing, as opposed to a mere selling, operation? The BOTB believes it has discerned a growing tendency among British exporters to go it alone, to set up branch offices or marketing subsidiaries.

Though often referred to as an agent, a distributor is, of course, a customer; he has been defined as a customer who has been granted exclusive or preferential rights to purchase and re-sell a range of products or services. The danger here is that the exporter too often

---

5   *Directory of British Export Houses,* British Export Houses Association, 69 Cannon St, London EC5N 5AB.
6   British Overseas Trade Board, 1 Victoria St, London SW1H 0ET.

regards him as only that, considering his own task complete when he has made the sale to the distributor. It is, as already mentioned, important to sell not so much *to* as *through* a distributor. The so-called 'whole-channel concept', the careful planning of the whole chain of distribution from manufacturer right through to end user, is just as relevant to the exporter as to the domestic marketer.

Overseas manufacture

Overseas manufacture may take any of the forms set out in Figure 5.2. It should be borne in mind that in very many countries a company establishing an assembly or manufacturing subsidiary may be eligible for significant cash grants, tax holidays and the like, often from different sources – say, national, regional and municipal. In some countries it is by no means a simple matter to locate all sources of financial assistance; thorough inquiry is essential.

Many of the alternatives suggested in Figure 5.2 are joint ventures, involving at least some degree of association with an organisation abroad. In *any* joint venture there is an inherent conflict of interest: each partner will inevitably wonder whether his reward is really proportionate to his efforts. Disagreements are yet more likely, however, in an international joint venture, simply as a result of national differences in culture, business practice and management styles, or possibly from inadequate communications. A licensing, franchising or other joint venture must therefore endeavour to cover all eventualities that might reasonably be expected to give rise to differences of opinion. For instance, in a joint-venture manufacturing operation, fruitful sources of friction are dividend policies, transfer prices of components from parents to the joint-venture subsidiary, and export sales from the joint venture to third countries to which the parent organisations may already be exporting.

THE MARKETING-MIX DECISION

In a short chapter such as this no attempt can be made to cover every aspect of the international marketing mix. All that can be done is to highlight some points of importance and perhaps draw attention to certain danger signals.

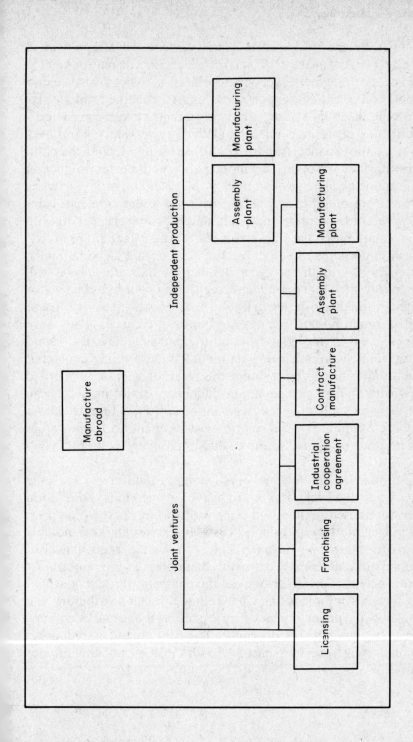

Figure 5.2   Distribution channels between nations (manufacture abroad): principal alternative channels

For instance, the UK exporter is often criticised for failing to meet the special product needs of his markets. The criticism may be valid in certain cases, though one wonders whether the critics always realise that marketing, including export marketing, is concerned with satisfying customer needs at a profit. The exporter must take a considered – and difficult – decision, comparing likely improvements in turnover and profit if the product is modified with, on the other hand, the often very significant costs of product modification and shorter production runs. Examples can be given of remarkable sales and profit increases resulting from modification in line with the needs of a particular market; yet some exporters may legitimately be concerned more with finding a market that has a *genuine* need for their standard product.

Just as important as the right product is a *name* for a good product. Around the world there are a number of individuals who will endeavour to filch that good name, registering your brand name for themselves and then offering to let you have it back – at a price. These so-called 'brand pirates' are a serious enough menace; much more insidious, and in the long-run more damaging, are the brand imitators, those who cash in on your reputation by offering similar but markedly inferior products under the same or very similar brand names, with similar packaging and labelling. Brand imitation can easily go undetected for years. Registration and use of brand names is not in itself enough; active efforts must be made to locate offenders.The price of a good international brand name is eternal vigilance.

Export marketing offers real opportunities for differential pricing, for charging what each market will bear. Yet even today some companies still quote one standard price world-wide, apart from differences in freight, duty and similar costs. In certain markets, notably commodities, they may have no choice. In most markets, however, such companies are simply depriving themselves of the opportunity to make increased profit, or to meet the competition. A serious, but far from rare, symptom is that when selling through distributors, you do not know the prices at which they are selling to the end customers. You may be sure that your distributor is getting the full market price. Are you getting your fair share? Or is he making a killing at your expense?

ORGANISING FOR EXPORT MARKETING

However many local sales offices you have, if your export operation is of any significance you will almost certainly be operating somewhere in the world through distributors or agents. It is almost platitudinous to emphasise the need for regular market visits, consistently by the same executive. Exporting is people, and you must staff up to the profit potential of the market so that you can exploit it fully.

What matters even more is what that executive does when he is there. Suppose, for instance, you are marketing a consumer product. Do you have a glad-handing salesman dropping in for a few days, calling on a few of the retail outlets, and motivating the distributor with a few encouraging noises? Or do you have a highly-trained marketer sitting down with the distributor and the local advertising agency to prepare some detailed marketing plans, based on facts and, where necessary, some careful market research? You cannot afford the latter? The sales potential cannot justify it? Then we are back to the question of whether you should be in the market at all. Perhaps you should, after all, be concentrating on fewer markets.

READING LIST

An introductory text: L.S. Walsh, *International Marketing*, Macdonald & Evans Ltd, 1978.

More extensive works: P.R. Cateora and J.M. Hess, *International Marketing*, Irwin.
G.E. Miracle and G.S. Albaum, *International Marketing Management*, Irwin.
Vern Terpstra, *International Marketing*, Holt, Rinehart and Winston.

6

Marketing to the middleman

Edward Walker, Consultant to the Forest Industries

Marketing to the consumer and to the retailer is already highly developed, often highly efficient and well documented. In comparison, marketing to the middleman is poorly developed and little has been written on the subject. Yet wholesalers, distributors, merchants and other types of middlemen play a vital role in the distribution of many products. More careful attention to the selection of middlemen and their continuing motivation by high standards of marketing can yield benefits to manufacturers out of all proportion to the effort and money involved.

THE CHANGING ROLE OF THE MIDDLEMAN

The role of the middleman varies from product to product and in many areas it is changing rapidly. In some industries the trend is to by-pass the middleman and distribute directly to the end-user, or retailer. But this is not always possible or even desirable; the middleman supplies the essential local stockholding and has the ability to serve many small customers that not even the largest manufacturing groups can afford. Excellent examples include cash and carry wholesalers serving small retailers and caterers; builders' merchants; electrical goods' wholesalers serving both the trade and retail outlets; timber merchants; paper merchants; and office supplies stockists.

 In these and other areas the structure of the middleman's business of wholesaling is changing radically. A number of large, powerfully backed national groups have been created and many smaller wholesalers have banded together to form independent buying associations. This rationalisation of trade will continue in the future, and will be encouraged by manufacturers adopting new policies of selective distribution which will increase the number of mergers within the trade.

The wholesaling trade is at present in a period of transition, gradually evolving more professional operational methods and changing its image from the 'superfluous' middleman to the aggressive marketer, thereby offering a key service. No longer will wholesalers immediately stock anything which is put on the market, even by their main suppliers, largely because profit margins have shrunk and the economy has contracted. Again, clear division is springing up between wholesalers who provide the market with a broad range of goods and a number of more specialised wholesalers who supply certain goods to specific categories of customer. This trend towards selective distributorship can also be expected to continue as more wholesalers act as importers and general distributors for Continental EEC firms.

WHOLESALERS EXPAND SALESFORCES

As more business goes direct or through manufacturer-owned outlets, the wholesaler has at last begun to look at ways of improving his efficiency by overhauling his stock control and general accounting and by rationalising and concentrating his product lines. The high cost of funding stocks is encouraging this rationalisation. Wholesalers are also taking a more positive approach to selling by expanding their own sales forces – a measure which is proving most effective, particularly where industrial or commercial buyers are concerned. The larger wholesaling groups have introduced the more sophisticated management techniques of their parent companies, whilst the smaller have turned to their trade associations for education, advice and training.

Inevitably the recent changes in wholesaling have created new problems for wholesalers which must be solved if they are to survive in the years ahead. Some of the problems facing wholesalers in many areas include:

(a) the mounting conflict between the traditional role of universal provider and the new role of selective stockist;

(b) the increasing complexity of products handled and the consequent requirement for product and application knowledge;

(c) the emergence of new competitive distribution systems and the resultant pressure on margins;

(d) the high costs of funding stockholdings and trade debtors;

(e) the prevalence of old, unsuitable and badly operated premises, and

(f) the difficulty in securing and keeping adequate managerial staff.

The new attitude of wholesalers towards manufacturers can be summarised as 'growth and profit through partnership between supplier and wholesaler'. Wholesalers want suppliers to look upon them as partners in a joint enterprise, where the suppliers are doing the manufacturing and the wholesalers are doing the stocking, selling and distribution on their behalf. Wholesalers do not like to be regarded merely as customers, but see themselves as a vital link in a chain which ends with the manufacturer's wares being delivered at the right time, to the right place at the right price.

For successful distribution through wholesalers or other types of middlemen, manufacturers must take far more account of this growing desire for partnership. As in any other type of business relationship there are two important prerequisites for success. The first is to select the right partner: wholesaler, distributor or merchant. The second need is to motivate the middleman to work with and for you, and this means high standards of marketing by your company.

SELECTING THE RIGHT MIDDLEMAN

Far too often, biggest is assumed to mean best when manufacturers select wholesalers or distributors. Although sheer size may have many attractions, it is not always the biggest organisations that are best qualified to act as distributors for specialised products. A disciplined approach is required in the selection of middlemen, and a straightforward but highly effective two-stage approach to the problem is readily available. It can be used equally well in export markets as in domestic markets.

The first step involves an audit of possible middlemen with the aim of narrowing down the list to those most likely to be suitable. Answers are needed to a number of basic questions which are listed below. The questions can and should be answered readily by any middleman who is keen to gain new accounts.

Basic questions on middlemen

1 What is the annual turnover of the organisation, and more specifically what is its turnover of products similar to those you want to sell?
2 Which competitive products are stocked?
3 What stockholding facilities are available and where are they located?
4 What selling and distributive facilities does the middleman possess?
5 How profitable is the middleman? This gives a good indication of the middleman's own business ability and stability.
6 How many potential customers does the middleman already serve and what success has been achieved in selling to the more important of them?
7 What terms are sought and what guarantees of turnover can be given?

Answers to these basic questions typically narrow down the list of potential middlemen on either a regional or national basis. All too often it is found that the middleman who sells himself best to potential suppliers is in practice the least well equipped to provide even rudimentary services, let alone devise or participate in imaginative marketing and promotional campaigns.

The second and critical step is to establish how the short-listed middle-men are viewed in the market place. This can only be done by careful interviewing of a sample of potential buyers of the product concerned, on a national or regional basis. Interviews should concentrate on rating the short-listed middlemen for a number of key aspects of their activities.

Market rating the middleman

1 How well known is he to existing and potential customers for the product?
2 With which products and suppliers is he currently associated?
3 How frequently do his sales representatives call on customers?
4 How regular and how reliable are his deliveries?
5 How knowledgeable is he about not only his suppliers' products but also about his customers' needs?
6 How efficient are his order taking, despatch and invoicing procedures?
7 How enthusiastic is he to win business and meet customers' special needs? How helpful are his catalogues, sales literature and advertising.

Only when these and several similar questions have been answered is a manufacturer armed with all the information he needs to select the most suitable distributor for his products. Only through careful and independent interviewing of buyers and potential buyers can accurate answers be obtained.

Motivating the middleman

The aim of marketing to the middleman should be to provide him with the continuing motivation to promote actively and sell your products in preference to those of your competitors. An active middleman working on your behalf can do much more than just meet the 'pull demand' created by your own promotion. He can, and must, create new business for you if the relationship is to yield optimum returns to all parties. Too few manufacturers devote funds to investigating ways of helping and motivating their distributors.

Even fewer firms have a 'marketing audit' conducted to find out what their distributors really think of them! Middlemen are not motivated by any one single factor – least of all by the size of discount or commission that they receive. Typically, it is the combination of product, service, financial and promotional factors (often but not always linked to exclusivity on a regional or national basis) that motivates the middleman. It is the marketing man's responsibility to ensure that the package is as attractive as possible, is honoured by the supplier, and is kept continually up to date to meet the changing needs of the market.

Once again market research can help identify those aspects of the supplier's package which are of most importance to the middleman and which, correctly structured, will ensure that middlemen are motivated to give maximum support. The techniques used involve interviewing, but this time of middlemen themselves. A structured sample of distributors is asked to rate various aspects of manufacturers' products and service. Such research clearly identifies which factors need most attention in motivating the middleman.

Confidential interviews can then go on to probe how well current suppliers meet distributors' requirements for each feature. The improvements needed in the suppliers's package can be identified, as well as the priority that should be accorded to meeting them. Much can be learnt about how well the competition performs in the eyes of middlemen, giving leads on good points to be followed and failings to be avoided or corrected. New motivational ideas can be tested and a free flow of communication established.

Motivation check list

Product features:

> Profit to the middleman
> Product technical design
> Completeness of range
> Price
> Packaging
> Labelling
> Product appearance

Service features:

> Supplier's loyalty to the middleman
> Rebates/discounts
> Exclusivity arrangements
> Reliability of delivery
> Office efficiency

Protection from inventory loss through obsolescence
Protection from price changes
Technical advice and service
Sales leads
Efficient complaint and enquiry handling
Special promotions
Sharing distributors' sales and promotional costs on an equitable basis
Advice on stock control and management techniques
Efficient product familiarisation training

Communications and promotions:

Quality, presentation and information content of catalogues and leaflets
Representatives
Usefulness of direct mail material
Exhibitions
Trade and consumer advertising
Regular checks on distributors' unvoiced complaints about either products, service or support

A check list of features which must be covered in this style of research is given above. All require attention by companies wishing to get the most out of their distributors. For the marketing man there are four key features needing attention.

The product and product range

For the distributor to do his job efficiently he must be convinced that the product and product range is correct for the market that he must serve. Outdated products or a limited product range restrict the distributor's potential market and make his job more difficult.

Distributorship agreements

If the middleman is to put effort into selling your products, he must be assured that his efforts will not be nullified by competition from the supplier's own direct selling operations, or by the activities of competitive stockists of the same product. The terms of agreement on these matters must be spelt out carefully and be seen to be fair to the distributor. He must know which accounts will be served directly by the manufacturer's own sales force and preferably given exclusivity in stocking and selling within agreed areas. Discounts and rebates should be at a level to yield the middleman an adequate margin to allow him to carry sufficient stocks and devote proper selling attention to the product.

Availability of the product

Whilst there are examples of non-stocking merchants (in the paper trade for example), it is typically the middleman's job to carry stocks. It is also the manufacturer's responsibility to ensure that fresh supplies are available and that the middleman is never left out-of-stock, particularly after a successful advertising or promotional campaign. It is now quite usual for manufacturers to commission regular surveys of wholesalers' and distributors' stock levels in parallel with forward demand forecasts.

Back-up services

Here are included technical advice and service, promotional support, provision of sales leads, help with market research and advice on stock control and management techniques. Once appointed, the distributor must receive continuing support from his suppliers if a true partnership is to develop. It is the marketing man's responsibility to ensure that support is adequate, effective and continuous. Work in this area has shown that too few manufacturers offer intensive product familiarisation courses for distributors' salesmen. This is particularly necessary for new salesmen joining a distributor, and when the manufacturer produces a new line.

An increasingly important role

Frustration borne out of disappointment with middlemen's efforts has encouraged too many manufacturers to incur the additional costs of direct distribution. But carefully selected and properly understood and motivated, the middleman can play an increasingly important role. It is time marketing management recognised this role and devoted more efforts to motivating the middleman, to understanding his problems and, above all, to investigating his reasons for not giving his whole-hearted support.

7

Marketing to retailers

Eric Morgan, Managing Director, British American Cosmetics Ltd

For several years after the war, marketing men liked to think that the retailer did not matter. They saw him as an almost mechanical channel of distribution whose only purpose was to allow the wise and seductive manufacturer to make contact with happy and persuaded consumers. Provided that goods were pushed into retail distribution, the marketing man's skills would pull them through into consumption. Some retailers contributed to this image of the effortless middleman, but the picture was really created by the expansive economic conditions in which almost any goods sold readily. It coincided with a period of greatly increased marketing awareness and training, and the recruitment of self-confident young men who were encouraged to be aggressive.

SIGNIFICANCE OF THE RETAILER

Times have changed. We have forgotten what expansion was like; most of our markets are actually declining in volume, although inflation in selling prices gives a spurious impression of growth. Competition is much more severe among manufacturers and among retailers – and some of the retailers have become part-time manufacturers, too. Consumers are far better educated about products and spend their money with more discrimination; they expect, and get, great freedom of choice. High inflation, together with shortages of cash and credit, forces the retailer to be more discriminating about his purchases;

61

inventory control has become a major concern of his business.

Many retailers are now running bigger businesses than they used to do and the professional manager can count as well as anyone else. All this has forced the significance of the retailer back upon us. It could be objected that he is still the effortless middleman, who is now the victim of circumstances instead of being their beneficiary, but this would be condescending and inaccurate. We can see that many retailers are very good indeed at understanding their customers, providing what they need and helping them to enjoy it. This calls for a new response from the marketing man.

ECONOMIC FLUCTUATIONS

Selling-in, once again, really matters – and very often it is not easy. Economic restrictions alone ensure that retailers will wish to buy smaller quantities and to restrict their inventory to lines which really sell through quickly. One of the most dramatic examples was seen in Venezuela, in the winter of 1979/80; after nearly three years of rigid price controls, restrictions were suddenly removed and prices shot up by 30 per cent. Retailers quickly ran out of money. The cost of borrowing was increased and credit was controlled, so they could not borrow money. Manufacturers also found it difficult to borrow. So purchasing was forced to slow down or stop altogether, as retailers liquidated their stocks. Best-selling lines went out of stock first, but the retailer did not re-order because he now had a chance to get rid of slow-moving items and turn them into cash. Eventually the retailer could start to buy again and, if he was sensible, he concentrated on best-selling lines and allowed the slower ones simply to go out of distribution.

The Venezuelan example was extreme, but something like it has gone on in many other countries, including Britain. The outcome is probably healthy, so long as consumers themselves do not run out of purchasing power. The retailer needs to sell his old stock at the new higher prices. This is not profiteering; it is the only way he can collect the money that he needs in order to purchase new stock. But if the state of the market is competitive and depressed, he may not be able to raise prices as much as he should.

This happened to retail jewellers in early 1980, when the price of gold had more than doubled. For many weeks retailers continued to sell their stock at the old prices because they simply could not sell it at all if they put their prices up to the new replacement price of gold. As this did not make sense either, the business virtually came to a halt. Some jewellers simply stopped buying, locked up their stocks and waited for the madness to subside. Fortunately for the jewellers, they had other things to sell, but the specialist manufacturer of gold articles was in serious difficulties.

PITFALLS OF EXCESSIVE DISTRIBUTION

The manufacturer must sell-in, that is obvious enough, but the selection of his customers is not so easy. Let us dispose of the idea that you do better if you sell to more and more retailers – you do not. The reason is clear. Markets are not indefinitely expandable. Once consumers can find the goods readily, and these goods are pleasantly offered with adequate ranges of choice, it is unreasonable to expect that consumer purchasing will increase further just because more retailers compete with each other for the market. Why should it? At some point distribution must reach its optimum.

This optimum might call for 200,000 outlets for baked beans or detergent, but it might be only 20 outlets for Rolls Royce. If you go beyond this optimum number, you simply reduce the amount sold by each retailer, so giving him a poorer income on your goods. He will be disenchanted with you. His stock will become stale. Excitement fails: consumers are turned off. The magic disappears. Several retailers then stop selling these over-exposed goods – probably sending their unsold stocks back to the manufacturer or, at least, refusing to pay for them until they are sold out. Such an exercise does nobody any good. Distribution can, of course, be inadequate but, once it has been built up to a satisfactory extent, any further extension is counter productive.

Selling excessive quantities to the retailer is similarly self defeating. It does not guarantee that he will make special efforts to sell your brands in order to eliminate the burden of high stocks. It might do this in some cases, but it is just as likely to result in a number of other, disagreeable situations. Some of your stock will go stale. Some will sit in the stock room and remind the retailer not to buy any more from you. Meanwhile he resents the trouble you are causing him and so he becomes a bad payer. You convince him that your brand does not sell well – he will return it to you, if he can get away with it. Alternatively, he may try to move the stock by means of drastic price cuts or other bargain offers. This may be harmful to the image and prestige of your brand and it will certainly be irritating to competing retailers who bought your brand from you in good faith, at normal prices. Such results are clearly undesirable. 'Adversary' positions like this should be avoided; they do not succeed, and they represent an awful way to live. It is much better to make your interests coincide with the interests of your retail customers; then both can prosper and enjoy it.

A NEW PERSPECTIVE ON SALES

Do let us understand what 'prosper' means. It is about money in the absolute. People do not live on percentages; a retailer makes money because he buys, sells at a profit, buys again, sells again at a profit and so on. He cannot buy more than he can afford, but the faster he re-sells his stock, the faster he can re-purchase and make another round of profits. The more he does this, the more money he makes. He invests the money in stock and he needs his stock to turn over as frequently as possible.

'Turnover' is interestingly ambiguous in English English; The Americans use it much better and do not make it synonymous with 'sales'. They use it to mean the number of times that stock turns over in a given period. The sales of a brand in a department store might be $100,000 per year, with a turnover of 6; this means that every two months, on average, the store sells its total stock of $16,700 worth of the brand. If everything could be controlled perfectly, the store would never hold stocks of the brand in excess of the $16,700 and just as it sold the last item, at the end of the two month period, it would take in a new delivery.

The Americans have another useful term – 'open to buy'. This means the investment which the store is willing to make in the inventory of a given manufacturer. Clearly, it is in the manufacturer's interest to manage this 'open to buy', so that it is invested in brands that sell well, because the manufacturer will then make new sales to top up the inventory, back to the 'open to buy' figure. By contrast, if the manufacturer made a sale which used up all the 'open to buy' but did so with products which did not sell through to the consumer, then no further sale to the retailer would be possible because there would be no 'open to buy' available. This concept is obviously different from the alternative of a monthly allocation of purchasing funds. 'Open to buy' is a superior concept because it relates the retailer's new purchases to the sales made by him; it ensures that the company which has done well can have a good chance of continuing to do well. It is just another example of 'To him that hath shall be given' – a principle which is much in evidence in retailing.

'Open to buy' has an interesting dampening effect on price changes. Sales managers normally can do the simplest arithmetic when they forecast the effects of a price increase; once they have decided whether or not to assume any reduction in the unit volume of sales, they just apply the new price to the agreed volume, and the value of the sales is found. (If there is no change in unit volume – and in times of inflation, we have seen price increases have much less effect on volume than they used to have – the amount of the price increase simply 'falls to the bottom line', which is to say that it represents precisely the resultant increase in profits.) However, under an 'open to buy' system, the total amount of money available for the inventory of the manufacturer's products is fixed until the date when the store next reviews it, probably in several months' time. Therefore, as the manufacturer sells in new stock, he can only sell in fewer units at a higher price, than had been sold out at the old price. This is an automatic volume restriction which has nothing to do with any reluctance that there might be, on the part of consumers, to buy at the new price.

All these ideas, and the tougher times that have brought them about, are quite good for us. They force us to think about what is really happening to sales and how money is really being made to work. It is self defeating, as we have seen, for salesmen to pump more and more stock into more and more retail outlets. It is similarly pointless for retailers to demand higher and higher profit margins and special discounts. The manufacturer cannot afford them. He has to live, too, and is subject to the same economic difficulties as his retail customer.

It behoves us, rather, to concentrate on moving the goods through to consumption. Let us build a franchise of interested retailers and loyal consumers. The whole cycle makes sense when consumers come back to repurchase, the retailer resells to them; the retailer repurchases and the manufacturer resells to him; the manufacturer remanufactures and repurchases materials. This enables the manufacturer to be more economic and so he prospers and offers a better deal to his customers. This pleases retailer and consumer alike and everyone benefits. The most dramatic example of this mechanism has been provided by electronic calculators, which now cost one-tenth of their price a few years ago and are now owned by almost everyone in the population. It looks as though microwave ovens are starting to move in the same direction.

INSIDE THE SHOP

In view of this need for fast and efficient turnover, it is not surprising that so much emphasis is put on activity inside the shop. This is not to say that all the activity is well thought through or is beneficial – there is nonsense among in-store activities, just as there is among TV advertisements. There are always very many ways of doing any good job badly. But display work has been studied for decades and is known to be extremely helpful. It is not particularly profound but is nonetheless true that a shopper is more likely to buy brand X if she can see it, if it looks nice, if the presentation is relevant to her and if she believes that she is offered value for money. So, merchandising demands that we know where to put brand X: into the right shop; into the right place in that shop; and on the gondola where your competitors are (ideally at the right height for easy vision and handling, in good light, where most of the people pass by, etc.) We cannot all put all our brands into just this ideal spot, but we must try. After all, some of our competitors are not paying attention and are not even attempting to compete for this space, while others are too weak to insist. 'To him that hath shall be given' applies in this respect too. The manufacturer with the most 'muscle' is the one whose products are the most important to the retailer; he is apt to demand special cooperation and privileges in the store, and he is likely to get them. Some people object that this merely makes the big bigger and that it restricts competition, but you can hardly blame the retailer for wanting to help the manufacturer whose goods produce the most profit. It is a fact of life and one which means that you should be concerned to be strong in those outlets which carry your goods; it is better to be important to your retailer than to be in widespread distribution with minimised sales per outlet.

INCENTIVES TO THE RETAILER

So there is competition among manufacturers for the support and good will of the retailer. Your scheme to promote your brand to the consumer may need, itself, to be promoted if it is to get into distribution at all. The old way was to give a bonus of money to the retailer. Later this switched to a bonus in goods. Then came personal incentives for the girls who actually sold the goods to the public. Then came more business oriented incentives, such as extended credit or consignment payment terms. Finally, perhaps, we see that the professional retail manager is offered answers to his particular problems. He does not want too much stock to occupy too much space but he does want rapid turnover (in the American sense). He is likely to feel cooperative towards promotions which sell substantial quantities during a limited period of time. This helps him to solve his problems. It also enables him to fit more promotions into the space which he has available in his store and in his calendar, and this makes him more competitive versus other retailers.

Other chapters in this handbook deal with planning what the promotional activity itself should be. There is a wide choice to suit different economic and competitive circumstances. Some promotions are just what they seem; a cut price offer, for example, is the simplest attempt to persuade consumers to buy this brand rather than another (or to buy larger quantities of it or to buy it sooner than one otherwise would). Other promotions appear to have one purpose but actually have another. The offer of a very expensive, mail-in premium, for instance may really be a dramatic vehicle for impressive display in the shop, while masquerading as a consumer offer. Some promotional offers have forgotten what they are for (such as the 'gift with purchase' when the gift is irrelevant to the purchased product and possibly even irrelevant to the purchaser). But no matter what the promotion, the retailer's cooperation is needed, and we all must realise that this is not automatically obtained. We have to be able to think in the retailer's terms, to be concerned about his problems and to find solutions to them if we hope to procure his participation and help in the promotion of our brands.

There are some other motivators which almost amount to 'licences to trade'. The most obvious – and the most abused – is cooperative advertising. The idea is that manufacturers and retailers share the cost of advertising the brand and also advertising the store where the brand may be found. Often the message in the advertisement is simply that brand X is on special offer at the specified store, and retailer and manufacturer naturally share the cost of the advertising between them. In practice, this can well prove to be an expensive disappointment. For instance, the manufacturer's 50 per cent contribution can be calculated on the worst rate (the single insertion price) of the newspaper or other medium concerned, whereas the retailer gets large quantity discounts from the medium, based on the total of all his advertising. Some retailers put more than one brand in the advertisement and if unwary manufacturers each pay 50 per cent the retailer is almost printing money. Obviously, a little caution can prevent these abuses.

Now we come to the advertisement itself. All too often the advertisements are placed in local newspapers whose printing is terrible and whose editorial ambience is unsuitable to your brand. The message in the advertisement is usually the wrong one; the retailer wants to push the bargain offer, the cut price etc., rather than the quality of the brand and information about its features and uses. It is very dangerous to give your advertising money to a retailer if he will not spend the money properly (perhaps because he does not really understand advertising or because he takes a very short-term view of the motivation of consumers). At least, the marketing man must try to control the editorial content of the cooperative advertisement, by providing layouts, matrices, radio tapes etc., and by insisting that they be used. Be prepared to spend enough time and to exercise controls so that your cooperative advertising expenditure has a chance of being effective, not just as a licence to trade, but as a sensible motivation of the consumer.

Other 'licences to trade' exist. In continental Europe, a firm favourite is the 'year-end bonus'. This is a payment to the retailer whose purchases of a manufacturer's products have achieved a pre-agreed annual total. Each year the target is negotiated, invariably demanding growth on the actual purchases in the previous year. Care needs to be taken in setting these targets, particularly because price increases alone can seem to produce growth, yet they cannot justify what is, in effect, an increase in retail percentage margin. Some marketing men find that the year-end bonus can be put to good effect, particularly to encourage a retailer to increase his purchases towards the end of the year when there might be a danger of his falling below the target. (This is a two-edged sword; if the retailer has already reached your target by early December, it may well be in his interest to stop buying your products while he concentrates on a competitor's, whose total is still below his target.)

'Natural rabatt' (e.g. supplying 13 units of a product but invoicing only 12) is a 'licence to trade' much used in Germany. It has nothing to recommend it because it cannot be used in any positive way. It is merely a means by which the retailer gets an increased profit margin. By contrast, the cash discount is coming to the fore again, pushed by the shortage of cash and the high cost of borrowing. A discount for prompt payment may well be worth the manufacturer's while, provided that he can prevent powerful retailers from taking the discount without actually remembering to pay promptly at all!

RETAIL CHAINS

In all of the foregoing discussion there is not very much difference between independent retailers as a class and retail chains as a class; we find all levels of intellect and all levels of probity. There is, of course, a difference of muscle. The big chain is more important to the manufacturer than the individual small independent. That is why many independents now bind together to form voluntary chains. These are frequently known as 'symbol' groups, because they usually adopt a name and a symbol with which to identify themselves. Some of them have brands of their own and the symbol features as their private label. Some groups are composed of totally independent cooperating retailers, while others have made some financial investment in their central organisation but, essentially, they are the answer of the independent entrepreneur to the large chain.

A group facilitates economic buying; this may be the negotiation of some overriding discount which shall apply to the independent purchasing by individual members, or it may depend upon the existence of a central buying office which actually purchases on behalf of members. Some central offices commit members to promotional programmes, while others execute advertising campaigns for the benefit of the whole voluntary chain. Almost every variation of organisation exists from one country to another and from one retail segment to another. Much of the pioneering work was done in the grocery field in Holland while Britain and Canada were active early in pharmacy.

A rather specialised form of the same principle is practised by the franchise chains (of which Kentucky Fried Chicken must be the best example). The franchised dealer usually owns his own shop and is personally responsible for its business results but, in return for fees, he is almost completely 'managed' by the central organisation which controls shop layout, product specification, pricing and promotion and which conducts a central advertising campaign. Franchising is growing, and actually includes perfumeries in Australia and motorcar mechanics in Britain.

It can be supposed that the strong central control, in a major retail chain, must give greater negotiation strength, provide better facilities and make more economic use of resources. This is probably true, so long as central bureaucracy can be kept under control. But it can also be argued that there is a much stronger motivation for the owner-manager to give service and to build a clientele, compared with the shop girl who is bored and watches the clock until closing time. This, in turn, is countered by the major training programmes of such companies as Marks & Spencer and by the joint ownership arrangement of John Lewis.

Chains are succeeding in unexpected quarters; in Germany, for instance, the Douglas chain consists of extremely sophisticated and exclusive perfumeries. This is providing honourable but very tough competition for the stylish independent retailer. Chains of discount stores produce less honourable competition, with their unauthorised and roundabout purchasing and their promotion of 'parallel imports'. These outlets do not build anything permanent or useful but merely spoil the consumer franchise which others have painstakingly built.

Chains not only offer private label goods (as in the major super-market chains) but some manufacture for themselves (consider the major own brands of medicines and cosmetics which are skilfully marketed by Boots). Others sell little or nothing but their own brands (e.g. Marks & Spencer). The manufacturer's relationship here is simply that of a contract manufacturer who makes to the retailer's specification but does not supply any brands from the manufacturer's own stable. Such very powerful retail companies obviously have a double relationship with the manufacturer; they can be his biggest customer and his biggest competitor at the same time. One might think that such situations could be abused, although monopoly laws and fair trading codes exist in many other countries to prevent this. In reality, the ethical standards of these major chains are very high and their trade practices are proper and constructive.

The retailer who turns manufacturer does need to re-think some of the basic economics. The straight retailer has to supply capital for his land, buildings, fittings and fixtures but, after that, he largely operates on his suppliers' money; goods can be received and sold on to consumers before the manufacturer has to be paid. The manufacturer, however, has to finance the stock, and this can easily represent working capital which is much greater than the investment in fixed assets. The retailer's own brand business, therefore, may give him extra sales and may give him a strong promotional image but it is questionable whether it offers him a very attractive return on the capital employed. In stringent economic times, we may well find that the retailer will do rather less of this sort of manufacture, because he will find that it is extravagant in its demands on his capital (and because the profit in absolute money, per article sold, is a good deal smaller than he could get from selling higher priced branded lines).

There is no point in the marketing man's complaining about competition from retailers, because it is a fact of life. It can even be helpful to the manufacturer by making a market lively and expansive. When it is unhelpful, the marketing man's duty is to try to persuade retailers to change their ways, but this should be a businesslike process. Above all, do not go to war with retailers, but find ways of making their interests lie in the same direction as your own. Not only is this more profitable but it is a much more agreeable way to earn your living.

PART II

DEVELOPING THE MARKETING STRATEGY

8

Marketing data

Ian Maclean, Director, Imac Research

If management is defined as 'the art of asking the right questions' there should therefore be considerable merit in providing the information to answer these questions. Within a company, the accountant has built up a massive volume of information on what the company is doing and what it costs. However, the process of developing similar flows of information about the external environment – the market in which the company operates, is still in its early stages. The problem is twofold. First, it is still being decided what questions should be asked and second, external sources of information are widely dispersed and of varied quality. The first section of this chapter is concerned, therefore, with the information flows required for marketing decisions and describes in outline where this information can be obtained. The second part describes in more detail the nature of each of the main sources of information.

SOURCES OF INFORMATION ON UK MARKETS

The information requirements can be grouped under five main headings:

1. How large is the market?
2. How is the market segmented by end-use industries, regions and size range of customers?
3. Growth of end-use sectors; growth or decline due to changes in the use of products and particular applications, e.g. the

substitution of plastic for steel and the increased volume of packaging materials used.

4 Factors influencing the share of a market held by a company.
5 Individual companies, both customers and competitors.

The information required under these headings is derived from a wide variety of sources. These sources are described in more detail towards the end of the chapter.

How large is the market?

Information on the level of output of a product or of an industry is normally available from other sources such as trade associations, special reports published at intervals in technical journals and proceedings of professional bodies, semi-official organisations such as the National Institute of Economic and Social Research, the National Economic Development Office and the nationalised industries.

The Government. The *Business Monitor* series is the principal source for detailed product information. There are some 160 *Business Monitors* embracing almost 5,000 products. The individual *Business Monitors* correspond broadly to the minimum list headings of the Standard Industrial Classification. The majority are issued quarterly and a small minority monthly. In addition to the production information, imports and exports are shown and where available there is a price index. These statistics are shown quarterly for the last four quarters and totals are given for the last two full years. The export and import figures are derived mainly from the customs and excise, but in certain sectors where the classifications are very different, export figures are shown on the same basis as production.

Business Monitors are available only on subscription, either individually or the entire series. The cost of subscription to individual monitors varies from £2 upwards per annum, and the cost of complete sets is now over £200 a year. The *Business Monitor* series is issued under three headings:

(a) production – relating to manufactured goods;
(b) service and distributive trades, and
(c) miscellaneous services.

The *Business Monitor* has replaced the five-yearly *Census of Pro-*

duction as the source of detailed product information. The census is now an annual event but restricted to figures relating to the total industry. Other statistical series providing information about market size include the *Monthly Digest of Statistics* and the *Annual Abstract of Statistics*. Certain statistics, however, appear only in *Trade and Industry;* an index to these statistics is published twice a year.

Trade associations. Trade associations vary widely in the extent to which they collect statistics, the publicity given to them, and the extent to which they are willing to disseminate information. The principal reason for collecting statistics is for use by trade association members, so that frequently information is not made available to outsiders. Even when it is supplied to non-members the detail is lost by the grouping of the figures into broad headings. There is also the problem that their statistics normally refer only to their members, and many trade associations do not have the full support of all the firms in their industry.

Other sources. Information on market size is provided intermittently in the reports issued by the National Economic Development Office, by articles written for technical journals and papers read to institutes and other associations. There is no basic guide to what is available, it is simply a question of contacting the journals and institutes active in the field being investigated. Commercial sources are beginning to close many of the gaps particularly on consumer markets, notably *The Marketing Manual of the UK* published by Mirror Group Newspapers, and the reports published by the Economist Intelligence Unit, Mintel, Keynote Publications and BLA's Market Assessment reports.

MARKET STRUCTURE

Information on the geographical distribution of manufacturing industry and the size distribution of companies is now made available as an *Annual Business Monitor*, PA 1002 and PA 1003 respectively.

The Private Contractors' Construction Census lists all the types of firm in the construction industry: builders, plumbers, painters etc. and also provides both the size of company and geographical breakdown.

Agriculture is covered by the *Census of Agriculture.*

The *Census of Distribution* covers retail and service trades, but the census is conducted only every ten years and the last census was for 1971.

Information on the number of premises under various classifications – shops, pubs, offices etc. is available from the *Inland Revenue Rating Statistics.* These have now been extended to include floor space.

The CSO publication, *Regional Statistics,* brings together in one convenient volume a very wide range of information on a comparative regional basis.

One of the most valuable sources of structural data is the employment data collected by the Department of Employment. Employment for each of the minimum list headings of the SIC is available for some 900 employment exchanges. Summary tables are published twice a year in the *Gazette*, and detailed information for each employment exchange area is available from the department's statistical office at Watford.

MARKET TRENDS

The industries into which a product is sold may be expanding or declining, and the use of a product in an industry may be changing. It is essential to separate these two effects because they are influenced by very different factors. There are situations when a declining end-use sector can still be an expanding market for a product, due to technical or economic change as, for instance, occurred with the demand for diesel locomotives on British Rail. The railways were a declining industry, but for a period there was a buoyant market for diesel engines. The reverse is also true. The market for metal-cutting gases has been rising rapidly, but the use of dissolved acetylene has declined due to its having been replaced by propane.

Trends in end-use sectors

This information is largely derived from the same sources as applied to size of markets, as historical series are normally available. For most purposes a five-year period provides an adequate time series, so a

Monthly Digest of Statistics or a Business Monitor series is normally satisfactory. The *Annual Abstract of Statistics,* however, provides a ten-year series, when available, and by piecing together the various Census of Production reports it is possible to go back to 1908. Post-war reports have been issued for the periods ending 1945, 1953, 1958, 1963 and 1968. The British experience of national planning has been disastrous, but the individual economic development committees of NEDO frequently produce excellent forecasts, particularly in the construction industry.

Technological change

Marketing is not concerned with how change occurs, but with the impact of change on our markets, and must therefore keep careful watch on the technical changes that are taking place. The government originates a very high proportion of the total research carried out in this country, some of the results being published through HMSO, but most in the publications of the various research associations.

Trade and technical journals and the proceedings of professional bodies are among the most useful routine sources for technical change information.

FACTORS INFLUENCING COMPANY MARKET SHARE

The influences that determine whether a customer buys from one supplier rather than another are difficult to evaluate and normally require a special market survey. The published information tends to be on the more general level of market intelligence. If we assume that the sequence is the attitude to a supplier and the supplier's products, the identification of the purchasing influences in the company, and the determination of the correct channels of communication to reach those purchasing influences, then in practice the published information tends to be of a general nature, especially on attitudes. This gap has been partly closed by the development of what are called multi-client market surveys in which a survey is carried out on behalf of several suppliers and the cost shared between them.

The information on purchasing influences again can only be established in relation to each individual company by specific enquiry, but the basic patterns are given in Hugh Buckner's book *How British*

Industry Buys. The channels of communication include the sales representative, journals, exhibitions, seminars, direct mail, and the relevant importance of each is again difficult to establish without special studies. The information in this area tends to be restricted to circulation figures for journals, attendance figures for exhibitions, and so on. A serious attempt has been made to improve the level of information available about, for instance, journals; and the media data form provides British advertisers with far more information than their continental counterparts.

INDIVIDUAL COMPANIES

The justification of marketing activity is in the sale of a particular product to a specific customer. It is therefore essential that marketing data should be considered in terms of companies as well as statistics. The Disclosure Acts prevent the government from providing information on the output of individual companies. Trade associations and other collectors of statistics also tend to follow this policy. There has, however, been one major breakthrough on the Census of Production. Companies were asked on the 1968 census returns if they would agree to their names being published as contributing to that census return; an average of 80 per cent of companies agreed, so now there is a thirteen-volume register listing companies under each minimum list heading. This register is particularly valuable as it provides a perfect match between a list of firms and the statistics on output for the census. Further editions have been published based on later census data.

Directories have been one of the main sources of company information, but there has been a tendency to compile them for the benefit of purchasers. Consequently, in many directories far more suppliers are shown against a product heading than there are manufacturers of that product. Directories are nevertheless extremely useful sources.

Government legislation provides the basis for much company information. All companies must register and their articles of association, together with annual report and balance sheet, must be lodged at Companies House in Cardiff where they are available for inspection. A visit to Companies House discloses a vast room containing the index to companies on an alphabetical basis and providing the required reference number. Armed with the reference number and a small fee the company files (on micro-fiche) will be brought to the enquirer after a suitable period of time – varying from 15 minutes to over an hour if there is a rush. The recent changes in company law provide for much more extensive information. It is now obligatory to provide information on employment and turnover (for companies over a certain size) and to provide separate returns for the different parts of a company where a company is engaged in significantly different activities.

The trade journals also provide valuable data on companies, but the problem is often confronted of finding the time to read them. There are two solutions. First, hand over a list of companies to a cuttings agency, who will provide you with a continuous supply of cuttings for a very modest fee. This approach naturally assumes that the list of companies on which information is required is known in advance.

Where this is not the case there are still short cuts, notably, the *Research Index* produced by Business Surveys Ltd, or McCarthy Information Services. The *Research Index* is a daily publication indexing articles from the main newspapers. McCarthy provides a service whereby cuttings are grouped under subject and company headings so that back information can be easily and rapidly obtained.

SOURCES OF INFORMATION

Each of the main sources will now be described in turn.

Government

Government information available is much more than just a collection of statistics. HMSO publishes a list of government publications on a daily, monthly and annual basis. In addition sectional lists are published covering material related to various departments and ministries. These have the advantage that they set out all available publications and not merely those issued during the previous week, month or year. The main problem with governmental information is to find one's way through it. Fortunately, this problem has been recognised and the government, in particular the Government Statistical Services, are now following an active policy of publicising their information. Among the more valuable government publications are *Profit from Facts* issued free by the Central Statistical Office. This contains a description of the way information has been obtained from within the government. There is a brief guide to sources of government statistics published annually, free on request, and a very comprehensive *Guide to Official Statistics is* available from HMSO, price £8.25 (1978 edition).

The old Ministry of Public Building and Works (now the Department of Environment) produced a massive inventory of construction statistics in 1968 that highlights just how much information can be made available. A special feature of this inventory was that examples of all the forms completed are shown so that it is possible to check exactly what information has been made available, an essential factor when checking the availability of information, as in the publication process there is often a tendency to aggregate and generalise. The Building Research Station at Watford, Herts, also contains a collection of construction statistics. Among the guides to other information of value in marketing, is a booklet produced by the National Reference Library for Science and Invention (the 'Patents Office') describing their activities and another providing advice on *Searching British Patent Literature.* There is a *Guide to the National Reference Library of Science and Invention,* and the Department of Trade and Industry have produced a special booklet *Technical Services for Industry.* This was in support of their industrial liaison officers, but now that this service has ceased it is unlikely that the booklet will appear again. A pity, as it is one of the most useful digests of information on government research centres, associations, and other sources which industry can turn to for technical information.

The principal government publications of interest are the old *Board of Trade Gazette* and *Ministry of Labour Gazette,* now entitled *Trade and Industry* (weekly) and the *Department of Employment Gazette* (monthly). A monthly publication *Economic Trends* provides comment on general movements in our economy, both overall and in major sectors, whilst *Statistical News* (quarterly) provides valuable articles on the developments that are taking place in our statistical system, and these have been far-reaching in recent years. Britain has a Central Statistical Office, but in the past this has been little more than a collecting point for data provided by other government departments. The broad pattern has not changed, but the emphasis is now different and the Central Statistical Office is taking a much more active role in bringing together the available statistics. Unlike many continental countries, the UK government's collection of statistics is decentralised into its various ministries. In order to help industry, enquirers are now encouraged to telephone the press office of the Central Statistical Office, if not sure how to proceed. The government also maintains a mailing list for people interested in being kept up to date with the latest developments. This service is free and if you are interested you should inform the press officer, Great George Street, SW1.

Semi-official organisations

There are a wide range of organisations in Britain that are neither run by the government nor in private hands, often designated by the term 'council' or 'board'. The most important of these is NEDO, the National Economic Development Office which operates through a series of councils. There is a publication *NEDDY in Print*, that sets out all the reports that are available. This is sent free on request and it is possible for one's name to be placed on the mailing list to receive new issues and supplements. The National Institute of Economic and Social Research provides a very useful review of the economy every year and from time-to-time produces reports on particular sectors. The British Standards Institute can often also provide useful information on markets, but to find out the full range of councils and other semi-official bodies there is a special guide produced by CBD Research Ltd, *Councils, Committees and Boards*.

Nationalised industries

The nationalised industries are worth mentioning separately as they are involved in basic sectors of the economy and therefore provide useful guidelines for a whole range of other products and markets. Furthermore, because they tend to be a monopoly within the industry, information is made more freely available than would be the case under competition. The *Statistical Year Book of the Iron and Steel Industry,* for instance, contains some of the best statistics on any industry, including input/output tables stretching back over the years.

Trade associations

The scope of the information services provided by trade associations varies widely, but it is always worth trying to see if they offer the data needed. These are listed in the CBD Research Ltd's *Directory of British Associations,* with a brief outline of their services. Unfortunately many trade associations interpret their roles too narrowly and fail to recognise that without betraying any secrets they could make available much information of the greatest value for suppliers to their industries.

Professional institutes

The institutes fall into two groups, those based on science and technology, and those based on management, but the lines are becoming a little blurred as the older technically-based institutes set up management and marketing groups.

In terms of publications the bulk of the output of the technical institutes is naturally technical, but again the more progressive of them are following an active policy of marketing their information to a wider audience, and an increasing flow of marketing-type information is now available. For instance, the best review of the air conditioning market in the UK appeared in the June 1972 issue of the *Journal of the Institute of Heating and Ventilating Engineers.*

The management institutes, particularly those of members of the marketing professions, make their contributions with information on marketing services. The Institute of Practitioners in Advertising publishes a wide range of booklets, for instance, on advertising conditions in each European country. The British Direct Mail Advertisers' Association produces a year book which describes the advantages of direct mail and lists the companies offering services, and the Industrial Market Research Association publishes a free *Guide to the Selection and Briefing of Consultants.* A full list of these organisations is given in the CBD Research Ltd's *Directory of Associations.*

Periodicals and newspapers

When the historian of tomorrow talks of the flood he will not be referring to Noah, but to the outpouring of journals and newspapers of all shapes and sizes that characterises the current scene. It is impossible to keep pace, so do not try. When you are investigating a new market sector get out BRAD – *British Rate and Data* or *Willings Press Guide* and select those journals covering your field of interest. You will find all the journals stacked away in the basement of the National Reference Library of Science and Invention, the old 'Patent Office'. A short cut is to use the *British Technology Index,* produced by the Library Association, to find which journals have published articles of interest to you. Journals can be obtained on loan from the National Lending Library but loans are only made to registered borrowers on special loan request forms. Journals and newspapers are also available from many public libraries and from the libraries of many industrial companies. A list of nearly 3,000 libraries is set out in the ASLIB Directory, volume 1, *Information Sources in Science, Technology and Commerce.*

Trade directories

There are some 20,000 directories in Europe, so finding your way to the one you want could be a problem unless you use CBD Research Ltd's publications *Current British Directories* and *European Directories.* CBD also publishes *Statistics Europe, Statistics Africa,* and a *Guide to European Companies.* These directories are source guides and absolutely essential for any marketing man's library. Another good guide is the *IPC Marketing Manual,* which contains four sections covering social and economic data, market-place data, media, and advertising.

While most directories cover specialised sectors of the market, there are a small number which aim to provide a full industry coverage. Again, these are listed by CBD Research Ltd *(Guide to Directories).* The main use of directories is for company information, and this requirement is also met by the information cards produced by services such as Extel and Moodies Services. The cards give a detailed analysis of individual companies' financial history and current situation, together with brief details of products.

Exhibitions and conferences

The value of exhibitions is that they tend to concentrate attention on a particular market sector. A full list of exhibitions and conferences to be held during the year is published in the *Exhibition and Conference Year Book.*

Commercial services

There has been a steady expansion in recent years of commercially produced marketing information, notably from the Economist Intelligence Unit, Mintel, Keynote Publications and BLA. A complete summary of the Business Monitor series is available from IMAC Research, with all 5,000 products included in one publication. The multi-client survey varies in price from a few pounds to several thousands of pounds. A list of these surveys is published by Industrial Aids.

Forecasting has attracted considerable attention and many surveys are now available, including the Henley Centre for Forecasting, Staniland Hall and the London Business School. One of the best European forecasts is published by Prognos Ag of Basle, Switzerland.

USEFUL ADDRESSES

Government

Central Statistical Office,
Great George Street, London SW1. 01-233 3000
Department of Employment,
8 St James' Square, London SW1. 01-214 6000
Department of the Environment,
2 Marsham Street, London SW1. 01-212 3434
Building Research Station,
Bucknalls Lane, Garston, Watford. Garston 74040
National Reference Library of Science and Invention (includes Patent Office)
Bayswater Division: 10 Porchester Gardens, London W2. 01-727 3022
Holborn Division: Southampton Buildings, Chancery Lane, London WC2. 01-405 8721
Department of Trade and Industry,
1 Victoria Street, London SW1. 01-215 7877
National Economic Development Office,
Millbank Tower, Millbank, London SW1. 01-211 3000
National Institute of Economic and Social Research,
2 Dean Trench Street, London SW1. 01-222 7665

Other organisations

ASLIB,
3 Belgrave Square, London W1. 01-235 5050
BLA Management Services Group,
2 Duncan Terrace, London N1. 01-278 9517
BRAD (published by Maclean Hunter),
76 Oxford Street, London W1. 01-637 7511
British Technology Index (published by Library Association),
7 Ridgemount Street, London WC1. 01-636 7543
CBD Research Ltd,
154 High Street, Beckenham, Kent. 01-650 7745
Economist Intelligence Unit,
27 St James's Place, London SW1. 01-493-6711
Extel,
1 East Harding Street, London EC4. 01-353 1080
The Exhibitions and Conferences Year Book – available from
York Publishing Company, 70 Abingdon Road, London W8.
01-278 4299
Henley Centre for Forecasting,
2 Tudor Street, Blackfriars, London EC4. 01-353 9961
IMAC Research,
Lancaster House, More Lane, Esher, Surrey. Esher 63121
Industrial Aids,
52 Grosvenor Gardens, London SW1. 01-730 5288
Keynote Publications Ltd,
23 City Road, London EC1. 01-588 2698/9
London Business School,
Sussex Place, Regents Park, London NW1. 01-262 5050
Mintel,
20 Buckingham Street, London WC1. 01-839 3276
Mirror Group Newspapers,
Holborn Circus, London EC1. 01-353 0246
Moodies Services,
6 Bonhill Street, London EC2. 01-628 9571
National Lending Library for Science and Invention,
Boston Spa, Yorkshire. Boston Spa 2031
Prognos AG,
Pelikanweg 2, Basle, Switzerland. (UK agents – IMAC Research)

Research Index,
PO Box 21, Dorking, Surrey. Dorking 87857
Staniland Hall,
42 Colebrooke Row, London N1. 01-359 6054
Willings Press Guide,
3 Holborn Circus, London EC1. 01-583 7403

9

Market research

Leslie Walsh, Sundridge Park Management Centre, Bromley, Kent

Market research has been defined as 'the systematic gathering, recording, analysis and interpretation of data on problems relating to the market for, and the marketing of, goods and services.'[1] From a technique point of view it is also useful to distinguish between consumer research (research directed at individuals, the ultimate consumers of a product) and industrial research (directed at organisations).

The data-gathering process relies on desk research and field research (principally postal questionnaires, telephone interviewing and the personal interview).

DESK RESEARCH

Desk research is the search for published, or existing available but unpublished, information. To the extent that 'desk research' suggests sitting behind a desk reading piles of books it is an unfortunate description; desk research involves telephone and personal interviewing. Further, it is a vital stage of almost any research project; the most self-evident truth in all marketing is that which exhorts us to undertake our (inexpensive) desk research thoroughly and exhaustively before embarking upon our (highly expensive) field research.

---

1 Ralph S. Alexander et al., *Marketing Definitions: A Glossary of Marketing Terms,* American Marketing Association, 1960.

There is, however, a very real snag: the sheer volume of data is discouraging even to the most dedicated researcher. The systematic approach towards desk research put forward in Table 9.1 will, it is hoped, go a long way towards solving that problem. It relies on a very limited number of 'guides to information sources', directories or similar publications which in themselves provide *no market information whatever* but merely act as signposts to other reference works or organisations that do. The recommended guides cover all the main avenues of enquiry: government, trade directories, trade associations, trade magazines, previously published surveys, libraries and company financial information. (In the interests of brevity and simplicity, the temptation to mention any publication that provides *market* information has been resisted; such information, if relevant, will be located through the information guides.)

But a researcher's best friends are often his competitors; it really is astounding just how much market, and not merely product, information companies will disclose in catalogues presumably intended for customers rather than for market researchers. So do secure copies of all relevant catalogues.

FIELD RESEARCH

The decision between postal questionnaires, telephone interviews and personal interviews will significantly affect both the cost and the value of the information obtained. The choice demands careful consideration, though it will be based largely on past experience and common sense. Table 9.2, which summarises the principal advantages and disadvantages of each method, should be of help in the selection decision.

POSTAL QUESTIONNAIRES

In consumer research, the response rate from individuals to postal questionnaires is low, sometimes abysmally so. This usually precludes their use in what might be described as the mass-market survey. In certain instances informants may be expected to have a degree of personal interest in the survey (e.g. when the target consists of

Table 9.1 A systematic and simplified approach to desk research by the use of information guides

Government statistics	Guide to Official Statistics	Her Majesty's Stationery Office, PO Box 569, London SE1
Directories	Current British Directories	CBD Research Ltd, 154 High St, Beckenham, Kent.
Trade etc. associations	CBD Directory of British Associations	
Trade and technical magazines	British Rate and Data	British Rate and Data, 76 Oxford St, London W1
Published research	International Directory of Published Market Research	British Overseas Trade Board, Export House, 50 Ludgate Hill, London EC4
	European Directory of Market Research Surveys	Gower Publishing Company Ltd, 1 Westmead, Farnborough, Hampshire
Specialist libraries	Aslib Directory	Aslib Publications, 3 Belgrave Sq, London SW1
Financial information on companies	Extel Statistical Services Ltd	37–45 Paul St, London EC2
	Dun and Bradstreet Ltd	PO Box 17, 26–32 Clifton St, London EC2
	McCarthy Information Ltd	Manor House, Ash Walk, Warminster

members of an association such as the Consumers' Association, or of enthusiasts such as hobby photographers). In these cases a postal survey may be appropriate.

In industrial research response rates to postal questionnaires may be expected to be very much higher; responses up to 92 per cent have been reported, though 20–25 per cent might be regarded as nearer the norm. With the latter level of response, however, the postal survey still risks a serious non-response bias. For this reason, even in industrial research, it is seldom used on its own; its role is more one of support to a programme of telephone or personal interviews. Often the larger informant companies are interviewed personally, with small companies, which it would be uneconomic to interview, being covered by postal survey.

As mentioned in Table 9.2, one of the main advantages of the postal questionnaire is its relatively low cost. It is, however, easy to underestimate that cost. Normally two separate items of cost should be taken into account: issue costs (paper, envelopes, printing, postage and clerical costs for both initial questionnaire and reminders) and researchers' time spent in questionnaire design, piloting, modification, and editing and analysis of returned questionnaires. The costs should, of course, be expressed not in terms of questionnaires sent out but in terms of returned completed questionnaires – which on a 25 per cent response rate would quadruple the final figure.

TELEPHONE INTERVIEWING

In countries such as the USA, where virtually every household has a telephone, the telephone interview is an acceptable tool in consumer research. In the UK the low proportion of telephones to households precludes the use of the telephone in any survey which aims at covering a cross-section of the whole population. In fact, consumer research by telephone interview is normally limited to those markets where it is reasonable to assume that telephone ownership is almost universal (perhaps holders of the major international credit cards) or to occasions where speed of contact is vital (such as advertisement-recall research, where a number of householders must be contacted within a very short period of time after the appearance of an advertisement on television).

In industrial research, by contrast, every commercial or industrial organisation of any significance may be expected to have a telephone, so that the telephone interview is especially appropriate. The cost of telephone interviewing depends heavily on the rate of successful interviews achieved per day. This rate will naturally vary widely between one survey and another, but as a general guide it might be adivisable to budget for a figure between eight and twelve interviews.

Table 9.2   Some advantages and disadvantages of the main alternative methods of data collection

Advantages	Disadvantages
Postal questionnaires	
Relatively low cost, especially if sample geographically widespread	Low response rate and consequent likely non-response bias
No interviewer bias	Limited nature and number of questions
Can sometimes reach otherwise inaccessible informants	Difficult to avoid misunderstandings
Telephone interviews	
Lower cost than personal interview	Low incidence of telephone ownership – sample unrepresentative for mass consumer research
Speed of interviewing	Interviews must as a rule be short
Much higher response than for postal questionnaires	Products, show cards etc. cannot be used
Personal interviews	
Volume of information obtained	Very high cost
Product, show cards etc. can be used	Possible interviewer bias
Rapport can be developed between interviewer and informants, ambiguities can be explained, misunderstandings avoided	Time required to complete interview programme

PERSONAL INTERVIEWING

As will now be evident, consumer research relies heavily on the personal interview. Some will be extended interviews ('depth interviews'), group discussions or other specialised forms of interview undertaken by trained full-time staff. The more usual type of interview in consumer research is the structured interview, where the interviewer (usually part-time) is required to adhere strictly to a formal questionnaire.

In industrial research, as has been seen, the personal interview is only one of several alternative methods of data collection. Nevertheless, it is of vital importance to virtually any industrial research project. The *structured* interview is relatively rare except for the really large-scale project. Most industrial interviews are either semi-structured or unstructured.

In the semi-structured interview the order and wording of the questions are predetermined in an interview guide, but most questions are open-ended, i.e. the informant is allowed to give his answers in his own way. In the unstructured interview, the interviewer merely has a list of topics to be raised. The respondent is encouraged to talk at length on whatever aspects of the topics are of interest to him; the interviewer remains very much a listener.

The demands of the semi-structured or unstructured interview are such that a trained high-calibre interviewer is essential. This will usually imply full-time company or research agency staff, at a very much higher salary cost. Further, the lengthier interviews and the distances between informant companies usually mean that two to four industrial interviews in a day is a good performance. Cost per interview is inevitably high – estimated even in 1978 at between £20 and £50 for an interview undertaken by in-company staff, and obviously much more for agency interviews.

SAMPLING

Consumer markets

In consumer research a sample may be taken from the total population relevant to the survey. Since this sample is only part of the parent population it cannot be expected to have *exactly* the same characteristics as that population. Nevertheless, *provided certain statistical principles are observed,* it can be taken as reasonably certain that the sample will adequately reflect the characteristics of the population from which it was drawn. An essential statistical principle to be observed is that a *random* sample must be taken from the relevant population.

At its simplest a random sample is one in which every item in the population has exactly the same chance of being selected for inclusion in the sample as any other item. It is *not* a haphazard selection process and usually requires the use of a table of random numbers (or random numbers generated electronically, as with the Premium Bond draws), though drawing well-shuffled tickets from a hat is adequate (as in the case of the village-hall raffle). For every item to have an equal chance of selection, it is necessary to have all items physically available (as with the raffle) or to have a complete list of the population (the 'sampling frame'). In the UK the consumer researcher is fortunate in having available to him at negligible cost two suitable frames for samples of the general population: the Register of Electors, and the rating records kept by local authorities.

Random sampling is expensive, and the consumer researcher will often rely instead on a quota sample: one purposely selected according to certain known and relevant characteristics of the population, these characteristics being reproduced in the sample in the same proportions in which they exist in the population as a whole. Characteristics typically of interest in consumer research include age, sex, occupation, social class etc.: all information readily available, at negligible cost to the researcher, from the Census of Population and other published data. With quota sampling it is no longer theoretically possible to evaluate the sampling error. It has been shown, however, that a properly controlled quota-sample survey can produce reliable results.

Industrial markets (assessment of market size)

The industrial researcher does not usually have access to a sampling frame adequate for the taking of a random sample. At first sight it might seem an easy matter for him to build up an appropriate sampling frame from relevant trade directories. However, directories will usually list enterprises (companies etc.) and not establishments (individual production units run by those companies). For any given product it will almost always be necessary to obtain data relating to establishments rather than enterprises, simply because many companies have so diverse a product range that data collected on enterprises would be relevant to the survey product only to a very limited extent. Most government statistics, such as the *Business Monitor* series, relate to establishments.

Furthermore, names are not in themselves sufficient. Some indication of size of establishments is virtually essential, to permit stratification by size, in view of the known fact that in many industries a relatively small number of companies is overwhelmingly dominant in terms of sales and purchases. Such size information is difficult to obtain, even in such simple terms as numbers of employees, and even by enterprise rather than by establishment. It will often be found in industrial research, therefore, that the cost of preparation of an adequate sampling frame is so high that the whole research becomes uneconomic. As a result, the principal applications of random sampling in industrial research are probably either *continuing* research programmes, where the initial costs of establishing the sampling frame (and the cost of updating) can be amortised over repeated enquiries, or research by government, which necessarily maintains detailed information files on enterprises and establishments. (Unfortunately, under the Statistics of Trade Act 1947, much of the information in Government files is confidential and the files are not available for general research purposes.)

For similar reasons any approach in industrial research akin to the consumer researcher's quota sampling will be out of the question. Some alternative approaches are required.

First, in certain industrial markets the number of customers is small. It is often economically possible to contact all of them, i.e. to carry out a census, not a sampling operation.

In other industrial markets, as mentioned, a very common characteristic is that a small number of companies is dominant, accounting for a very high proportion of total purchases (the so-called Pareto's Law). The Pareto distribution is heavily relied on in industrial research. It is often possible, at no significant expense, to identify merely the major enterprises and establishments of relevance. The sum total of purchases of the survey product by these larger organisations will *not* provide a *total* market figure, but will give an incontrovertible figure for a *minimum* market size. This may well give adequate guidance in terms of the action to be taken on the research results.

So far we have considered only an approach to *customers* in order to assess market size – naturally enough, since the market size is merely the sum total of their purchases. However, in industrial markets there is always a chain of demand which typically might go from raw material supplier to component manufacturer, then to machine or equipment manufacturer (often known as original equipment manufacturers or OEMs), possibly through industrial distributors, and finally to the end user of the equipment. In such markets, though the number of end users may be impossibly high, there are far fewer OEMs. Each of these has a global view of the end user market, which consists of their own customers, and they can provide invaluable information to the researcher.

The industrial researcher, therefore, will approach OEMs as a matter of routine, and will often take his inquiries further up or down the chain of demand, to distributors, component suppliers, and even raw material suppliers – not forgetting competitors, though in this case, for obvious reasons, the information obtained will usually require cross-checking with other sources.

Despite all these alternative approaches the fact has to be faced that in certain industrial markets the problems of assessment of market size are sometimes insuperable, at least at any economic price. However, much is being done. The government, in close co-operation with the Industrial Marketing Research Association[2], has in recent years significantly improved its industrial statistics and is contemplating, by the mid-1980s, access by private enterprise to its own computer-based data (only those not subject to disclosure restrictions, of course). Meanwhile, private enterprise is playing its part. Dun and Bradstreet's [3] *Market Facts File* covers some 200,000 UK *enterprises,* with broad size groupings, in terms of numbers of employees, for about 75 per cent of them. Market Location Ltd, [4] of Leamington Spa, offers a data base of some 130,000 locations which, they believe, represents 95 per cent of UK manufacturing *establishments,* plus a substantial listing of commercial premises such as warehouses and transport depots. Broad size groupings, again by numbers of employees, are available for about 85 per cent of their listed establishments. The thinking industrial marketer will take good care to keep himself up to date with current statistical developments in industries of interest to him.

2   Industrial Marketing Research Association, 11 Bird St, Lichfield, Staffs. WS13 6PW.

3   Dun and Bradstreet Ltd, 26-32 Clifton St, London EC2P 2LY.

4   Market Location Ltd, 17 Waterloo Place, Warwick St, Leamington Spa CV32 5LA.

COMMISSIONING A MARKET RESEARCH PROJECT

By definition, market research is moving into the unknown, sometimes by well-tried and established procedures and occasionally by experimental techniques. It is not, sadly, a product you can examine before you place your order. Often you will not really know what you have bought until the final report is submitted.

Further, it takes two to produce a successful research project: a competent researcher and a competent marketing professional commissioning the research. Research agencies in the UK are held in very high regard as thorough professionals in their task. It is up to the marketer to match their standard.

A vital first stage in any project is the definition of the problem. An intending research sponsor should define that problem in detail and *in writing*, decide whether or not research will assist in solving it, consider the various alternative answers to which the research might lead, and consider what *action* will or will not be taken in the light of these answers. A research project that will not result in some clearly defined action should not be commissioned.

Once the intending research sponsor is satisfied as to the practical value of the project, he should prepare a clear written brief for the agency. This should include a statement of the problem as originally defined, details of any relevant market information already available in company records, an outline of the information the research is required to produce and an indication of the degree of precision required. Insistence on a high degree of precision can lead to a dramatic increase in research costs. A sponsor should always ask himself whether such precision is really necessary in the light of the action to be taken on the research results.

Inquiries should be sent to no more than three agencies as a rule. Preparation of proposals is an expensive item and agencies soon lose interest in a client who issues enquiries wholesale. The three agencies are best chosen on the basis of previous satisfactory experience of their work, or perhaps by recommendation. It will usually pay to examine the *International Directory of Market Research Organisations,* published by the Market Research Society.[5] The written brief

---

5   Market Research Society, 15 Belgrave Sq., London SW1X 8PF.

should be handed to each agency and should form the basis of an initial face-to-face discussion prior to the submission of proposals.

Those agency proposals will provide a clear idea of the final cost of the research. At this stage the whole project should be reconsidered. Is it still worth proceeding in the light of the action to be taken on the results?

If it is, then the research agency should be selected after consideration of the written research proposals, the staff who will *personally* undertake or supervise the project and, in the case of consumer research agencies, their arrangements for briefing, supervising and controlling the part-time field force (e.g. ratio of supervisors to interviewers, training of interviewers, instructions on quota-sampling procedures, supervisor re-visits to respondents, postal check-backs with respondents etc.). Price is the last, and least, of your considerations.

It is at this stage that so many marketers make a fundamental mistake: they sit back and wait for the report. Close liaison with the agency as the research proceeds can only be helpful to both sides. This should involve not only a start-up meeting at which all agency staff are given a full briefing on the marketing background to the research, but also subsequent progress meetings. One such progress meeting should certainly give final consideration to the questionnaire before field work commences. This is the sponsor's last chance to ensure that the right questions are being asked *before* real money is spent.

Finally, a report alone is never enough. Agencies should be asked to present their findings at a presentation meeting, hand over copies of the report at that meeting, and ideally, once the report has been mulled over, attend a final discussion on its implications for action.

READING LIST

Consumer research

An introductory text:	A.H.R. Delens, *The Principles of Market Research,* Crosby Lockwood.
More advanced text-books:	P.M. Chisnall, *Marketing Research: Analysis and Measurement,* McGraw Hill.
	A.H. Davies, *The Practice of Marketing Research,* Heinemann.
	K. Elliott and M. Christopher, *Research Methods in Marketing,* Holt Blond.
Standard reference works:	R.M. Worcester and J. Downham (eds.), *Consumer Market Research Handbook,* Van Nostrand Reinhold.
	R. Ferber (ed.), *Handbook of Marketing Research,* McGraw Hill.

Industrial Research

A general text:	A. Wilson, *The Assessment of Industrial Markets*, Cassell/ABP.
A more detailed handbook:	A. Rawnsley (ed.), *Manual of Industrial Marketing Research,* Wiley.

10

Product planning – a new perspective

Simon Majaro, Director, Strategic Management Learning and Managing Partner Simon Majaro Ltd, International Management Consultants

The marketing concept is no longer a new concept. It has been in existence as a creed for over a quarter of a century. Yet although it has become an increasingly important activity within many firms it is disappointing to observe what a superficial hold the marketing creed, as a way of life, has attained. A 'way of life' means that marketing is a force that must pervade the entire firm, not just a single function called 'marketing'. It must transcend functional areas and every decision maker in the organisation, regardless of his or her level and functional affiliation, must be vigilant of the needs of the customer who is likely to be satisfied by the firm's offerings.

Peter Drucker summarised this simple notion many years ago by saying: 'Until the customer has derived final utility, there is really no "product"; there are only "raw materials" '. In other words the production people must be involved; the R & D department must be aware of the customer and his needs and so too must the personnel and finance functions. The paramount objective is to ensure that the customer derives final utility and satisfaction; without them there is no 'product'.

It this statement is true, one is entitled to ask a very fundamental question: 'What is the product?' This question represents a very subtle shibboleth. The reader may recall the biblical story of Gilead-ites who could identify their enemies by asking them to say 'Shib-boleth'. Whoever responded by saying 'Sibboleth' was an enemy and was slain. The inability to pronounce the test word correctly betrayed the person's nationality. Ask a person: 'What is your "product"?' and the answer will help you to judge the level of understanding and commitment that the interlocuter has towards the 'marketing concept'.

THE VARIOUS FACES OF THE 'PRODUCT'

A product has many faces. What the manufacturing person sees can be very different from what the marketing person should be seeing. Let us take an example. A company manufactures ball bearings and roller bearings in a vast assortment of sizes, alloys and configurations. The production manager will respond to the question: 'What is your product?' by simply saying 'Ball bearings and roller bearings'.

The marketing man should be punished if he gives the same reply. To him the product or products are 'anti-friction' devices. They are aids to the reduction of friction in a number of machines or instruments, such as motor cars and machine tools. The marketing man will know in detail the various sectors of the Standard Industrial Classification and will be able to enumerate the needs for anti-friction devices of each of the sectors listed. Where there is no friction there is no need for the product, or to be more precise there is no product in Peter Drucker's terms. This example is quite simple. Let us look at more complicated cases.

A pharmaceuticals company manufactures a number of drugs. By the nature of the industry and its level of technology the drugs represent complex chemical compounds. The production people and the R & D people are very tempted to define the product in units of the 'wonder drug' that the firm produces. The enlightened marketing person will describe the product in terms of the illness which the drug combats or the discomfort which it alleviates. The production oriented man will boast about the units of the antibiotics which the firm manufactured in a given period; the truly marketing oriented person will talk about the number of pneumonia sufferers who were cured by 'our product', and when attempting to measure the firm's market share he will do so in relation to his perception of the market, namely the number of pneumonia cases that occur in the course of the year.

Normally the more intricate the product and the more sophisticated the technology the greater the chasm between the perceptions of the product among the various functions of the enterprise. Obviously the R & D person who has been instrumental in the development of a highly innovative analgesic would prefer to talk about the complex chemical molecule of the product, rather than its headache alleviation characteristics. They are of course both right, but the R & D man talks about the physical properties of the product; the marketing man talks about what the product does for the consumer. In marketing terms the latter utility is the one that really matters. Unless you have a headache you are not in the marketplace and the product has no relevance to you. If you do have a headache you become passionately interested in the product, not because it contains the x or y wonder ingredients but simply because it will alleviate your condition.

A manufacturer of diesel engines will tend to talk about the number of units, the size of the units and the number of cylinders he has produced in the course of the year. 'What is your product?' will inevitably be answered with 'Diesel engines of 50 h.p. or 75 h.p. etc. configuration!' The marketing man should say 'we manufacture energy producing units of a particular design as an auxiliary facility in process plants, or ships or hospitals and at a cost per unit of electricity of x pence etc.' The marketing person must respond to the question as if he were the buyer of the product.

The message should be fairly clear. The marketer who has absorbed the marketing concept as a way of life will always seek to identify the product in terms of what it does for the customer and the cost/benefit it is capable of generating for the consuming environment, whether it is an industrial environment or a domestic one.

THE 'PRODUCT' – A NEW DIMENSION

Much has been written about the product life-cycle and what happens to sales and profitability during its course. The concept is a useful one but one of its pitfalls is the fact that we often forget to identify the product in terms that are really meaningful to the marketing process. The product may be progressing well towards 'growth' in the context of its technology or manufacturing processes, yet it may have reached its 'saturation' point in terms of its market or segment penetration. The two levels of performance are not necessarily congruent. Let us take an example.

A manufacturer of running shoes supplies the fraternity of professional and quasi-professional joggers with specially-designed shoes that provide arch support when running or sprinting. The sales follow a classical pattern that indicates that a 'product life cycle' is in operation. As a result of the ravages of competition and the fact that the product has reached the saturation point in the cycle pressure on margins is heavy and erosion of profitability is taking place. Nonetheless, rather unexpectedly the life cycle takes a twist upwards and sales are starting to boom again. The obvious implication is that the laws of gravity have been defied and that the theory of the product life cycle should be relegated to academic manuscripts only.

What has really happened is that the 'marketing ecology' has changed. A new market has sprung up for the firm's product: the amateur joggers, people of all ages who have read about the health value of jogging and decided to join the throng of early morning enthusiasts. In truth what has happened is that a new market has developed and to all intents and purposes the product has acquired a new face and should be treated as a new product. On this basis one would have a product for the professional runner and one for the enthusiastic jogger. The physical product may be the same but the marketing product will be different and each will deserve its separate analysis vis-à-vis the life cycle evaluation.

In the light of this it is instructive to re-examine the earlier example from the pharmaceuticals industry. Imagine that Stanton Chemicals manufactures an antibiotic product, Stantalyn, which is used effectively in the treatment of a wide range of infections. If the product is looked at as a technological package its life cycle could be traced on the basis of its overall sales and profitability. On the other hand, we can rightly assume that each infection type represents a separate market with the result that one can plot the life cycle performance in relation to each sickness. Thus, without getting too involved in the technicalities of a complex industry, one can have a product life cycle in respect of each identifiable 'indication': infections of the throat, ear, lungs, bile duct etc. Each 'indication' will have its own product (with or without different brand names) and each one of these products will have its own life cycle.

The situation can be further embellished by saying that the drug used by children in relation to one kind of illness is a different product from the one used by adults. Thus we finish by getting a three-dimensional matrix of product/market/segment *vectors*.

It is quite possible that the product will need to undergo a slight differentiation process, such as the production of a sweetened syrup for children, to facilitate absorption or swallowing, but essentially the product characteristics in technical terms are probably unchanged. Thus this illustration would suggest that we have many products as shown in Figure 10.1, and not just one. If this is so, we can now look at the new dimension of the product life cycle by plotting the cycle of each 'vector' in turn, as illustrated in Figure 10.2.

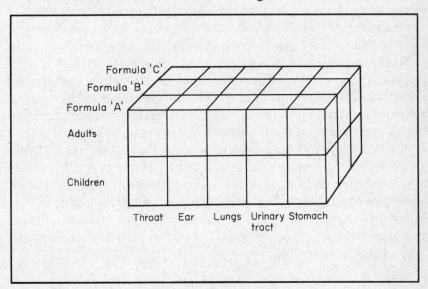

Figure 10.1   Product/market/segment vectors

This concept opens a new perspective for the marketer inasmuch as the product life cycle gains a meaningful and more practical dimension. The product becomes the instrument of satisfaction for each market segment and it is the progression of the product in relation to each sub-market that is being monitored. The marketer who learns how to monitor the product in this way will also acquire the skill of applying the most appropriate marketing tools for each stage of the 'vector' life cycle.

'Vector' in mathematics means a quantity having direction as well as magnitude, denoted by a line drawn from its original to its final position. To the marketer 'vector' means the market segment which is 'satisfied' by a specific product. The segment in question may be capable of 'satisfaction' by a number of products offered by the firm. Each 'product/segment' unit of activity is a vector. In other words what is being suggested is that instead of talking about the progress of a product or a brand along the life cycle one should plot the behaviour of the vector life cycle, namely the 'utility rendered to a specific market segment'. Thus if a diesel engine manufacturer has designed a small power generating plant that can supply energy for a factory and also propel a vessel, he has two distinct 'vectors': the supply of energy to a plant; and the supply of propulsion to ships. The physical and technical product may well be the same but in marketing terms two separate vectors exist and their development will probably take totally separate patterns towards growth and success.

Top management often expects the identical performance from all its products. In many instances this is neither possible nor justifiable. Different vectors have to cope with totally different marketing environments and to expect the same level of results from such environments just because the physical product is the same is illogical. The level of competition, the cost/benefit requirements and the distribution problems can tilt the balance in favour of one product/segment and make the other one look unattractive. Marketing people understand this much better than accountants or production people. The latter feel that a machine is a machine and the level of profit it provides to the selling company is the same irrespective of who uses it and what it is being used for.

MARKET SEGMENTATION REVIEWED

The theory of market segmentation has taught us that very often a company does better by devoting its efforts and creativity to developing a marketing programme specifically designed to appeal to a segment of the market rather than to the market as a whole. The theory goes on to say that having studied the firm's strengths and weaknesses in some depth the marketer decides to seek to satisfy a selected part of the market rather than attempt to be all things to all men. However, when approaching the market with a segmentation

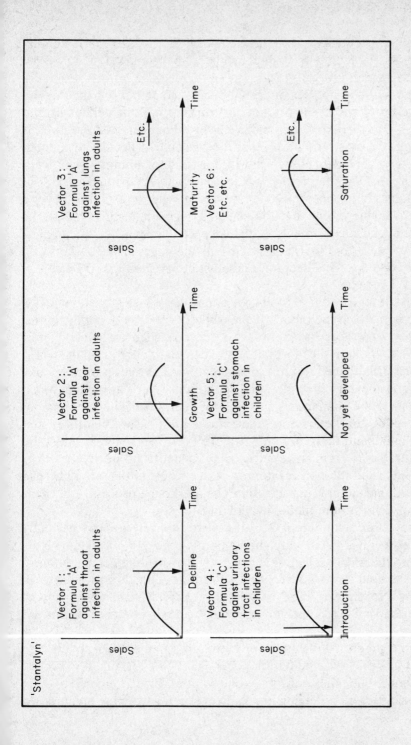

Figure 10.2 Vector life cycles

policy it is necessary to recognise that it is essential to gain a signific-ant portion of the sub-market whilst a small market share of the totality would have sufficed.

Segmentation policies often fail for the simple reason that having decided to segment the market and concentrate one's effort in that area, one has acquired too small a share of the segment in question. It is therefore vitally important that the person who decides to concen-trate on a segment should seek to dominate or obtain a significant part of that segment. The would-be segmenter should carry out thorough market measurement studies in order to establish beyond all reasonable doubt that the selected segment justifies the firm's attention. After all, having opted for a part of the market instead of its totality one takes the risk of 'placing all one's eggs in one basket', and before taking such a decision one must be satisfied that the strategy selected is right.

Market segmentation offers considerable scope for creativity. It is an area in which the innovative marketer can identify opportunities which competitors have missed or have decided to ignore. Thus, when one looks at the more successful car manufacturers in the world such as BMW, one soon recognises that the real reason for their suc-cess was the fact that they had identified a very attractive, albeit small unexploited market segment. However, in selecting one's target segment for marketing development one must ensure that three fun-damental conditions are adhered to: (a) the segment must be measurable; (b) is must be sufficiently substantial to justify the effort to be invested therein; (c) it must be accessible in the sense that the institutional systems that facilitate the marketing process (e.g. chan-nels of distribution, media availability) exist.

These three conditions are of course interrelated and perfectly logical. Yet it is sad to watch how often fairly experienced marketers fall into the trap of selecting segments which do not meet one or more of these conditions and consequently fail. A further pitfall lies in attempts to 'cheat old age' of a declining product by simply differen-tiating it vis-à-vis a specific segment which happens to be on the decline as well.

In our modern and very competitive environment it is not enough to assume that a segmentation policy is per se a formula for success. One must refine the concept beyond what we have attempted to do in the past. Before indulging in product planning we must break down the market into consuming-oriented and cost/benefit oriented sub-markets or 'vectors'. Obviously there is nothing to stop the marketer from standardising a product for a cluster of 'vectors', but it must be by design and not by accident. This is not dissimilar to the kind of problem that one encounters in international marketing where the effective marketer seeks to identify the needs of each country but then attempts to standardise the product for as many countries as lend themselves to such standardisation.

For example, suppose a large transport company has decided to specialise in the field of carrying very heavy cargoes (over 150 tonnes per cargo). This is in itself a segmentation policy inasmuch as the firm has opted out of the very competitive field of transporting ordinary cargoes. One hopes that before embarking on this strategy, which demands a very heavy 'infrastructure', the company has gone through the process of measuring the size of the market for heavy cargoes and found it to be substantial in marketing terms. Furthermore, the firm should have established that the segment in question is accessible.

The strategy may prove to be successful but if the firm wishes to pursue the logic of this argument a step further it must undertake a vector analysis. That would help to ensure that the marketing effort is more directly geared towards the real marketing opportunities and that the product is totally congruent to the needs of each vector.

How should the company go about it? They should analyse step-by-step in quantified terms who needs to carry very heavy cargoes. The Standard Industrial Classification offers a useful division of the industrial scene. Thus the mining/quarrying and the chemical and shipbuilding industries are all relevant vectors, and each one probably needs a different product. Moreover, some of these many vectors will offer better marketing opportunities than others.

If one could plot all these opportunities on a 'dart-board' type chart (see Figure 10.3) the best will fit into the 'bull's eye' centre; the next on the adjacent circle and so on. Once the implications of this philosophy are grasped by the creative marketer, he or she will have acquired an excellent tool for planning. First, the product will be more directly designed to meet the best vector's needs. Second, the promotional mix can be geared towards the most attractive target audience. Third, the sales force can be directed towards the 'bull's eye' buying environment. It is a totally different story from sending a sales force in search of people who need to transport very heavy cargoes.

ORGANISATIONAL IMPLICATIONS

It is worth exploring the organisational implications of what has been suggested. Many companies have so-called product managers or brand managers. Quite a few of these firms must reflect upon the real role of these managers and its appropriateness to a truly marketing oriented business. In many situations these managers are the hidden manifestation of a bias towards the product as seen by production people rather than the one seen by marketing people. What, for instance, is the marketing relevance of a flooring product manager in a firm that manufactures and supplies flooring for domestic, industrial and institutional markets? Surely what such a company needs is a domestic flooring *market* manager, an industrial flooring *market* manager and an institutional flooring *market* manager.

The word 'market' is emphasised because the product as such does not exist until such time as the market/segment/vector in question exists. It is the needs of the market which the manager has to satisfy and not the needs of the product. In seeking to meet the needs of the market the marketer has to develop a total marketing mix and not only a product. By calling him or her a product manager we simply fog the issue and detract from the importance of the job.

It is not suggested that the role of product managers has disappeared. In many firms such managers are most appropriate and their role is an important one. At the same time it is recommended that before opting for a structure that encompasses the product management concept top management must explore the alternatives and consider the relative merit of each in relation to the marketing aims of the firm. In fact in certain circumstances one can envisage solutions which embrace both product management and market management in a matrix[1] combination.

The whole essence of the matrix approach to organisation development is based on the theory that two vital, albeit slightly overlapping structures can coexist. One of the structures is traditional, hierarchical and results-oriented. The other structure is coordinative, integrative and in many instances seeks to impart a truly marketing-oriented dimension to a system which by its very nature is

---

1   See Simon Majaro, *International Marketing – a Strategic Approach to World Markets,* George Allen & Unwin, ch. 11.

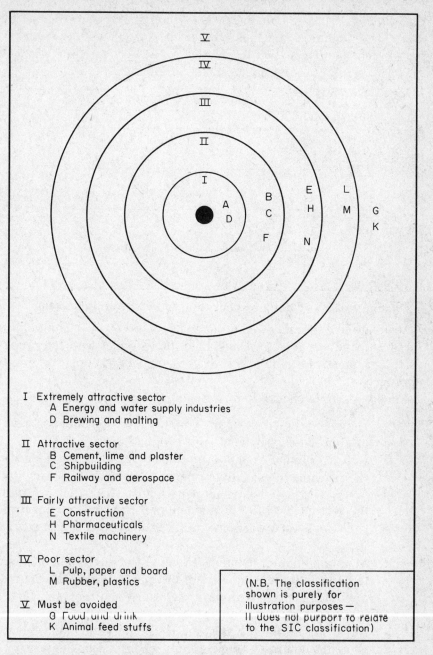

I Extremely attractive sector
   A Energy and water supply industries
   D Brewing and malting

II Attractive sector
   B Cement, lime and plaster
   C Shipbuilding
   F Railway and aerospace

III Fairly attractive sector
   E Construction
   H Pharmaceuticals
   N Textile machinery

IV Poor sector
   L Pulp, paper and board
   M Rubber, plastics

V Must be avoided
   G Food and drink
   K Animal feed stuffs

(N.B. The classification
shown is purely for
illustration purposes —
It does not purport to relate
to the SIC classification)

**Figure 10.3   The relative attractiveness of 'sub-markets' for a 'heavy-
cargoes' transporter**

less capable of being dynamically so. Referring back to the earlier example of Stanton Chemicals, one can envisage a matrix type organisation like the one shown in Figure 10.4.

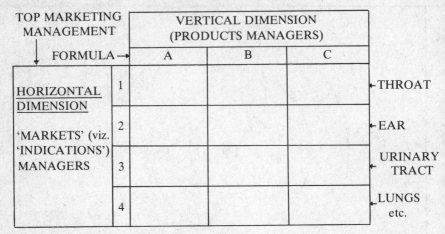

Figure 10.4   Matrix organisation for Stanton Chemicals

A structure like this may well prove to be the best way of combining the more traditional way of managing the product with the much more progressive, albeit more complex, marketing oriented approach.

Finally a simple checklist for the more enlightened reader:

1 Do not attempt to structure your organisation until you have established clearly what your products are.

2 Before defining what your products are, attempt to identify the size and accessibility of the various market vectors that your company is best equipped to satisfy. The 20 per cent of the vectors that offer 80 per cent of the results for your firm will direct you towards the most sensible and effective structure.

3 Maintain enough flexibility in your structure to enable you to cope with the dynamism of the marketplace. The matrix approach to organisational structuring can offer such a flexibility in many situations.

4 Never forget that the most successful marketing takes place when the company knows exactly who it is trying to satisfy.

11

Making a Marketing Plan

John Stapleton, Executive Director, Marketing Tuition Centre

Every marketing activity is an investment in time, energy and money. Few companies would spend thousands of pounds on, say, a purchase of capital equipment without a full investigation into its justification, the alternatives available, and the expected return on expenditure. Yet every year the vast majority of companies allocate a substantial part of their revenue to marketing actions without fully assessing the value or likely return on that investment. By introducing the disciplines arising from marketing planning a company should be able to ensure that the costs of marketing show an equitable return and are subject to measurement in the same way as all other business investments.

Many executives believe that the costs of marketing form an additional expense that has to be borne in order to sell their goods. Whilst it is true that many companies use certain tools of marketing for this purpose, it is true also that the most successful companies accept marketing as an essential and integral part of the company's total commercial operation, for it is an essential cost in just the same way as production or finance.

Companies often avoid marketing planning procedures because of the effort needed to express their forward policy in a written form. Executives commonly consider that their time is too valuable to spend on anything other than pressing operational problems; those that face them from day-to-day. In fact, the manager who devotes his time to dealing with current administrative detail is almost certain to have ignored proper planning in the past. For if properly prepared the marketing plan will contain sufficient details of the company's policy and operational strategy for the implementation to be undertaken by an assistant. As the many alternative courses of action are programmed it is merely necessary for the assistant to activate the appropriate remedy or decision. Only unusual situations need be dealt with by the manager.

The first step in preparing a marketing plan is that of producing the information necessary for decision making. Usually, a company will have within its own administration and control system the raw material necessary for the plan's foundations. In addition, there is an abundance of published information which is made available by government departments, para-governmental bodies, institutions, associations, and the national, trade, and technical press.

Marketing research is an activity which has yet to be fully exploited by the majority of companies. It has so far only been used by companies that have recognised that their existing information sources are inadequate. Because of the scale of operations that now confront the typical businessman it is essential that investment decisions are based upon relevant information, so reducing the number of variables and, hence, business risk.

STANDARDS FOR MEASURING PERFORMANCE

For a marketing-oriented activity to produce lasting results the entire operation has to be systematically planned. By producing basic information in written form and establishing goals and aims for the future the company is creating standards against which actual performance can be measured. Documentation of detailed policy actions then provides the basis for monitoring and controlling the company's operation. Future trends may be predicted through the investigation of all factors that are likely to influence company results.

It is, however, unusual for future opportunities to be easily isolated or even defined. The possibilities are infinite, but it is essential that the most promising are fully investigated and the potential assessed. It is particularly important that the man responsible for planning be a senior executive, for the full appraisal of market opportunities will enable that executive to gain far more intimate knowledge of the workings and the environment of the business operation than could be achieved from a lifetime of working within the close confines of the limited philosophy and procedure of one company. The executive will be able to learn about the interactive forces that affect the company, the industry and, more important, its markets.

In studying the company's future market the businessman will try to discover basic needs for which there is no satisfaction or possibly where there is an inadequate match. It is by discovering the peculiar needs of each existing and potential customer that the enlightened company starts its marketing-orientation. It is upon such special needs that the foundations are laid. Looking at the market and listing the operational needs of each industry, then measuring the extent of each need and then the value that the market places on overcoming the problem gives an indication of the potential – in volume and in profit opportunity.

THE NEW PRODUCT DEVELOPMENT PROGRAMME

From this stage the company will embark on a new product development programme in an effort to resolve the problems that face the market. Once a satisfactory product has been produced the basis for a promotional campaign is already apparent, as the original market assessment will have shown the prospects either by size, industry or location, and the product feasibility studies will have indicated the most appealing stimulus to demand for advertising and field selling purposes.

It must be apparent from these observations that success in marketing cannot be achieved overnight except by coincidence or good fortune. Often a minimum of three years will be required before the first hopeful signs become apparent. Successful use of certain marketing activities alone does not automatically mean a company is marketing oriented. This situation frequently presents management with an almost insoluble problem. As the whole company has to become involved with marketing principles for success to be possible, it is unlikely that a new recruit hired for his expertise will be able to win sufficient confidence from colleagues by results in the time span that is normally allowed a new manager.

There is usually only one man in a company who can inspire the confidence and support that is necessary and who will automatically have the authority to implement the total changes that may be justified, and he is the chief executive. Introducing satisfactory marketing-orientation is more likely to be successful if the present chief executive delegates most of his daily activities to an assistant or to senior line managers and devotes his entire energies to planning, than if a manager is appointed with such responsibilities.

DETERMINING COMPANY OBJECTIVES

Few company executives have ever formally determined their company's business activity. If they have it is often specified in terms of the means by which the business activity is achieved, e.g. printing rather than communications; or the end-product, e.g. aero-engines rather than propulsion; or by convention, e.g. insurance rather than security. The only sure means of defining the business activity is by thinking in terms of applications for a product, for whilst products, no matter how successful they are now, are heading for eventual decline, the need will usually remain – to be satisfied by the latest innovation. Determining the appropriate business activity is the first essential step in the marketing plan. In this first step the executive will establish the parameters within which his efforts should be confined initially, but will also rely upon the know-how, expertise, market reputation, and resources the company has accumulated during its history.

At the preliminary planning stage the company will need to decide upon the course that it wishes to take and the stages that have to be reached during each step in the journey. These objectives have to be achievable and yet sufficiently challenging to enable executives and staff to take pride in their fulfilment. The aims and goals of each company have to be expressed in the marketing plan in a way that is beyond dispute whilst capable of measurement and comparison. The only medium that achieves these standards is money – the means by which company prosperity is valued. The prime requirement for the survival and development of any business is profit. Too many managers still regard profit as the amount of money that is left over after all the operating expenses have been met. This view almost has connotations with a death wish, for profit is the prerequisite of all business activity and as such must be the first cost to the business.

PROFIT IS THE FIRST OPERATING EXPENSE

By writing in the profit required as its first operating expense the company recognises its major priority and then gears all its other objectives to ensure the acquisition of that profit. The sales volume needed, the orders to be won, the tenders or quotations to be sent out, the inquiries to be solicited, and all the means by which they are obtained are secondary objectives to be achieved before the prime objective becomes possible – in practice.

Any objectives of this sort must be based upon certain assumptions. It may have to be assumed that raw materials will continue to be available or that the government will not cause a market to dry up following an Act of Parliament. Whatever the objectives they will depend for their satisfaction on certain events happening or not happening. These assumptions are incorporated in the plan with a cross-reference to the strategies that will have to be implemented or the tactics employed should the assumptions become invalid. The strategies a company adopts are the means by which the company approaches its market opportunities and by which it adjusts its resources to exploit those opportunities. Its tactics are the methods it uses to meet short-term situations or more frequently the steps it takes when in immediate contact with customers.

In documenting the preliminary marketing plan it is also necessary to list all the major problems that have faced the company during its immediate history, as well as those that are expected to confront the company in the future. At the same time it is prudent to list all opportunities that have been under consideration with the expected profit return, when they are to be achieved and under what circumstances. Both problems and opportunities are then subjected to the same appraisal as the objectives and assumptions when the company strategies are built into the plan.

Every company struggles to improve its profit performance and any attempts planned for the period of the marketing plan, in detail for one year and in outline for five years, should be included. It is possible that improved productivity at the plant will make it possible for the company to improve its profitability through increased sales volume. Sales may be improved either by additional expenditure on marketing actions or by reducing price in an effort to expand the total market. It is by marketing planning that a company can be sure that whatever action it chooses will be based upon facts and information obtained from the marketplace.

Every action and every decision taken by the company executives will have an effect somewhere in the business. It may be favourable, it might be unfavourable. In formulating a marketing plan the company will be formalising its actions, weighing its alternatives, and deciding the most appropriate route open to it. Unless each marketing decision is made with the full and detailed consideration of the known, likely and possible effects upon the business, the investment that marketing actions require will be unmonitored and the management will have lost effective control of a major asset and the benefits that should accrue from that asset.

DEVELOPING THE MARKET PLAN

Preparing a sales forecast, the basis of the total marketing plan, is not just a matter of looking at past sales and trying to establish trends, but a conscious effort to look into the future and assess potential sales opportunity.

A company has started to be objective about its future when it attempts to evaluate the future and forecast what the market will require in the way of new or improved products. Most companies, in making long-range sales forecasts, choose a period varying between five and twenty years, while more detailed sales targets are usually prepared for the financial year immediately ahead. Many products which will be available in five years' time are already on the market and firmly established in the product range. It is often possible to use such historical sales performance as the basis for projections into the future, but only as the basis, for such projections are dependent upon future events being similar to events which have happened in the past. Allowance must be made for changes due to economic circumstances and changes in competitive forces within the industry under investigation.

Comparison of movements, either short-term fluctuations or medium to long-term trends, can often be achieved using the published economic data. Sometimes, acceptable degrees of correlation can be traced and these tied indicators will be useful parameters in forecasting.

The sales forecast can be as sophisticated or as simple as is justified by the business. The small to medium-sized business is usually better placed than its larger competitors for maintaining close contact with its markets and can use elementary methods of forecasting which often produce better results than the methods employed by larger firms, where customer contact has become more remote because of larger lines of communication.

While the larger company will normally handle the research necessary to prepare a sales forecast by using its own personnel, the smaller concern cannot justify the expense of recruiting and retaining specialist staff. Where such forecasts are prepared, outside agencies are usually brought in for the task and, in recent years, multi-client projects have been evolved to cater for this demand. As the cost of research is spread over several sponsors, the research organisation can afford to employ highly skilled staff and carry out projects in some depth across a wide front. In addition, the research organisation is often able to prepare a report confidential to each client concerned.

BIAS TOWARDS ONE'S OWN COMPANY

Any sales forecast is subject to numerous influential factors, each of which must be isolated and measured. Some factors will have more effect than others and the forecaster must attempt to isolate and grade those factors according to their significance in such a way that weightings can be applied and an acceptable forecast determined within tolerable limits. In forecasting there is inevitably some bias towards the forecaster's own company and this must be avoided otherwise operating budgets, based on the forecasts, will be over-estimated, adversely affecting profitability.

It is also necessary to predict trends in related industries which provide indirect competition to the company's own products and which could have a bearing on the growth rate of the industry concerned. It is here that the forecaster can discover opportunities for product innovation or new product development. Since new products are the lifeblood of a company, their discovery, development and subsequent production programming are necessary parts of the sales forecasting procedure.

To maintain a constant growth rate it is essential that every company estimates the life cycle of each of its products and introduces new products at the apex, or earlier, of an established product's life cycle in order to continue company growth. New products should not be introduced in a haphazard manner, but properly planned to fit the firm's expansion programme.

Price cutting, the most often observed tactical device in the struggles against competition, is a negative approach unless done from a position of strength with the company anticipating growth in the market and increased consumption achieved as a result of the price stimulus.

New markets are occasionally created following new legislation by government. Such changes can also be the cause of a substantial growth or decline in established markets and are often put forward as attempts to improve the social and/or economic life of the nation. Sudden changes in taste or fashion can cause sudden shifts in demand. Climatic changes can seriously affect sales of products which rely on extremes of temperature for their sales volume. Economic recessions, strikes or industrial disputes often bring in their train changes in purchasing habits.

CONTINGENCY PLANNING

Fortunately, many of these factors are predictable. There will certainly be any amount of published comment indicating possibilities. Research into future events is sometimes sponsored by trade and professional bodies; many thousands of words are produced by numerous authoritative writers in scores of newspapers, magazines, and trade and professional publications. These reports can be of tremendous value to the businessman seeking an insight into the future.

While one cannot forecast accurately what is going to happen, plans can be laid to cover any eventuality in advance of the event, at different levels of effectiveness. If the consequences of events are quantified in purely monetary terms, the businessman will be able to equate consequences with sales volume and, thus, profitability. Where necessary, contingency plans can be brought into operation.

It is true to say that many manufacturers take their products for granted and rarely investigate the uses to which they are put by customers, or how relevant they are to the customer's applications. Research can establish whether new features introduced by the manufacturer in good faith in the belief that they provide a plus for the buyer are not really required and not used, although paid for by the customer in the original selling price. It is possible, of course, that customers may not have realised the significance or relevance at the time of purchase.

In assessing product performance the businessman needs to relate application to product characteristics. Several companies have developed their share of the market as a direct result of providing a superior finish or excellent design. Buyers are often impressed by tales of long life for some mechanical item and sometimes make buying decisions in favour of such devices because the cost can be amortised over several years' operational life.

In arriving at the final assessment based on established standards relating each factor to every other factor, the researcher can compare the total significance of these in terms of market share and will be able to relate the performance of individual companies according to factors on which they concentrate. Comparison of results is the only certain way of monitoring company performance in a competitive commercial environment. The standards established in the appraisal of competitor profiles provide the foundations for a full analysis of market shares. Companies desiring to break into a completely new market will need to examine the extent to which policies adopted by those already serving this market have been successful.

Having obtained full information on total market size it is necessary to assess the extent to which the market can be penetrated either by winning a share of the existing market or by concentrating on growth and winning the business which would otherwise have gone to present suppliers. Once this work has been done the company can make a full and realistic evaluation of the marketing budget necessary to achieve its objectives.

It may be easier in some industries to take business from established suppliers than to expand the total market. In other projects it may be more feasible to opt for developing the growth market potential than to get involved in a battle with those already active in the market. Only when the business activity of the company has been decided should any attempt be made to measure the total market and to prepare a reasoned definition of the market.

DEFINITION OF THE TOTAL MARKET

Many people are confused about the total market for a particular product. It is the total amount of money spent in satisfying a need, irrespective of the products which satisfy that need. This means that all types of food are in competition with one another, the various forms of transport are competitors, and all aids to business efficiency are locked in combat for the purchaser's money.

The market situation for any given company or industry is continually changing and violent fluctuations can occur in market shares from day to day. Over a period shifts in the pattern of demand will become evident and it is imperative that a check be kept on such trends. Steadily rising sales turnover is not, in itself, a true indicator that a company is making the best use of its potential. It is quite possible for a company to achieve reasonable increases in sales year by year yet find that it has a rapidly diminishing share of the market. It will be losing sales opportunities unless sales volume is rising at least as rapidly as that of the industry as a whole.

A company also needs to keep track of its competitors' market shares and be able to explain any change that becomes apparent. There must be a reason why a competitor is expanding his market share faster than anyone else. If, on the other hand, a competitor with a strong marketing team is seen to be losing out on a market share, it could be that he has decided to diversify because of a forecast over capacity or a decreasing growth rate. It is for these reasons that it is vital to carry out constant analyses of market share at frequent intervals, even if in a simple form, rather than rely on occasional extensive research projects, no matter how sophisticated.

Confusion sometimes arises when referring to marketing research and market research. The former is the activity which examines all the elements which make up marketing practice, including markets, products, channels of distribution, pricing behaviour and opinions. Market research is only one element of marketing research, albeit the most widely known and practised.

When it comes to getting the goods to the customer, different companies use different channels of distribution. While some use stockists or distributors, others deliver direct to the retailer or even direct to the ultimate consumer. Different channels of distribution achieve different levels of success in selling their suppliers' products, and their effectiveness can be critical to the sales volume achieved by any one company. Channels of distribution in the consumer field have undergone considerable change in recent years. The development of supermarkets and self-service stores has progressed very rapidly in some areas of retailing, more slowly in others. Some companies have achieved considerable growth through the provision of mail order facilities, while others have built their share of the market through new selling methods such as party plan or vending machines or through selling direct to the household.

In the industrial field there have not yet been such fundamental changes in the pattern of distribution, although some changes have become apparent, e.g. leasing of factories and capital equipment, and the use of time sharing for data processing equipment.

CONTROL OF DISTRIBUTION

It is not generally realised that the cost to industry of distributing a product may range between 5 and 60 per cent of the final selling price, depending upon the nature of the product and the method of distribution selected. Active control of distribution can reduce these expenses and allow a substantial increase in profitability. Many related activities could be improved following an improvement in actual distribution.

The marketing executive must endeavour to reconcile the needs of the customer for a full service with his company's requirements for the provision of an economic level of service. If he decides that the most appropriate way to win sales from a competitor is by providing a superior distribution service, then that is a deliberate expense incurred in the marketing budget as an alternative to other marketing activities and expenditure.

Because of the forces of competition, demand for any one product from one source can vary considerably. It is the distributive function to provide a contingency against wide fluctuations in demand, and the businessman's responsibility to develop a distributive pattern to cater for those deviations from the norm. Some are more predictable than others and the product mix from the factory must be adjusted to cope with the demand.

Properly controlled, the distributive system can protect a company against giving customer dissatisfaction and will enable it to achieve a high level of productivity by ensuring economical production runs according to predetermined planning.

MONITORING THE MARKET PLAN

No matter how carefully a management may plan, some objectives will always be more difficult to achieve than others. Marketing planning is not a panacea for all commercial and industrial problems.

Ideally the marketing plan will include any action which may have to be taken to avoid diminution of profits. Even if actual performance exceeds all expectations there should be built-in provisions for the favourable conditions which have become apparent. If proper care has been taken to structure the marketing plan the contingency section should be straightforward, being no more than the detailed consideration of alternative courses of action. The contingency plan should include action which may need to be taken in the short term to minimise or maximise the possible consequences of deviation from the schedule as well as the medium to long-term action necessary to exploit a changed environment.

To ensure that the right action is taken at the right time – to ensure best results – it is essential that a barometer of company and industry performance is developed. Steps must be taken to monitor actual results against forecast company sales and forecast market shares.

There are several specialist organisations which provide, at reasonable cost, performance comparisons within an industry. If one of these organisations is used, the company needs to develop only an internal early warning system. This can be done by plotting orders received by major product groups against the purchasing industry by standard industrial classification.

In the shorter term, signals can be provided by relating actual inquiries, quotations, orders received, and sales by major product groups against the forecast. Then if the average timelag between inquiry and order is, say six weeks, and between order and delivery is four to six weeks, the company will have, automatically, nearly three months' notice of an imminent fall-off in sales. Care must be taken to ensure that conversion ratios between each stage do not vary, or that if they do adjustment be made accordingly.

Whilst it would not be wise to institute remedial action as a result of one deviation from plan – for occasional fluctuations do happen – once a trend becomes apparent, the cause should be established and appropriate action taken. In addition to showing industrial performance as a whole, some specialist comparison organisations quote the detailed performance of unspecified companies against which the performance of one's own firm can be measured.

Here, the company should be able to judge the extent to which it will be able to exert influence on the market. If the entire industry is suffering the same deteriorating position, it is probably wise to curtail any plans for expansion unless there is a clear indication that the present circumstances can be favourably exploited. The timing and extent of any cutback in this area should be provided for in the contingency plan, which should show detailed profit and loss statements for 70, 80, 90, 110 and 120 per cent actual performance against forecast. Each of the detailed accounts should include the appropriate departmental budgets and head counts. The major driving principles must be to preserve net profit and indemnify future profits. These considerations often prove incompatible in practice and a working compromise may be necessary. Sometimes, profit comes from the last 15 to 20 per cent of sales, after overheads have been covered, and when costs become marginal. Under such circumstances a reduction of 20 per cent in sales volume will warrant, perhaps, a cut of 30 per cent in expenditure in order to maintain net profit at par value.

A company can sometimes avoid the disaster of a temporarily poor market position by acquiring another company. A study of competitive profiles in the marketing plan, followed by detailed investigation of suitable partners, may disclose a competitor which could supplement, or ideally complement, the company's own operations.

Although the possibility of making a takeover bid will almost always be considered first, realistic management must not discount the advantages of soliciting a bid for one's own company, as this may be more prudent.

Detailed consideration of both rationalisation and diversification policies should form a logical part of any contingency plan. There is nearly always conflict between the sales department, anxious to meet individual customer requirements, and the production department needing long production runs and the elimination of time-consuming 'specials'. Some firms reconcile these differences by adopting a market segmentation policy, producing 'specials' for each industry group. They then become so well-established within these industries that they achieve long production runs of these so-called specials. While these firms concentrate their efforts on the part of the market for which they are best suited, others have diversified into other activities in order to absorb their surplus production capacity.

Where there is a possibility that an imminent scientific breakthrough will bring product obsolescence, companies affected should attempt to concentrate future plans on less vulnerable fields of operation. A side-step into a related industry or technology is a natural and logical move for most companies as their technology and management expertise can then be put to profitable use.

INVESTMENT IN COMPANY RESOURCES

Although the need for improved efficiency and productivity has long been accepted by manufacturing processes in industry, and a similar need recognised for some time in the marketing function, it has never been satisfactorily resolved in the latter because of the difficulties of reconciling accounting principles with a business function which is considered part art and part science. While many marketing activities operate under disciplines not widely appreciated – let alone understood – by management, the practice of marketing is still an investment in company resources. If control is to be maintained marketing will be subject to the same accounting appraisal as any other form of investment.

The cost of handling orders of varying sizes must be ascertained if stock levels are to be controlled with great accuracy. It may be found more profitable to refuse orders selling below a price-level considered to be uneconomic. Such selective selling often increases profitability. Location of warehouses, planning of sales territories and routes of salesmen can be organised, using accurate cost statistics rather than intuition. Improving direction and supervision of salesmen through the setting of performance and activity targets can result in increased selling and operating efficiency.

Management in many companies is not always able to recognise that its products or services are mediocre or even inferior to others on the market. Where such blindness exists the company is unlikely to introduce new methods or procedures to assist in rectifying or overcoming the problem. In the same way the firm is unlikely to experiment with new ideas or make a fresh approach in an attempt to improve its future prospects. In these circumstances the only avenue left for that firm is to continue in its own fashion no matter how much the position may deteriorate.

Because of the pace of technological change, a greater demand is manifesting itself for information to be employed in decision making. Investment decisions become more and more complex as businesses grow. The businessman must endeavour to forecast growth potential, and the factors likely to influence his company's penetration of that potential, in an attempt to reduce the risk facing every business enterprise.

Companies should be able to identify the influences on their major activities and show how they are being controlled to the benefit of the entire organisation. The extent to which the information provided is relevant to the company's needs should be assessed. Executives need to eliminate unused material being prepared and to discover additional information previously unknown. Such research into the marketing effort will help to ensure that an economic level of expenditure is being maintained. Appropriate marketing policies should ensure that all products are developed according to the needs of the market and resources are not wasted on products which the market shows are unsatisfactory.

COMMUNICATING PROFIT RESPONSIBILITY

One of the important developments in marketing consumer goods is the change in emphasis to impersonal selling techniques such as advertising and point-of-sale display. Personal selling still has the most important role in industrial marketing. Improvement in the function and performance of industrial sales forces justifies more attention than is now perhaps necessary in consumer goods selling efforts. These salesmen cannot be expected to sell the ideal product mix without guidance and direction nor differentiate between product profitability. In any organisation the level of profit responsibility must not only be decided but also widely communicated to ensure the satisfactory implementation of the most critical of business activities.

The marketing plan and all its ancillary documents must be used by executives as a day-to-day control and development manual. The planning process must not be treated as an annual political exercise suffered by busy executives concerned with other tasks. Planning, organisation, direction and control are basic management jobs and, in a successful marketing-oriented company, will fill the management's working days. Each manager needs to understand the interactive nature of the individual tasks which have to be completed during each period of the marketing plan.

The timing of each step, at all levels and in each function, is critical if the total plan is to be satisfactorily coordinated and the anticipated results achieved. A flexible attitude to planning principles needs to be adopted so that management recognises the need for contingencies and their control within corporate strategy.

Unforeseen events create a different scale of priorities, and flexibility in policy interpretation as allowed for in the plan must be recognised if the company's interests are to be best served. The results of monitoring actual performance against forecasts have a definite value in personnel development and in operating efficiency, as does the preparation of forecasts itself.

The chief executive of any marketing-oriented company retains the final responsibility for marketing policies. The marketing manager gives advice in the field of marketing and may well carry a line responsibility. If the marketing concept is to be adopted the entire company and, in particular, the management team must be oriented towards customer satisfaction. And this is the essence of planning in marketing. For the end result – the marketing plan – is not so important as the benefits gained from the input. The effort, study, appraisal, and evaluation of the business environment provides the major bonuses from the preparation of the plan and it all starts from considering customer needs.

In the foreseeable future most companies will become increasingly involved in computerisation. Even if not directly concerned as users, companies will become involved by the extent to which suppliers, competitors, and customers become geared to electronic data processing. Every businessman must appreciate how the computer can be applied to marketing problems. He needs some appreciation of the effects of computers on present-day and future marketing decisions.

Future growth potential of computer-linked terminals making computerisation possible and economic for many smaller firms will certainly assist in the scientific application of marketing. The day is not far off when a company's entire planning process will be subject to computer storage and processing.

12

Developing and launching a new consumer product

Peter Kraushar, Chairman, Kraushar and Eassie Ltd

THE FAILURE RATE

Whenever one considers new products, there is immediately talk of the risks, the problems, the failure rate. There have been many requests for figures about the failure rate. What is it? Is it going up? Is it going down?

These are very difficult questions because there are so many problems in defining a new product and in defining success or failure. It is likely that very few executives, even in the company that launched a particular product, know five or ten years later how it has performed in relation to the initial criteria and the investment put behind it.

Probably the most comprehensive study ever carried out on failure rates was an analysis of 7,500 grocery products launched in the years 1959–74.[1] They were categorised as successes if they were still listed in Shaws Price List for August 1975 (see Table 12.1).

It is obvious that the date of the launch affects the proportion of products extant at any particular time. Thus only 16 per cent of 1974 launches had disappeared by August 1975 because there had not been time for this to happen. Otherwise the study showed that about one-third of all products disappeared in the first two years and

---

1   Kraushar, Andrews and Eassie Ltd, *New Products in Grocers*, London 1976.

Table 12.1 Products on the Market, August 1975

Launch year	Successes Number on market in August 1975	% of launches
1959	56	24
1960	72	22
1961	70	19
1962	98	23
1963	121	23
1964	100	23
1965	88	22
1966	127	40
1967	160	37
1968	140	39
1969	161	40
1970	167	41
1971	232	42
1972	325	63
1973	398	64
1974	442	84

eventually the number remaining settled down at 20–25 per cent of those launched.

It is probable that in the last few years the failure rate has not been so high. Companies have launched fewer important new products; they have cut down in particular on risky ones, often outside their area of expertise; they have improved their methods of evaluation; they have not made as much initial investment as before. For all these reasons the rate of failure has fallen and it is possible that out of ten consumer products launched nationally 30–40 per cent are successful in meeting profit criteria. What is certain is that there is considerable variation in this between different companies. Levers, United Biscuits, Birds Eye and a handful of other companies can undoubtedly claim a success rate higher than this while there are many consumer goods companies which still find it difficult to launch any successes at all.

Why do so many new products fail? Again reasons vary, but the main ones are as follows:

1   Companies are organised for today's business, not tomorrow's: therefore new products suffer from insufficient attention, priority being given to the company's current products.
2   Lack of objectivity: a new product project generates a momentum within a company which is difficult to stop and it is then looked at with rose-tinted spectacles.
3   Inaccurate evaluation: product/market research, financial evaluation, marketing evaluation are often done scantily, especially if there is time pressure, or it is just too difficult to predict what will actually happen in the market place.
4   Lack of sales force resources: most sales forces have been cut considerably in recent years and they find it difficult to cope with new products unless very careful attention is previously given to this area by management.
5   Inadequate distribution: the wholesale and retail trades have rightly become more selective than ever before and some new products have not obtained enough distribution to achieve adequate consumer penetration.
6   Inadequate consumer appeal: poor product quality, high price in a price-sensitive market, confused presentation, lack of enough advertising support are all frequent reasons for failure.

DEVELOPMENT POLICY AND CRITERIA

As a starting point, it is vital for the company to establish a development policy including financial and other criteria. This seems obvious but even large and sophisticated companies often do not have such a policy or, if they have it, it is not communicated to the relevant executives. What is the point of knowing where the company wants to go, if those involved in decisions on the company's future are not aware of the policy? The policy itself should be concise and should allow some flexibility. It should also be reviewed regularly, probably annually.

Ideally, analysis of the company's business and its strengths and weaknesses should take place, in order to establish:

(a)   the future of the current business;

(b)   whether there is likely to be a gap between profit require-
      ments (if so, when) and what is likely to be generated by
      current products;

(c)   opportunity for cost cutting in order to reduce the profit
      gap;

(d)   quantification of the profit gap in terms of development
      needs;

(e)   financial resources available for development;

(f)   the main assets that the company can bring to develop-
      ment, i.e. where it is strong and are there any areas where it
      has potential competitive strengths, and

(g)   any relevant weaknesses that need to be borne in mind and
      possibly reversed.

Following such an analysis it should be possible to establish a policy
covering:

(a)   definition of business area the company is/will be operating
      in;

(b)   development time scale;

(c)   attitudes to acquisitions versus internal development;

(d)   maximum capital available for
        (i) acquisition,
        (ii) internal development project;

(e)   minimum size of acquisition;

(f)   minimum turnover for a new product;

(g)   return on capital requirements;

(h)   attitudes to investment/payback policy, and

(i)   any other relevant criteria.

SEARCH FOR MARKET OPPORTUNITIES

Perhaps the most difficult problem a company faces is how to allocate
priorities and where management time and other resources should be
channelled. Some companies study every possible opportunity in
depth without cutting down to a short list of the most suitable ones, so

they produce nothing except paperwork. In other companies an idea catches on and it cannot be stopped however badly it performs in research, often because there is nothing else to take its place.

It has been found useful, therefore, to use numerical screening systems, in order to screen different markets as well as different concepts in one particular market. Such a system is no magic formula for success, but it has many advantages:

1 It allows evaluation of a large number of opportunities, yet enables the company to concentrate quickly on the best ones.
2 It is a disciplined approach which takes some of the subjectivity out of such decisions.
3 All the opportunities can be compared on the same basis.
4 It is possible to understand in what ways one opportunity is better than another.

Table 12.2 shows a typical, though simplified, example of a market screen.

Such a system pinpoints the problems and opportunities in each case; thus the example shows baby foods to be a very poor market, canned meat to suffer from both lack of profit and poor sales trends, while fruit juice has the best score for a food company because it is a reasonable market and it is suitable for internal resources. Greeting cards and toys are far more exciting markets, but do not fit in well with internal resources; acquisition or a joint venture would solve this, if either were within the scope of the development policy.

MARKET EVALUATION

Once a short list of possible market areas is established, it is clearly necessary to prepare an evaluation of the market in each case. There are many obvious standard headings such as market size, trends, products, prices, margins, companies in the market, distribution profile, trade attitudes, consumer attitudes, consumer profile, usage, profitability, main problems, main opportunities, initial conclusions. Such automatic headings are, however, not enough for development purposes; it is usually also worth considering the following:

Table 12.2 Example of a market screen.

Factors	Maximum score	Baby foods	Canned meat	Fruit juice	Greeting cards	Toys
Market size	15	4	14	7	15	15
Past growth	10	1	2	9	6	5
Profitability	20	8	2	13	18	19
Competition	20	6	8	15	16	16
Chance of originality	20	5	7	9	14	17
Seasonality	5	5	3	3	1	1
External total	90	29	36	56	70	73
Fit for:						
Company production	25	2	5	5	0	0
Sales force	20	8	14	14	7	7
R & D	10	7	7	7	2	2
Branding	15	2	8	9	1	2
Distribution	10	6	8	8	5	5
Internal total	80	29	42	43	15	16
Total score	170	58	78	99	85	89

1 How easy is it to obtain the market information? If it is, then any market opportunities are likely to be quickly available to hundreds of other companies.
2 What product failures have taken place in the market in the last 10–15 years? Why have they failed? Such information could be invaluable, as so often failures are repeated and companies just do not learn enough from the past (for example, Cadbury, Schweppes and Batchelors did not seem to learn enough from Nestlé's failure with Nestea).
3 What successes have taken place in the market and what are the reasons for their successes?

4   How does the market compare with that in other countries? Are there interesting different products in, say, the US, Japan, Scandinavia?

5   What is the price sensitivity in the market? Is there scope for higher priced, added value products?

6   Can the market be considered in a very different way from the usual standard classifications? For example, bath additives were a very small and uninteresting market in the UK, until manufacturers stopped thinking in terms of bath cubes and bath crystals and began to talk of luxurious products for the bath almost irrespective of the product formulation. The difference between the two approaches may seem small, but at the end it could provide a clue as to whether there is potential for development.

Such market data should be available from a combination of desk research and key interviews with the trade. Using executives experienced in key interviews can yield a wealth of highly valuable information. Such interviews are usually the most important factor in evaluating a market.

HOW TO ENTER THE MARKET

Following the market evaluation, it should be possible to see if it is worth proceeding further; if it is, the two main routes are through acquisition or internal development. Acquisition search and evaluation is outside the scope of this chapter: internal development almost invariably leads to the need to find distinctive and important new product ideas – which is very easy to say, but very difficult to execute.

In general, initial research (in the form of large gap analysis exercises, problem tracking studies etc.) is not cost effective in leading to distinctive and important new product ideas. It has been found more useful to generate ideas based on market knowledge and assumptions, develop the better ones and then validate the assumptions made by means of concept research.

While it is usually vital to find a distinctive concept, it must be a simple one which does not require a great deal of consumer education. If an idea sounds obvious once expressed, it is likely to be a good one, e.g. Weetaflakes, a wheat flake breakfast cereal instead of corn flakes – a simple concept which has nevertheless proved successful for Weetabix. There is no magic formula for idea creation but the following approaches have been found useful:

1 Obtain the 'feel' of the market: this may require some market research, but usually desk research, possibly augmented by key interviews, is enough.
2 Search for market gaps: search for opportunities through simple grid analysis, market segmentation, gap analysis based on existing market data.
3 International product search: successful products abroad do not necessarily repeat their success in the home market, but they can lead to useful ideas. A failure abroad can lead to an interesting product for the UK.
4 R & D/production ideas: it is important (but not always practised) to involve the technical personnel wherever possible; R & D often have relevant ideas and it can be useful to unearth old R & D suggestions/projects which have never been progressed for various reasons; what can be produced on underutilised plant may be another starting point.
5 Synectics: lateral thinking, in conjunction with the more 'logical' approaches, often leads to the more original ideas.
6 Lateral brainstorming: there has been some development of an approach combining the best aspects of lateral thinking with traditional brainstorming. Such sessions can often be quicker and so more cost effective than formal synectics.
7 Consumer creative groups: companies have been experimenting with different forms of creative groups, including target consumers as well as executives to develop more finished concepts and to react to ideas in a creative situation. In practice this does not work as well as it ought to, because typical consumers are not creative and, if one seeks atypical consumers, one might as well use marketing and technical executives!

CONCEPT DEVELOPMENT AND RESEARCH

Once it is agreed that an idea is worth researching, it must be shown to target consumers in such a way that they will understand it fully. This usually means that it should be explained on a concept board which gives the main points about the idea; initial packs could be used instead in situations where the pack itself is particularly important, e.g. in many toiletry markets. In addition, where possible, the consumer should be shown and even asked to use/eat a physical representation of the product, in order to have a better idea of what the company has in mind.

In practice, these procedures are not difficult in most food and drink markets; the initial product development can be done in a rudimentary way and kitchen samples can be used for such research. In toiletries again the product examples can be obtained, usually without too much trouble. In household chemical products – polishes, laundry products, DIY, gardening – the problems can be more difficult, but 'fudging' the products on the basis of what is already on the market is often possible.

In durables, on the other hand, where the design element is critical, this is a real problem, because the cost and time needed to develop a prototype make it difficult to have several different ones developed at the same time. Nevertheless, use of photographs or initial drawings is rarely satisfactory and it is important to have at least one prototype which can be shown to target consumers; thus car clinics have been extremely popular for all new car development.

When there are many concepts for the same target market, it can be helpful to carry out pre-sort concept groups. This makes it possible to discuss up to twelve concepts with consumers in outline form, in order to narrow down to five to six concepts which are worth covering in depth in subsequent concept research. In the concept research, which usually takes the form of group discussions, it is vital to have a very experienced researcher to lead the discussion. Only by so doing is it possible to differentiate between reactions to the concept in general from the way in which it has been expressed in both creative and product form. Inexperienced researchers find this differentiation difficult, but it can certainly be done in practice, so that such initial concept research should provide important indications as to whether there is an opportunity and, if there is, on the most profitable path to be followed technically and commercially.

In summary, a typical concept development project could look as shown in Figure 12.1

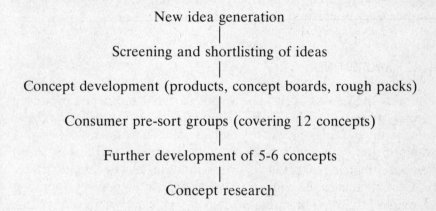

New idea generation
|
Screening and shortlisting of ideas
|
Concept development (products, concept boards, rough packs)
|
Consumer pre-sort groups (covering 12 concepts)
|
Further development of 5-6 concepts
|
Concept research

Figure 12.1   A typical concept development project

STAGE BY STAGE PLANNING AND EVALUATION

Once there is a definite new product concept with initial consumer interest in it, it is likely to be developed by means of a staged process which must vary considerably according to the type of product concerned and the risk and opportunity at each stage. Some of the stages are likely to be simultaneous, others sequential; some can take under a day, others years. A typical programme is shown in Figure 12.2, but it can only be treated as an example.

Ideally there should be a senior project leader within the company who has the personality and the authority to 'pull the project through' an organisation which is likely to be unconsciously against him. He must represent the very difficult combination of realism and enthusiasm, so that he can kill the project at any time if it does not meet criteria and enthuse everyone else if it does. In the latter eventuality he must have the backing of top management to ensure that he has full cooperation from technical development, sales management, financial, production, distribution and management itself, so that the new product has the right amount of priority. For example, at Heinz the marketing of soup is, in a way, child's play compared with the launch of, say, creamed rice, and it is significant that Heinz only made headway with new products in the early 1970s when Tony O'Reilly appointed his most senior manager to be in charge of new rather than of existing products.[2]

TEST MARKETING

Because of the risks likely to be involved in launching a new product it usually pays to test it first in a limited area. Mini-van research, as developed by Unilever, can at times be a substitute means of bridging the gap between product research and national marketing, but a proper area test market in realistic conditions has two main virtues.

First, it teaches the company how to handle the new product, as it provides a pilot plant situation. This is particularly important if the new product is outside the company's previous expertise; for example, there have been strong rumours that Procter & Gamble is entering the sanitary protection market in the UK and, despite the company's knowledge of this market in other countries, it is natural that it should go into a test area to learn how the UK market operates and to become familiar with the production, marketing and selling requirements and the relationship between all these factors.

Second, test marketing provides a basis for future sales and profit forecasts, though these must be treated with care, because no one area is typical and the market varies from one year to the next. Test market performance must obviously be more reliable for future forecasts than estimates based on artificial research alone. This is particularly true if the test is long enough to allow for a settled pattern of repeat buying to take place.

Test markets are rarely possible in the case of durables, but there are times when it is possible to import a limited number of products or to obtain sufficient from another source for an area for one large customer. It is always worth considering such methods of cutting the risk.

---

2   Charles Lowe, paper presented to Marketing Society annual conference, 1973.

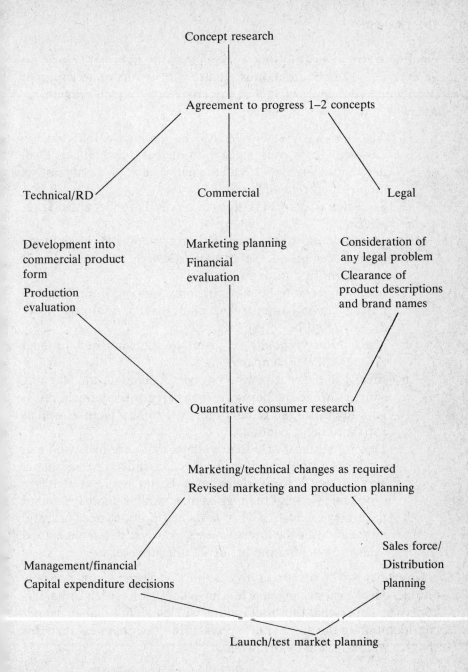

Concept research

Agreement to progress 1–2 concepts

Technical/RD   Commercial   Legal

Development into
commercial product
form
Production
evaluation

Marketing planning
Financial
evaluation

Consideration of
any legal problem
Clearance of
product descriptions
and brand names

Quantitative consumer research

Marketing/technical changes as required
Revised marketing and production planning

Sales force/
Distribution
planning

Management/financial
Capital expenditure decisions

Launch/test market planning

Figure 12.2   Stages in the development of a new product concept

THE LAUNCH

Finally, at the end of all this work, comes the national launch. In practice not enough attention is paid to it; it is also quite wrong to consider it as the final step in the project – it is still only the beginning! A few points are worth making:

1 The national launch needs to be planned a long time in advance. Some companies will not accept any launch, even in a limited area, unless all the details are agreed at least six months beforehand.

2 The sales force must be given a very full product and market briefing.

3 The trade must be given a full presentation of the thinking behind the product, the main research and test market results and the future aims.

4 Forecasts need to be made of consumer and trade penetration each month or every two months and monitoring procedures should be set up accordingly.

5 High priority should be given to the launched product throughout the company.

6 Ideally the executive who has been behind all the planning should also be the person responsible for the launch; this is vital to ensure the required level of commitment as well as for the sake of continuity.

7 Despite all the work done to date, there are likely to be at least some problems. If the product has indeed passed all the hurdles satisfactorily there must be no panic at the first problems; some of the biggest new product successes found it hard going at first. The launched product needs careful nurturing over the first few years to ensure that it has a good chance of joining the list of significant successes.

No reader will be so naïve as to imagine that a brief chapter on new product development can make him an expert in this crucial area. It is hoped, however, that this brief outline will lead him to much deeper consideration of the more vital aspects. If this does happen, then this chapter will have been worthwhile.

13

Developing and launching a new industrial product

Professor Michael J. Baker, Department of Marketing, University of Strathclyde

For many years it has been argued that there are more similarities than differences between industrial and consumer marketing so that it is divisive and often counter-productive for practitioners in either field to ignore practice and experience in the other. Nonetheless, in the particular, it is clear that there are important differences in degree which merit separate consideration and treatment. In the preceding chapter Peter Kraushar has dealt with many of the key concepts related to new product development and the same ground will not be covered again – the primary objective is to focus attention on some of the more distinctive features associated with the marketing of new industrial products.

Clearly, within the scope of a book of this nature, it is only possible to provide a brief overview of some of the main factors and the reader is strongly recommended to consult some (or all) of the books listed in the reading list at the end of the chapter in order to gain an appreciation of the complexity and richness of this field of marketing activity.

The chapter itself is developed in the following manner. First, the importance of new product development to the firm's survival and growth as the major plank in its competitive strategy. Next, the reasons why users and markets resist innovation with the result that many new products are deemed to be failures. Arising from this analysis, some guide lines are proposed for identifying early buyers so that the firm can develop the most effective launch strategy to ensure rapid penetration and development of the market for its new product.

THE IMPORTANCE OF NEW PRODUCT DEVELOPMENT

While it is true that demand does exceed supply in certain markets this is largely confined to new markets for new products. In more traditional and familiar markets, such as those for steel, ship-building, car tyres and even cars themselves, potential capacity far exceeds effective demand with the result that firms compete with each other for the customer's favour. Classical economics would have us believe that this competition would focus on price, but the reality is that manufacturers choose to recognise that demand is not homogeneous and so seek to differentiate their product to match more closely the needs of specific subgroups or market segments. Clearly if the manufacturer is successful in distinguishing his product in a meaningful way, then he provides prospective users with a basis for preferring it over other competing alternatives and so creates a temporary monopoly which allows him a measure of control over his marketing strategy.

The desirability of exercising some control over a market rather than being controlled by it – being a price maker rather than a price taker – is self evident. The wisdom of doing so is equally compelling, for a number of surveys have shown conclusively that while price ranks third or fourth in the selection criteria of most industrial purchasing agents product characteristics or 'fitness for purpose' invariably ranks first.

For these reasons product differentiation has become the basis for competition between suppliers competing for a share in a market and this explains the importance attached to product development by most firms today. It also helps to explain why new product development (or innovation) has become increasingly sophisticated and much riskier than it used to be. This is because, with so many more firms investing heavily, minor features are quickly copied or made obsolete by more radical changes. In the same way, the accelerating rate of change has had a similar effect on major innovations so that the average life of products is becoming shorter and shorter (compare, for example, valves, transistors and microprocessors as basic inputs to computing devices). Thus many firms are faced with the apparent paradox that if they do not innovate they will be left behind, while conversely if they do the probability of failure is very high and this could ruin the company too. As Philip Kotler has put it:

> Under modern conditions of competition, it is becoming increasingly risky not to innovate .... At the same time, it is extremely expensive and risky to innovate. The main reasons are: (1) Most product ideas which go into product development never reach the market; (2) many of the products that reach the market are not successful; and (3) successful products tend to have a shorter life than new products once had.

With regard to the first point it is clear that discarding products during development must impose some cost. However, there is a great deal of advice on this phase of development and it is believed that companies have become much better at weeding out weak ideas earlier in the development cycle and so minimise losses from this source. Similarly a shorter life might be preferable to a long one if one can generate similar volumes of sales, because the discounted value of present sales is greater than future ones and early capitalisation of an investment gives the firm greater opportunity for flexible action. This point will be developed later.

Much the most important cause for concern is the fact that many products are not successful at all. In these cases not only has a company incurred all the development costs but it has also incurred the marketing costs of launching the new product, not to mention the possible loss of goodwill on the part of the users who discover the product is unsuccessful and likely to be withdrawn from the market.

THE NATURE AND CAUSES OF PRODUCT FAILURE

While claims concerning the incidence of new product failure are commonplace, few such claims are based on hard evidence. Those that are usually conflict with one another, due to the absence of any agreement about precisely what is to be measured, so that trying to quantify the proportion or value of failures is largely a matter of speculation. However, managers are agreed that the number and cost of failures is high and are anxious for advice as to how they can reduce this risk. In order to do so it will be helpful to propose a simple definition of failure and then see if at least the major causes of it can be identified.

A simple definition of failure is that this is deemed to have occurred when the innovator so decides. While this may not appear to be very helpful, it should help to clear the ground by making it explicit that success and failure are comparative states and there is no yardstick or criterion for deciding when one ends and the other begins. To argue otherwise would be to claim that all firms subscribe to the same managerial objective – for example, a return of x per cent on capital employed – and clearly they do not. It follows that your failure might be someone else's success and attempting to define the states precisely is a sterile exercise.

This is certainly not true of establishing the perceived causes of failure because by so doing it should be possible to develop guidelines and tests for identifying and avoiding these in future. Unfortunately, relatively few firms appear to be willing to document their failures and there is a marked dearth of case history material on the subject. Many years ago (1964) the National Industrial Conference Board in the United States conducted a survey as a result of which it offered the following list of factors underlying failure in rank order of importance:

(a) inadequate market analysis;
(b) product defects;
(c) higher costs than anticipated;
(d) poor timing;
(e) competitive reaction;
(f) insufficient marketing effort;
(g) inadequate sales force; and
(h) inadequate distribution.

Over 50 per cent of all respondents cited the first three reasons.

A more recent study was carried out by Roger Calantone and Robert Cooper of McGill University in which they asked managers in 150 industrial companies in Quebec to categorise the nature of the causes leading to market failure: 'those products where sales had failed far short of expectations'. Table 13.1 summarises the responses to this survey and reveals strong support for the findings of the 1964 study.

Table 13.1 Specific causes for poor sales performance (N = 89)

Specific cause	Percent of product failures	
	Main cause	Contributing cause
Competitors were more firmly entrenched in the market than expected	36.4	13.6
The number of potential users was overestimated	20.5	30.7
The price was set higher than customers would pay	18.2	33.3
The product had design, technical or manufacturing deficiencies/difficulties	20.5	25.0
Selling, distribution or promotional efforts were misdirected	15.9	23.9
The product was the same as competing products . . . a 'me too' product	14.8	25.0
Did not understand customer requirements; product did not meet his needs or specifications	13.6	26.1
Selling, distribution or promotional efforts were inadequate	9.1	31.8
A similar competitive product was introduced	10.2	22.7
Were unable to develop or produce product exactly as desired	11.4	19.3
Competitors lowered prices or took other defensive actions	12.5	13.6
Timing was too late	8.0	13.6
No market need existed for this type of product	5.7	18.2
Timing was premature	6.8	13.6
Government action/legislation hindered the sale of the product	2.3	3.4

In between these studies Andrew Robertson and his colleagues at the Science Policy Research Unit at Sussex University conducted an analysis of a series of 34 new product failures and concluded that their main cause was a lack of market orientation.

While the evidence may not be as extensive as one might wish the conclusion appears inescapable – failure is the consequence of managerial ignorance or, worse still, managerial neglect. Ignorance because there is a very extensive managerial literature, based on well documented practice, which emphasises the importance of thorough market analysis as an essential prerequisite of any new product development; neglect because it is management's responsibility to keep itself informed of the best current practice and, if one is well informed, it is difficult to conceive how one could excuse commercial failure in a variety of ways which fundamentally all come down to the same thing – inadequate market analysis.

Several other chapters in this handbook provide advice on aspects of market analysis and measurement all of which is applicable to industrial marketing. Accordingly it will be assumed that the reader is informed and responsible and will put to good use the advice contained in these chapters. Unfortunately while this will greatly enhance the probability of success it cannot guarantee the eradication of 'failure' for one or other of two basic reasons.

First, failure is defined in terms of not achieving a target sale volume within some prescribed period of time, usually determined on the basis of the time necessary to earn a satisfactory rate of return on

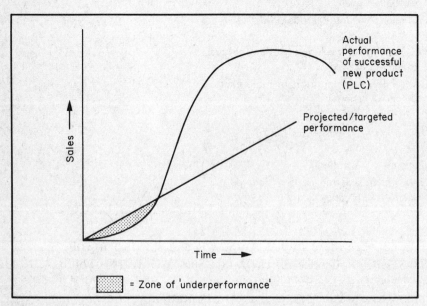

Figure 13.1   Product life cycle and projection of expected sales

the capital employed. The difficulty in applying such a criterion is that the great majority of managers tend to use a straight linear extrapolation when projecting future sales despite the fact that all the available evidence on the sales performance of successful new products points convincingly to some form of exponential growth. The theoretical expression of such a phenomenon is the well known product life cycle concept which postulates that all products pass through a life cycle characterised by slow initial development. This is followed in turn by a period of rapid growth and a period of maturity or stability, whereafter sales will begin to decline unless management takes positive steps to extend or even rejuvenate the mature phase. Such a product life cycle is reproduced in Figure 13.1 together with a straightforward linear projection of expected sales. From this figure it is abundantly clear that in the initial phases the new product will consistently underperform against the target – indeed the gap between the two will increase. Depending upon the time scale involved it seems quite likely that many managements will withdraw a product from the market because of its apparently deteriorating performance (the gap between 'projected' and 'actual') without ever knowing whether it would 'take off', in which case actual sales would later greatly exceed those projected.

Of course this is the major criticism levelled against the PLC concept – it can only tell you what the sales performance of a *successful* new product will look like – it cannot tell you if any given product experiencing difficulty in penetrating a market would be successful if you persevered with it.

The second reason why existing advice on market analysis and new product development will never result in a 100 per cent record of success is that there is another important factor which has been omitted from conventional analysis and which accounts for a significant proportion of failures. This factor has been described in a number of ways, the most familiar of which is 'resistance to change'. But, however we describe it, it is an expression of managerial attitude towards new products and it helps to explain why such products make slow initial progress when first introduced to a market.

It is vital that managers responsible for launching new products should understand why prospective customers may be slow to appreciate or accept the benefits claimed for such innovations. Clearly, if one possessed such information then it might be possible to devise strategies to overcome these difficulties. Basically, the problem seems to be that while most managers feel that they can pre-identify the most receptive market for an innovation the evidence is that by and large they are not very good at it. With the benefit of hindsight it is not difficult to see why company *A* could not seem to make up its mind about the benefits of adoption while company *B* accepted it almost immediately. The question is can we identify any patterns in the reactions of companies to new product propositions which would enable us to pick out the *B* companies in advance? The next section summarises some of the factors which should be taken into account.

MANAGERIAL ATTITUDE AND 'RESISTANCE TO CHANGE'

It has been suggested that a major problem with economic theory is that many laymen mistake its models for reality. Much the same problem seems to beset our attitude to industrial purchasing decisions for, while it is argued that consumers (usually 'silly housewives') may act irrationally, it is unquestioningly accepted that firms follow the precepts of economic rationality and make decisions which maximise a price/quantity relationship in the manner prescribed by economic theory.

My own view is that *all* buyers use objective criteria in determining which purchase will give them the most satisfaction i.e. they behave 'rationally'. Unfortunately, such a process frequently fails to enable a prospective buyer to come to a decision for the simple reason that after exhausting all the available objective criteria he is still left with two or more apparently equivalent alternatives and has to make a choice between them. As a theoretician we can assume away this problem by stating that if two or more products are objectively the same then they *are* the same and it does not matter which we choose. In the real world it is not like that at all – Daz is different from Omo, Rover is different from Mercedes, Goodyear is different from Dunlop, JCB is different from Caterpillar and so on. In the absence of any means of distinguishing between close substitute products life would become intolerable for we would live in a state of constant uncertainty. Thus the reason products are perceived as different is because we believe them to be so (usually with more than a little help from their manufacturers) and it is this belief or attitude which determines how we make purchase decisions.

But subjective factors do not only influence final purchase decisions when we are required to make a choice between what otherwise might be considered objectively identical products, they also influence our perception of the objective factors themselves. Thus it is not a question of what the seller claims are the attributes of a product or the benefits which will flow from its adoption that is important, but the prospective buyers' interpretation of these claims and there are numerous reasons why their views may differ. For example, James Bright cites twelve major sources of opposition to innovation and it is significant that only two of these, (c) and (f), make any pretence to economic objectivity:

(a)   to protect social status or prerogative;
(b)   to protect an existing way of life;
(c)   to prevent devaluation of capital invested in an existing facility, or in a supporting facility or service;
(d)   to prevent a reduction of livelihood because the innovation would devalue the knowledge or skill presently required;
(e)   to prevent the elimination of a job or profession;
(f)   to avoid expenditures such as the cost of replacing existing equipment, or of renovating and modifying existing systems to accommodate or to compete with the innovation;
(g)   because the innovation opposes social customs, fashions, tastes, and the habits of everyday life;
(h)   because the innovation conflicts with existing laws;
(i)   because of rigidity inherent in large or bureaucratic organisations;
(j)   because of personality, habit, fear, equilibrium between individuals or institutions, status, and similar social and psychological considerations;
(k)   because of a tendency of organised groups to force conformity;
(l)   because of reluctance of an individual or a group to disturb the equilibrium of society or the business atmosphere.

There is now a very considerable body of evidence which confirms beyond doubt that industrial buyers are just as subject to the processes of selective perception and distortion as are individuals making purchases for their own needs and it follows that industrial sellers should follow the example of their consumer counterparts in seeking to develop a better understanding of the factors which shape and influence the buyers' attitudes and behaviour. The final section of this chapter attempts to isolate certain guidelines which may prove helpful in this task.

IDENTIFYING THE INDUSTRIAL 'EARLY BUYER'

From the foregoing discussion it should be clear that:

1   Commercial failure is usually the result of delay in building up an acceptable sales volume.
2   The sales of a new product grow exponentially so that after an initial slow start successful products 'take off' and sales grow very rapidly indeed.
3   There is an inherent resistance to change and it is this which delays early sales.
4   While one may define a new product's economic and technological characteristics in objective terms these characteristics are viewed subjectively by prospective purchasers.

If we accept these conclusions then it seems reasonable to hypothesise that the first persons to buy must perceive the innovation more favourably than those who defer a decision or else reject the new product. It follows that if this is so then there must be a significant advantage in being able to pre-identify potential early buyers for it will then be possible to target one's initial sales efforts at them. As noted above most sellers would argue that they already try to do this, but if their pre-selection is based upon their perception of who is likely to benefit most from purchase then it is unsurprising if this differs from the potential user's view.

For example, many innovators concentrate their sales efforts upon market leaders or those with the greatest potential demand for the new product on the basis that they have the most to gain. They also have the most to lose and it is this alternative interpretation which invariably predisposes the bigger company to proceed cautiously. This is not to say that they will not be among the first to buy, because given their scale of operations large users can often afford to buy an innovation solely to test it without any final commitment to it either way. Conversely small companies may need only one unit of the innovation if it is a piece of capital equipment, or may have to standardise upon it if it is a raw material or component with the result that they are wholly committed and have to make the innovation work. Other things being equal then smaller companies have a greater commitment to any innovation they adopt and so will make strenuous efforts to make it successful.

Smaller companies are also likely to respond more quickly for the simple reason that decision making is more concentrated than in large companies and does not have to proceed through a heirarchy of committees. Further in the smaller company it is usually simpler to discover who the key personnel are – the 'gatekeepers' who allow in or exclude information on new products and the opinion leaders who gain job satisfaction through influencing their colleagues' views on specific matters such as the technical merits of a new piece of machinery. The benefit of being able to identify key individuals is obvious because we can then get to know them as such and achieve a much better knowledge of what conditions their perception.

Extensive research has shown that the firms most likely to respond quickly to new products are those which are experiencing some difficulties or problems of their own. For example, Jim Utterback of the Massachusetts Institute of Technology found in a study of five industries in Europe and Japan that 'successful projects were seen to be related to a fairly or highly urgent problem faced by a firm', and this conclusion is confirmed by numerous others. In broader terms then innovations are likely to appear more attractive to unsuccessful firms than to more successful firms. The conventional wisdom tends to favour the more successful, if for no other reason than that they will be able to pay, and this increases the probability of delay in market penetration.

A third factor of considerable help in pre-identifying receptive firms is determination of their policy on depreciation and replacement. Most innovations are substitutes for something else and it is clear that a need to replace may give rise to the urgency discussed in the preceding paragraph. Certainly, if organisations are actively reviewing replacement possibilities there would seem to be a greater likelihood of their being willing to evaluate a new product than would be the case if they are entirely satisfied with their present supplier or installation. Most firms have explicit depreciation and replacement policies, and time taken to determine these and the stage in the cycle at which individual firms are placed could repay handsome dividends in identifying the most receptive market segment.

A study of replacement policies may also uncover opportunities for joint product development, an approach which work by Eric von Hippel has shown to have a very high success rate. Most firms are flattered that their suppliers should take an interest in their likely future needs and are often willing to participate in joint product development thus making it quite clear what benefits users are seeking and also providing facilities for field testing and trials. In addition, one of the most persuasive arguments to encourage the purchase of a new product is to be able to point to its successsful use by someone else (another risk reduction strategy).

Collectively all the foregoing factors emphasise the need to know your customers and to put yourslf in their shoes when considering the perceived merits of an innovation.

Most new products are introduced by existing firms into existing markets and this is obviously much less difficult than is the case when developing an entirely new market. In the latter instance the same advice still applies, but much of the information will be more difficult to come by and may have to be inferred from other indicators. In such circumstances considerable benefits can be obtained by regarding the market development phase as a capital investment project (like R&D) and offering inducements to early buyers which help reduce the high perceived risk of being first. For example, it is possible to limit the financial risk by leasing or sale or return clauses, and running-in problems can be reduced by providing technical assistance and a generous policy on losses due to start up difficulties. Alternatively, it is possible to join forces with a supplier/distributor with a proven track record in the market and benefit from its marketing skills.

SUMMARY

In the scope of such a short chapter we can only scratch the surface of an enormous subject. Hopefully the discussion will encourage reading of the specialist books, some of which are listed below, as well as underline the relevance of the other chapters in this handbook. Marketing is a highly complex activity in which the practitioner has to combine a multiplicity of factors to meet a dynamic and continually changing situation. Nowhere is this more true than in the case of new product development, yet it is an activity which we cannot afford to avoid if we wish to remain competitive. It follows that any guidance on how to improve our success rate is to be welcomed and it is hoped that this chapter has provided some insight into the more important factors.

READING LIST

Michael J. Baker, *Marketing New Industrial Products,* Macmillan, London 1975.

Michael J. Baker and Ronald McTavish, *Product Policy and Management,* Macmillan, London 1976.

Michael J. Baker (ed.) *Industrial Innovation,* Macmillan, London 1979.

James R. Bright, *Research, Development and Technological Innovation,* Richard D. Irwin, Homewood, Illinois 1964.

Roy W. Hill and Terry J. Hillier, *Organisational Buying Behaviour,* Macmillan, London 1977.

Robert D. Hisrich and Michael P. Peters, *Marketing a New Product,* Benjamin/Cummings Publishing Co. Inc., Menlo Park, California 1978.

Edgar Pessemier, *New Product Decisions: An Analytical Approach,* McGraw-Hill Inc. New York 1966.

Merlin Stone, *Product Planning,* Macmillan, London 1976.

Brian Twiss, *Managing Technological Innovation,* Longman, London 1974.

14

The organisation of the marketing function

Michael J. Thomas, School of Management Sciences, University of Lancaster

INTRODUCTION

Organisations should serve the purposes for which they have been created. This chapter is firmly based upon the assumption that the purpose of any marketing organisation is primarily to serve customer needs. At the same time it is recognised that the marketing organisation is a vehicle for the company, and in particular for the chief marketing executive, to achieve the goals and objectives of the company.

Marketing executives have two parallel responsibilities. They have to make operating decisions whereby short-term marketing programmes are implemented, and they have to make a vital contribution to the strategic decisions which guide the company into the future and which ensure its long-term survival in the face of social, technological, environmental and, in particular, competitive change. Good marketing organisation must accommodate and be responsive to the needs of both operating and strategic decision making.

Very few companies in the United Kingdom are marketing companies. Though many chief marketing executives will happily state that they have embraced the marketing concept, such evidence as we have about marketing organisations in the United Kingdom[1] sug-

---

1   See 'Marketing organisation structures', pp.161–2.

gests that only a small number of companies are organised to implement it effectively.

Too many chief marketing executives are preoccupied with operating decisions, when they should be concentrating on strategic decisions. Too many marketing executives are concerned with the short term rather than with the long term, with individual customers rather than with market segments, with sales volume rather than with long-term profit. Marketing organisations in the 1980s must be focused on long-term survival, on exploiting long-run opportunities. They must examine how these can be turned into new products and markets, and how strategies can be developed that will ensure long-term growth in markets both at home and overseas.

There is no substitute for market orientation as the ultimate source of profitable growth, and the only way to be market oriented is to make sure that the organisational structure of the company is focused on its major markets.

Most companies, even some sophisticated companies, think with some conviction that they are market oriented, whereas in reality they are product and production oriented. There is no guarantee, for example, that a company that uses the product management system[2] will be market oriented, for, not surprisingly, many product managers can be very product oriented. In contrast with companies that think they are market oriented are those that have been forced into new organisational orientation as a result of pressure from very large customers, such as retail grocery chains which require that the companies they buy from use a specialist approach. Such an approach is referred to variously as national account selling, special accounts marketing or trade marketing. Similarly, companies that do business with the government, particularly with the Ministry of Defence, have had to develop specialised marketing approaches in response to the unique buying and contracting procedures of the customer.

The logic of such changes in organisation can easily be applied to other markets, both consumer and industrial. A number of companies have made an initial step towards market orientation by differentiating between consumer markets and institutional or commercial markets, developing marketing units to deal with each type of market. Some companies differentiate between distributors and orig-

---

2   See 'Product management organisation', p.163.

inal equipment manufacturing customers. Some companies differentiate between classes of distributors, organising their approach to distribution on the basis of the different markets served by different classes of distributors. Ironically, some companies are product oriented in their approach to the home market, but market oriented in their approach to overseas markets, an organisational approach forced on them by the special requirements of overseas markets and customers.

There is no one best way in organisational terms to implement the marketing concept, and what follows is not simple prescription. Rather, a series of questions about the marketing organisation will be posed and explored; questions that should enable the chief marketing executive of any company to explore the extent to which his marketing organisation is marketing oriented. It should be said that market orientation is first and foremost a state of mind and the chief marketing executive plays the key role in developing strategies, plans and organisation to implement the marketing concept.

The chief marketing executive is responsible for guiding his company into market orientation. He is responsible for serving the needs of established markets, for serving new needs in established markets, and for searching out new opportunities in new markets. What type of marketing organisation might best serve his needs?

WHAT SHOULD DETERMINE THE NATURE OF YOUR MARKETING ORGANISATION?

The Basic Principles of Organisation

Eleven principles of organisation are frequently cited[3] as general guidelines for any organisation. They are not immutable but provide a sound basis for organising any management task. They are classified into four basic elements:

1   *Objectives*. The objectives of the enterprise should be clearly stated and understood.
2   *Activities and groupings*. The responsibilities assigned to a

---

3   See H. Stieglitz, *Organisation Planning: Basic Concepts, Emerging Trends*, National Industrial Conference Board, New York 1962.

position should be confined as far as possible to the performance of a single leading function. Functions should be
assigned to organisational units on the basis of homogeneity
of objective.

3   *Authority*. There should be clear lines of authority running
from the top to the bottom of the organisation, and accountability from bottom to top. The responsibility and authority
of each position should be clearly defined in writing.
Accountability should be coupled with corresponding
authority. Authority to take or initiate action should be
delegated as close to the scene of action as possible. The
number of levels of authority should be kept to a minimum.

4   *Relationships*. There is a limit to the number of positions that
can be effectively supervised by a single individual.
Everyone in the organisation should report to only one
supervisor. The accountability of higher authority for the
acts of subordinates is absolute.

The external environment

Markets. The nature of a company's markets will help to determine
the nature of the organisation. Where there are relatively few
markets, a market oriented, functional or market management
oriented organisation is appropriate. Where the number of market
groups is large, and none is very powerful, a product oriented, product management system is appropriate. A geographically dispersed
market, particularly one involving overseas markets, will require
some form of geographical organisation, though this will be combined with product or market management. Customer rather than
market orientation may be appropriate, particularly when customers
are few in number, requiring negotiated sales and/or a high level of
after sales service.

The business environment. The type of business engaged in will
influence decisions about appropriate marketing organisation. A
company producing fast moving consumer goods is not likely to be
similar in organisation to a firm selling high technology products to a
small number of industrial consumers. The role of advertising, for
example, will differ greatly between two such environments, and in so
far as the marketing organisation will to a degree reflect the relative

importance of each of the subfunctions of marketing (sales, advertising, new product development, after sales service etc.) we would expect each marketing organisation to differ. Finally, if the rate of change in the markets being served is high, we would expect a marketing organisation to be flexible and responsive to change. And, since there are very few mature, unchanging environments around, most organisations must have this flexibility.

Customer requirements. The buying practices of customers become a crucial influence on marketing organisation. Where large customers buy through a central purchasing office, when large retail and wholesale chains negotiate 'deals', and where the government is a principal customer, then market orientation is required – the customer is the market.

The internal environment

Management style influences organisational design and structure, and history cannot be treated as bunk in thinking about the redesign of organisations. Implicit and explicit top management attitudes will to a degree determine the pattern of individual and group action, of centralisation and decentralisation.

Product policy. As product lines proliferate, simple functional organisation must give way to product and market orientation.

People. Organisations are living things, and human attitudes help determine what an organisation does. It is people not organisation charts that give life to an organisation. One reason why few companies have implemented (in any meaningful way) the marketing concept, is that the same people who held management positions during periods of production or sales orientation have remained in positions of responsibility when the marketing concept has been embraced.[4] The organisation charts in many companies have changed, job descriptions have been rewritten, but the same people are in place. Changes in organisation must not ignore people, but

---

4   See, for example, P. Kotler, 'From Sales Obsession to Marketing Effectiveness', *Harvard Business Review,* November/December 1977, pp. 67-75.

must be designed to achieve their objectives through effective management of people, sometimes requiring painful shifting or removal of people if the organisational change is to be meaningful.

MARKETING ORGANISATION STRUCTURES

No substantial research on marketing organisation in British companies has been undertaken since a British Institute of Management study published in 1970.[5] The findings of that survey based upon data supplied by 553 companies suggest that in the majority of the companies surveyed the marketing department is organised functionally. Table 14.1 shows the titles of personnel reporting to the chief marketing executive. It can be seen that the data apparently show that the product management system is confined to 10 per cent of the companies reporting.

Table 14.1   Percentage of personnel reporting to chief marketing executive.

Sales manager/general sales manager	50
Advertising manager/commercial manager	15
Export managers	15
Marketing manager/marketing director	14
Field sales manager	13
Salesmen	12
Sales administration managers	12
Product/brand managers	10
Customer service manager/technical service manager	8
Public ralations managers	7
Distribution managers	5
Sales promotion/merchandising manager	5
Market research personnel	5

5   Information Summary 148, *Marketing Organisation in British Industry,* BIM 1970.

However, the majority of companies (59 per cent) reported that their marketing activities were organised around their product line, though, as Table 14.2 shows, multiple responses suggest that a combination of methods (product × geographical area, for example) must exist.

Table 14.2   Basis for breaking down marketing activities (per cent).

Products	59
Geographic area	44
Combination of above	39
Customers	32
Others	8

TYPES OF ORGANISATIONAL STRUCTURE

Functional organisation

This is the most basic structure, embracing the activities of sales, advertising and sales promotion, marketing research and product planning. In large organisations, where a divisionalised structure is used, the functional marketing structure may be utilised within each division, as well as at corporate level.

The advantage of this form of organisation is its relative simplicity, but its very simplicity makes it suitable for firms which sell relatively few products in relatively few markets. When products and markets grow in complexity and diversity, then severe strain is put on the functional organisation. A modification of the simple functional organisation which does respond to our previously expressed concern for the importance of strategic market planning is shown in Figure 14.1.

Product management organisation

The growing complexity of the product lines offered by a company is likely to reduce the effectiveness of the simple functional organisation. Then, a product line organisation becomes feasible and relevant, and in the large fast moving consumer goods companies the use of a product manager system is of proven relevance. Such a system is by no means to be confined to such companies, however.

In the largest companies, when divisionalisation takes place, each division may be organised around a major product or product group. The brand manager structure in one division of Beechams is shown in Figure 14.2. A generalised form of a product or brand management system is shown in Figure 14.3.

Market management organisation

It was stated initially that the purpose of any marketing organisation is to serve consumer needs, which is the meaning of the marketing concept. Growing market orientation may require an organisational response as described above, viz. greater attention to the product-market fit by use of a product manager system, or a system that concentrates on the needs of particular markets and use industries or channels of distribution. The term 'trade marketing' has been used to describe this organisational approach (particularly in the grocery products trade), though there is little evidence that concentration on key accounts has as yet forced any fundamental change in marketing organisation – the product manager system can adapt to key account orientation. However, market orientation is vital to implementation of the marketing concept, and the organisational implications of market orientation must be carefully considered. Where markets are sufficiently differentiated from one another, and potentially large enough to warrant special organisational focus, then some changes in organisation will logically follow.[6]

Geographical organisation

Organisational units structured on the basis of geography are rele-

---

6   For an interesting American example see M. Hanan, 'Reorganise Your Company Around its Markets', *Harvard Business Review,* November/ December 1974, pp.63-74.

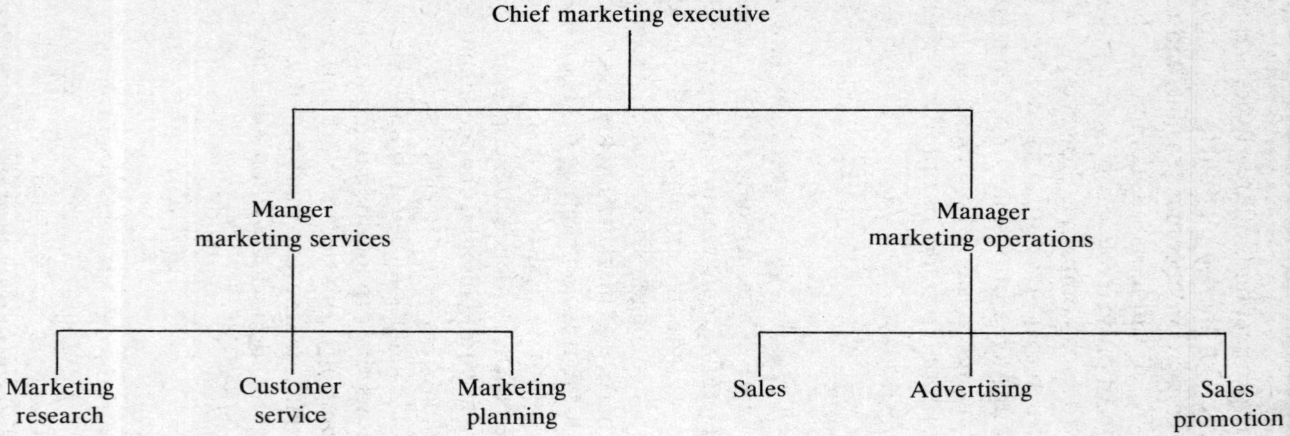

Figure 14.1 Modification of functional organisation

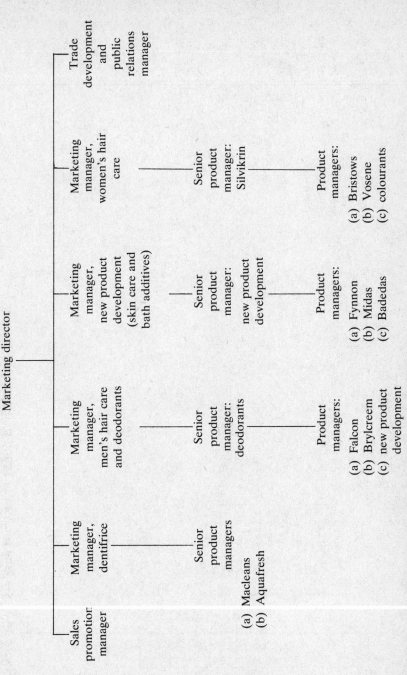

Figure 14.2 Example of brand management structure

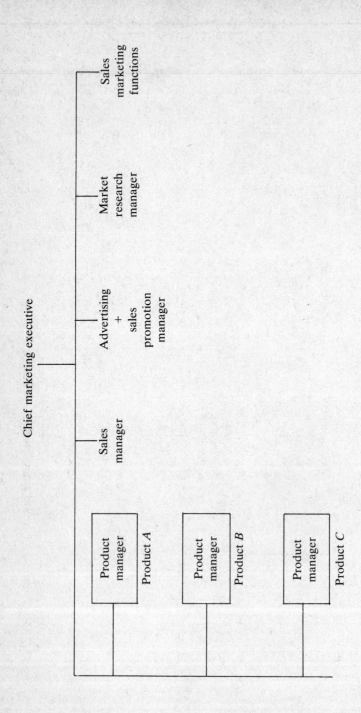

Figure 14.3　General product or brand management system

vant primarily to large organisations marketing their products and/or services on an international scale. Geographic organisation on this scale usually contains within each geographic entity organisations reflecting functional, product, or market type organisations.

Customer-oriented organisation

A marketing department based on customer orientation will not differ in essentials from an organisation based on markets, but where a few very large customers exist for a company's products, consideration must be given to a customer-oriented organisation.

PRODUCT OR MARKET MANAGEMENT?

The most likely dilemma facing chief marketing executives is how to develop their marketing organisations beyond the relatively simple functional structure that serves so many companies. This section summarises the major advantages and disadvantages of a product or a market management system of marketing organisation.

The product manager system enables a multi-product firm to bring a total business management orientation to each product or brand it manufactures. The core responsibility of the product or brand manager is to develop an annual marketing plan geared to the needs of his product, and designed to enlarge its market share and profitability. The product/brand manager is the product/brand champion. The product/brand manager in his annual planning should be concerned with his total marketing opportunity, but his strategic thinking will inevitably be limited in scope, since he is employed primarily as an operations manager. Product/brand management has limitations in the strategic sense, and characteristically brand managers are interested in their own brands, to the exclusion of much else. New product development fits poorly into the brand management system.

Only where the product defines the market, where the product manager and market manager are synonymous is the danger of product orientation avoided. Alternatively, in markets where customers are few in number, there is likely to be little danger of product managers being out of touch with significant market developments. But, where a company's products are used by many different types of customers, or in many different ways; where customers' needs are rapidly changing, and new markets are likely to emerge; where technology is available to produce new solutions to customers' problems; and where a company's offering is a mixture of product(s) and service, then a market management orientation must be seriously considered.

SOME QUESTIONS TO ASK ABOUT YOUR MARKETING ORGANISATION

1 Is current marketing strategy innovative and data-based, clearly expressed and continually re-examined?
2 Does your company have a detailed annual plan, and long-range plans that are continually re-examined and updated?
3 Do contingency plans exist, and how effectively can the company react to changes in the environment?
4 Is the company organised to serve the needs of chosen markets, both at home and abroad, as the means to obtaining long-term growth and profits?
5 Is the company prepared to segment its markets and develop different product offerings for each segment?
6 Does management take a systems view of resource management – is a balance struck between the needs of the marketing mix (sales effort, advertising, product quality, service), the major functions of the company (manufacturing, finance, marketing) and the external environment (customers, distributors, suppliers)?
7 Are the main marketing functions in the company (sales, advertising, product-line management, new product development, after-sales service) managed and controlled in an effectively integrated manner?
8 Does marketing work closely and effectively with research and development management, with manufacturing management, with the purchasing department, with physical distribution and transport management, with accounting and finance, to the end that all departments cooperate in the best interests of the company?

9   Is new product development an effectively organised unit, closely integrated with the strategic planning of the company?

10 How well informed is marketing management about its present and future markets? How recent are market research studies of customers, of buying influences, of changes in distribution channel behaviour, of competitors' performance?

11 How well and how regularly is sales potential and profitability calculated for each market segment, sales territory, product, channel of distribution and order size?

12 Is each area of marketing expenditure regularly analysed for cost effectiveness?

If the answer is an unequivical yes to each of these questions, you ought to be managing an effective marketing-oriented company. Any hesitation in answering any of them suggests that the relevant aspects of organisation and marketing orientation ought to be closely examined.

READING LIST

H.M. Baligh and R.M. Burton, 'Marketing in Moderation – The Marketing Concept and the Organisation's Structure, *Long Range Planning,* vol. 12, April 1979.

V.P. Buell (ed.), *Handbook of Modern Marketing,* McGraw Hill, New York, 1970.

E.R. Corey and S.S. Star, *Organisation Strategy: A Marketing Approach,* Harvard University Graduate School of Business, Cambridge, Mass. 1971.

R. Hayhurst and G. Wills, *Organisation Design for Marketing Futures,* George Allen and Unwin Ltd, 1972.

R.W. Lear, 'No Easy Road to Market Orientation', *Harvard Business Review,* September/October 1963.

T. Levitt, 'Marketing When Things Change', *Harvard Business Review,* November/December 1977.

M.T. Wilson, *The Management of Marketing,* Gower, 1980.

15

The legal framework

Malcolm Carlisle, Assistant Legal Adviser, Colgate Palmolive Ltd

This chapter summarises briefly the very wide range of legal factors affecting the marketing of a company's products. Of necessity it is a considerable simplification, but its value should lie in making the broad principles clear and in providing a pointer for more detailed reference. The chapter is divided into sections covering business rights in products, contractual obligations, responsibility for product quality and performance, codes of practice and a short section on miscellaneous legal requirements.

PROTECTING YOUR INDUSTRIAL PROPERTY RIGHTS AND RESPECTING THOSE BELONGING TO OTHERS

Patents

Before launching a new product consider whether there are any original aspects which may be patentable. Patents are in essence a limited monopoly granted by a government to an inventor (or to that inventor's employer) in return for making an invention (whether it be a product or the process by which that product is made) public by publishing its specification at the Patent Office. Ownership of a patent in the UK prevents others from copying your invention for a period of 20 years.

The UK law on patents was revised recently by the Patents Act 1977. It provides that inventions may be patentable if you can show that they are original (i.e. are not obvious to a person reasonably skilled in the field of the particular invention) and have not previously been made public either in this country or elsewhere in the world.

In particular, it will not be possible to obtain a patent if you have used, sold, distributed or otherwise publicised your invention in virtually any country prior to applying for a patent. However, an improvement to an existing formulation, product or manufacturing process or a novel use for a well-known substance, may be patentable.

Registered designs

Your new product or its packaging may have a particularly unusual and interesting appearance. The features of the shape, configuration, pattern or ornament of that appearance may be sufficiently original to be registered, thus granting you a monopoly of its use for up to 15 years. Once registered no one may use the same design and you can stop anyone from doing so even if their imitation of your design was inadvertent. If you wish to register a design in the UK you must apply to do so before using the design publicly (e.g. by sale or advertise-ment) in the UK. However, the law at present allows you to register a design in the UK which has already been publicised in another country but not here. As mentioned below, your industrial designs may also be protected by copyright owned by you in them. However, the advantage of a registered design is that, unlike infringement of copyright, you can stop even unintentional and innocent imitation of your design.

Copyright

Copyright is a protection granted automatically, without the need for any registration, to prevent the deliberate copying of artistic works. It may cover films, photographs, drawings, music, and the written word, although in the latter case there must be something more substantial than just a brief advertising slogan such as 'Guinness is good for you' for copyright to exist. Clearly where you are having such artistic work done for you, for example pack designs, television advertising copy, or advertising photography, you should make sure that the copyright is given to your company. In particular your advertising agents should automatically assign to you any copyright in their work for you.

Copyrights are often extremely complex. For example, there may be rights belonging to different persons in the same work. In the case of a pop song the copyright in the sheet music and in the recorded version of that music may belong to separate people. Similarly different people may own the copyright to the same artistic work in different countries. Thus, if you buy the right to use a copyright, it is essential to investigate very carefully that the seller really owns what he is offering to sell.

Copyright may also exist in industrial designs, for instance in engineering drawings, or the external appearance of a product.

The copyright in artistic works lasts 50 years from the death of the author, whilst that in industrial designs lasts 15 years from the first industrial application. To stop others from infringing your copyright you have to show that they were deliberately or recklessly copying it, since it is always possible that two 'artists' may independently create the same thing. Compare this to design registration where proof of copying is not required.

Trademarks

Trademarks consist of words, symbols or devices used to distinguish your products from those of another company – for example 'Ford', 'Schweppes', 'Terry's' or 'Ajax'. They should not be confused with generic words which simply describe things – for example 'motor car', 'tonic water', 'chocolate' or 'scouring powder'.

Good trademarks can be of immense value and it is important not to use them in a way that simply turns them into generic words. Aspirin, linoleum, petrol and kerosene all used to be trademarks, the exclusive property of their originators, but are now everyday words.

If you treat them properly you should always be able to stop others using your trademarks on products. A few basic rules are:

1   Use a trademark as an adjective and try to make it stand out, rather than using it on its own. For example, refer to our 'Double Dealer' calculators and 'Easy Money' abacuses.
2   Try not to change the spelling of trademarks or use them to make new words (e.g. 'Easy Money-type'), and do not play around with a trademark design, for example by altering it to fit in with your advertising.
3   It is often useful to identify trademarks on packaging, for example by printing a note: 'Double Dealer' and 'Easy Money' – trademarks.

As in most countries, many trademarks in the UK may be registered. Registration is available for marks which are invented words, are not descriptive or laudatory of the goods concerned and do not have surname or geographical significance. The main advantage of registration is that it enables you to stop other people from using that trademark (or one confusingly similar to it) on the goods for which it is registered. By contrast if you do not (or cannot) register your trademark you can only stop others from using it if you prove that you have a public reputation in that trademark and that your competitor was 'passing-off' his goods as yours.

Remember that trademarks are designed to distinguish a particular trader's goods from another's. Suppose Company *A* makes a variety of calculating machines, and owns the trademarks 'Double Dealer', 'Four Flusher' and 'Easy Money' in respect of calculators and the like. That does not mean it can stop a competitor from using the same or similar words on quite different products for which Company *A*'s trademarks are not registered and for which products it has no reputation. Thus Company *A* could not prevent Company *B* from marketing its 'Double Dealer' egg timer.

Other people's rights

Obviously it is possible for your competitors to have industrial property rights which could be infringed by your marketing activities. Accordingly it is essential that you discuss with your legal department at the earliest possible stage what precautionary measures should be taken to avoid a new product launch being interrupted by a writ from a competitor. For example, it may be necessary to carry out patent and registered design searches before introducing a product. If a new trademark is to be used it is necessary to search the Trademark Registry to try to ensure no one has already registered it. If possible a company should complete its own registration before using the trademark. Thus it could cost our imaginary company £20,000 to buy itself out of the difficulty encountered through ignoring Fagin Computers Ltd's registration of 'Easy Money' for adding machines when launching the 'Easy Money' abacus. Remember that it can take many months to 'clear' a new product for sale.

Passing-off

This is an old-established legal remedy designed to stop one manufacturer capitalising on the reputation of another. To give an example of how far this remedy can go, there was a string of cases in which the champagne producers of the Champagne area of France successfully stopped Spanish producers from describing their sparkling wine as 'Champagne' and thus benefiting from the reputation of the French product.

The law of passing-off exists to protect a trader's property in his good will and reputation. Passing-off may occur where there is a representation made by a trader in the course of business to potential customers which injures or causes loss to another trader's goodwill or business – for instance by attracting business away from you – by deceiving other people into buying his goods, believing them to be yours.

Thus you must always be sure that in name or appearance your product and advertising is not so close to a competitor's product as to be likely to confuse people into thinking that your product is made by your competitor so that you benefit from his reputation. You should examine the competition closely to avoid such confusion.

CONTRACTUAL OBLIGATIONS

In the course of your marketing activities you will be involved in a variety of contracts. These will range from agreements for outside manufacture, special promotions, sale of products through distributors to the provision of refreshments for the weekly marketing management meeting. A basic outline of contract law is therefore necessary.

Formation of contracts

Contracts are formed by a definite offer by one party being firmly accepted by another. It is not enough to respond to an offer by a counter-offer: that may be part of the negotiations leading to a contract, but it is not the contract itself. It is also necessary to distinguish between 'offers' and 'invitations to treat', i.e. invitations to others to make an offer which you may accept. For example, advertisements of goods for sale or displays of goods in shops are normally invitations to treat; in such a case the contract occurs when the actual sale agreement is made. The shopkeeper accepts your offer to buy – it's not vice versa.

Once an offer is accepted it must be clear that the parties intended it to be a legally binding arrangement. This will normally be the case between businesses, or between a business and its clients. However, between private persons agreements are often purely social arrangements, binding in honour only, and there is no intention that they be subject to the court's jurisdiction.

Normally a contract must be supported by consideration or value on both sides. In other words apart from the agreement itself, there must be a quid pro quo for all parties – as where goods are exchanged for money. Unlike some countries the UK courts will not enforce an agreement where one party promised to do something for nothing. The exception to this rule is when a contract is executed under seal: in such cases a gratuitous promise can be made legally binding.

The terms of a contract

A contract will consist of a number of terms. Where the contract is wholly in writing these will be easily ascertained. Where it is wholly or partly verbal, there may be argument as to what the exact terms are. It is most important to remember that legally binding contracts can be made either in writing or verbally. The lack of a written document has no effect (except in special cases) on the validity of a contract; it only makes it more difficult sometimes to find out what the contract is about. Try not to lose sight of this fact during any negotiations. It is often useful in correspondence during such negotiations to refer to the fact that agreement is 'subject to contract', i.e. that a binding agreement will exist only when a written contract is completed.

Apart from express terms (which are those specifically agreed by the parties) there may in addition be other terms, which were not specifically included, but which are implied in the contract. Sometimes such terms are implied in order to make business sense of the contract. In other cases terms may be implied by statute, and in particular you should note in this context the Sale of Goods Act 1893 and the Unfair Contract Terms Act 1977.

Performance of a contract

Contracts will hold obligations for all parties to them. When each party has fully performed his obligations the contract is said to be discharged and is at an end. However, where one party fails properly to perform his obligations, he may be exposed to an action by the other parties to force him to do so or to compensate them for his non-performance. In such a case, the parties can also reach a fresh agreement which allows the defaulting party to discharge his obligations by doing something different from what he originally agreed.

In practice the day-to-day performance of contracts will often differ from the strict contractual terms, and the parties will tacitly agree to this. However, do not underestimate the value of a carefully drafted written contract in the event of a dispute arising. Remember that if matters go wrong the defaulting party can be exposed to an action for damages (monetary compensation) or performance of the contract. For instance it might be possible to insist on the supply of components under a fixed price contract long after inflation has made that price uneconomic to our suppliers and very attractive to ourselves.

Advertising agencies

Finally it may be useful to remind you of the unusual position of advertising agents in English law. Historically, they were the agents of the media – hence their name. Although the word agent implies that they are the servants of their clients, the companies who engage them, and act only within the bounds of the authority given them by their clients, the fact is that by custom and practice advertising agents are presumed in England to act as principals unless the contrary is stated. Thus, without specific authority from their clients, advertising agents can enter freely (but at their own risk) into whatever arrangements they feel are best for their clients. If you wish to ensure that your agency does not act in this way, but is limited in part or whole in the action it can take without your specific authority, it is important to make this clear in your contract with your advertising agency.

HAVING REGARD FOR THE CONSUMER

The law has shown increasing regard for the rights of the consumer over recent years and this trend is likely to continue for a while to come.

Negligence and product liability

English law imposes a duty on everyone to take all reasonable care to avoid doing something which he can foresee may injure those whom he can reasonably anticipate being affected by his action. This, in essence, is the principle established in the well known case of Donoghue v. Stevenson, when a young lady recovered damages from the manufacturers of a bottle of ginger beer which she had drunk and which contained a decomposed snail.

The practical consequence of this principle is that companies such as ourselves must do everything reasonably possible to avoid harm coming to those whom we can foresee using our products. This involves safety testing and the issuing of any instructions and warnings necessary for the safe use of our products.

In common with other countries, England has looked at the question of introducing strict liability of manufacturers for damage caused by their products. This would mean a consumer would be entitled to compensation from a manufacturer or supplier for any loss or damage shown to be caused by a product, whether unforeseeable or not, and whether or not the manufacturer or supplier had been negligent. Such a system was recommended by a Royal Commission in 1978. Also the EEC authorities have been working for some years to introduce such a system throughout the Common Market. The latest draft directive was published on these lines late in 1979 and this will probably be adopted by the EEC and then implemented in member countries, including Britain, in the course of the 1980s.

In this context of product liability remember that in 1977 the Unfair Contract Terms Act rendered invalid all notices or terms of contracts which attempted to exclude liability for death or personal injury resulting from negligence. It also provided that liability towards consumers for damage to their property caused by negligence can only be excluded by a notice or contract term so far as to do so is reasonable. One should not, therefore, take too much notice of the absolute disclaimer for liability printed at the entrance to many cloakrooms disclaiming all responsibility for loss or damage to property left there.

Sale of Goods Act 1979

This Act consolidates the original 1893 Act and subsequent amendments. Its main purpose is to give a purchaser certain implied warranties as to the quality of goods bought by him. Those warranties include the assurance that the goods must match their description – a gold watch must be gold and not gold plate; that they must be reasonably fit for their purpose – a lawn mower must be capable of cutting grass. Products must also be of merchantable quality, in other words they must be of the quality reasonable buyers would expect having regard to the nature of the goods and the price paid.

By virtue of the Unfair Contract Terms Act 1977 it is not possible to exclude these warranties when dealing with a consumer, and they may be excluded vis-à-vis another business entity only in so far as it is reasonable to do so.

Trade Descriptions Act 1968

The fundamental purpose of this Act was to protect the consumer from misleading statements about products or services. If, in the course of trade or business, a false indication as to certain matters (including their size, weight, origin, nature, performance or composition) is applied to any goods otherwise than by mistake or accident, the person applying that indication is guilty of an offence. The false indication must be such as is likely materially to mislead an ordinary person. Similar provisions apply to false indications about services.

The Trade Descriptions Act pays particular attention to indications of price and specifically makes it an offence to indicate a price in such a way that suggests a product costs less than it actually does.

Retail prices and bargain offers

For many years it has been unlawful to impose minimum retail prices. However, it is still lawful to impose maximum retail prices and to recommend retail prices. Indeed manufacturers' recommended retail prices are often the only practicable as well as legally acceptable benchmark for bargain price offers, such as '10 p. off RRP'. Most industries are free to use recommended prices as the basis for such offers. However, the Bargain Offers Order 1979, as well as attempting to regulate the way in which bargain offers are made so as to reduce any risk of consumer confusion, also prohibited certain industries from basing bargain offers on recommended prices.

Consumer Credit Act 1974

This Act codifies the law on credit and hire purchase. It regulates virtually all credit business up to a specified limit (currently £5,000) and requires every business offering credit or hire facilities to consumers to obtain a licence from the Director General of Fair Trading. Ancillary businesses such as debt collectors and mortgage brokers are also required to be licensed.

Weights and Measures Act 1979

The law affecting the declaration of weight or volume of goods in the UK was largely revised by the 1979 Act in order to give effect to EEC law on the subject. Whereas before 1980 any declaration of contents had to amount to a guarantee of minimum contents to the consumer, with effect from 1 January 1980 it is generally sufficient to show only that batches of product contain on average not less than their declared weight or volume. There are, of course, provisions to ensure that no one package has too great a deficiency.

Fair Trading Act 1973

This Act aimed principally to promote increased economic efficiency and to protect consumers against unfair trading practices. The first part of this objective was dealt with by reconstituting the Monopolies Commission into the Monopolies and Mergers Commission and revising its powers to control monopolies and mergers in industry. The second objective was met by creating the office of Director General of Fair Trading and the Consumer Advisory Protection Committee, as well as giving the government power to make statutory orders on a wide range of consumer trade practices.

The Government has now passed a new Competition Act which further enhances the investigatory and regulatory powers of the Director General and the Monopolies and Mergers Commission in the interests of ensuring competition between businesses is not restricted.

CODES OF PRACTICE

In addition to law, this country is noted for its tradition of self regulation in industry. The centre of the system is the Advertising Standards Authority, an independent body financed by a levy on advertising expenditure. The authority has a Code of Advertising Practice Committee which is responsible for producing the British Code of Advertising Practice, the so-called CAP Code. This code contains guidance on a large range of general and specialist fields of advertising and seeks to balance the needs of industry, consumers, society and fair business practice. A sub-committee also produces the British Code of Sales Promotion Practice which deals specifically with the way in which competitions, premium offers and other sales promotions should be conducted. The sanction for infringing these codes is non-acceptance of advertisements and promotions by the media which adhere to the codes. However, on a day-to-day basis, the ASA is normally able to persuade advertisers voluntarily to comply with the codes.

The Independent Television Companies Association also publishes and enforces its own code for television advertising, and its sanction is to refuse to accept a particular commercial. Finally, the International Chamber of Commerce also produces codes on advertising and sales promotion practice.

MISCELLANEOUS

Limitations prevent coverage in detail of all the laws relevant to marketing activities. However, one or two special legal controls should be mentioned very briefly.

The Medicines Act 1968 introduced government control by licensing of all manufacture, import and sale of medicines in the UK, as well as controlling the promotion and advertising of medicines.

Food manufacture was one of the earliest industries to be control-led by law. The Food and Drugs Act 1955 and regulations made under it regulate the whole food industry.

Cosmetic Products are controlled by the Cosmetic Products Regulations 1978 which enact EEC law on the subject in the UK.

The impact of EEC law will be clear to you from the above information and marketers should anticipate a steady increase in EEC law in pursuance of the EEC objective to harmonise the laws affecting trade and competition throughout the EEC.

PART III

MARKETING IN ACTION

16

Packaging as a Marketing Tool

R.N. Theodore, Economist and Consultant at Peat Marwick Mitchell

The importance of packaging in the UK economy may be judged by the expenditure of £3,500 million in 1979 on packaging materials, which is equivalent to 2.25 per cent of the gross domestic product. The reader may think of the number of packages his or her family buys each week, and so recognise its marketing potential.

Nearly all manufactured and processed goods require packaging protection in their journey through wholesaler, retailer or distributor to the final consumer. But packaging is not just a question of protection, its role is increasingly one of embodying selling power in its design. Packaging, through use of graphic and structural design, will help establish the identity and provide information on package contents and facilitate handling for both the consumer and those associated with distribution. Finally, packaging may be used to provide a persuasive argument for purchasing the product it contains, particularly at point of sale.

For packaging to be effective it must fulfil all the above functions as a contribution to overall profitability. Thus, packaging is an integral part of marketing strategy.

DEVELOPMENT OF PACKAGING COMMUNICATION

The history behind the merchandising of consumer goods, particularly foodstuffs, underlines the developments of packaging as a marketing communications tool.

Foodstuffs and essential household products required little or no pre-packaging in the nineteenth century, and choice was influenced by the visible quality of a product, or the consumer accepted whatever was offered in return for the limited income available. Much adulteration of foodstuffs was also common. As the country progressed towards industrial maturity pre-packaging became an important factor in the transport and storage of goods, as localised markets developed into national ones. As more competing products appeared in the local store the consumer, who was enjoying a rising real income, was permitted a greater choice. It was therefore necessary for the manufacturer to influence that choice. The manufacturer, by introducing the concept of 'branding', sought to build a personality into his product with which the consumer could identify. The brand name was usually that of the producing company and implied a guarantee of the advertised quality from a prominent display on the package.

The twentieth century has seen the consumer being offered a growing number of packaged goods within the retail store. Meanwhile manufacturers have found that there is a limit to the volume that can be sold of any particular product, either because of satisfied demand or because marketing costs escalated beyond marginal profitability. Increased sales were therefore sought by expanding the range of products offered and introducing different varieties of the same basic product or other related products.

It was intended that consumers liking one product would try others of the same brand name. Product ranges of a wide variety of foodstuffs, such as vegetables and desserts, were expanded. The result was that the brand name alone would not suffice on the package. It was necessary for the product name to be given a prominent feature on the package, which was further aided by an illustration of the contents.

CHANGES IN CHANNELS OF DISTRIBUTION

The next phase in the development of the package design was seen in the growth of supermarkets and self service departments. This dispensed with the need for a shop assistant who had acted as the salesman at the point of sale, advising the customer and confirming his or her choice. It was the package and the 'silent salesman' that now had to sell the contents.

The consumer in the supermarket is faced with a choice of over 3,000 products and will probably spend an average of less than half an hour choosing those required. Unless the consumer knows precisely what he or she wants, the purchase of a product will be an impulse reaction. A survey undertaken by *Marketing* magazine a few years ago revealed that very few shoppers entered supermarkets with a shopping list. Thus, once inside the store the package has a vital role in generating a sale. To generate an impulse purchase the package has to communicate the benefits to be derived from the product contained. Even if the consumer has a definite view of an intended purchase, which may have been encouraged outside the store, the package, in less than the second it is viewed, must be recognisable. Package design then, is now oriented towards the consumer in order that a sale might be effected or a choice of selection confirmed.

The three phases in the development of package design have been described by Volckaert[1] as brand related, product related and consumer related. Although consumer-relatedness occupies the main emphasis today, the factors of brand-relatedness and product-relatedness are still vital ingredients of the package design. Besides expressing the consumer benefits to be derived from the purchase of a product, a package must still identify the producer and provide information relating to its contents. Consumer-relatedness may not necessarily play the primary role as consumer benefits may have been projected through advertising media, e.g. television. This will then allow the packaging to promote the brand or its contents. Often the menage will reinforce the advertising theme. The decision will depend on the marketing strategy chosen for each particular product.

Implications for packaged goods

The principles of package design practised by the companies successful in selling through the supermarket network have important ramifications for other products not already sold in this manner. Already, more than 70 per cent of the nation's grocery bill is incurred

---

1   J. Volckaert, *Package Design: Facing up to the Market,* International Trade Centre, 1969.

through the supermarket, and, meanwhile, self-service has penetrated the department store and even the corner shop. More important still is the growth of self-service departments in the form of hypermarkets and discount warehouses where consumer durable goods are becoming prominent items. Those companies that will prosper in such circumstances are likely to be those which have recognised the crucial role of packaging in the selling process.

Companies engaged in marketing industrial products must also appreciate the significance of package design. Good protective packaging is imperative where the high value of the product or its precise design specifications are concerned. Although the graphic design of packaging will not be important, except for establishing a strong brand identity, the structural design aspect is a significant factor in providing a marketing 'plus' in the form of customer service. Packaging may be especially tailored for particular end-use markets, made more easily transportable on the customer's premises or even aid the disposal of the package. It is possible that packaging as part of marketing strategy will become just as important for industrial goods as it has for consumer goods, for it is increasingly recognised that the principles of consumer behaviour are not dissimilar from those in the environment of the industrial market.

PACKAGING IN THE MARKETING MIX

Continued industrialisation has created a somewhat uniform economic system with standardisation in production and similarity between producing units. This has tended to equalise the price and quality amongst competing products and this, in turn, has diverted marketing efforts towards advertising, promotion and packaging. However, a successful marketing strategy requires a balance between these factors, and it is essential that packaging should be weighted accordingly.

Advertising's impact is seen to be declining in a relative sense. Some companies are finding that reductions in their large advertising budgets are having a negligible effect on sales and that their money brings in a better return in other areas, one of them being packaging. Kimberly-Clark is reported to have experienced this when repackaging its facial tissues resulted in an extra 2 per cent of its brand's share of the market. However, the point is not to play down the role of advertising since advertising is still important in getting the customer to the point of sale. It is the function of packaging to clinch the sale and maintain an after-sales impact. It is often quoted that no advertisement is ever read as often as the package. Not only is the package viewed in the store, where it bears out the original advertising message, but in many cases it is viewed in the home during the period of consumption.

The close association with advertising is not the only role that packaging may be required to fulfil. Two further roles may be identified. Many product/packages do not have heavy advertising support, either because of limited budgets or because it may be impractical to advertise all product lines. It is here that the package must contribute the full sales impact. The second role is that of packaging which may be subordinated to point of sale displays. Here, the package merely confirms the choice made by the purchaser.

PACKAGING AS AN AID TO SALES AND DISTRIBUTION

So far, packaging has been discussed mainly from the viewpoint of a marketing communications tool. Before considering the components of package design and how they can be combined into projecting the required sales message, it is necessary to examine the situations in which packaging may be utilised to increase sales, reduce costs and contribute to profitability, and to improve distribution.

It has already been mentioned that the price and quality of many competitive products have been equalised making them almost homogeneous; in fact, leading to oligopolistic-type competition. A price-cut in an effort to increase sales will most likely be met by competitors. They will however be less likely to react to a new package design.

The package of a product may be used in an effort to extend the product life-cycle. Updating design may help to give the pack a more contemporary image. It is increasingly difficult to come up with completely new products, but any variety of packaging innovations can be introduced which offer features a consumer wants and will be willing to pay for – a form of product innovation. This may be exemplified by the growing number of convenience products, e.g.

ringpull cans for soft drinks and aerosols for hair-sprays and deodorants. The convenience factor is not limited to the consumer. Wholesalers and retailers will look more favourably on products with packages which are easy to stack, price, mark, display and identify.

New features of a package help to maintain the interest of the trade in the product concerned. They will also provide extra help for the salesmen to use in selling to the trade. In the toy industry, re-packaging has been described by one senior executive as more important than innovation.[2]

Seasonal fluctuations in demand may be smoothed out through packaging. The canning and deep freezing of some perishable products, like strawberries, enable all-the-year-round consumption.

The package design for a particular product may be varied in order to expand the market by appealing to different market segments.

Detailed appraisal of the current performance of packaging may reveal that cost reductions are possible through an alternative packaging form, e.g. plastic pots as opposed to glass pots for cosmetics. The application of multi-packaging to low profit margin mass-consumption food products allows more worthwhile price reductions than when one pack is sold on its own. This is of particular interest in premium offers.

The introduction of new packaging can extend the life of a product. Besides reducing wastage, this will render savings in distribution costs. Golden Wonder Crisps, in presenting the product in a plastic film bag as opposed to the conventional glassine paper bag, was able to extend shelf-life to a period of weeks rather than days.

The size of a unit pack may be scaled in proportion to the shipping case with dimensions which may be scaled in relation to the transport container used for distribution. Thus maximum use of available space may be made.

Attention to packaging may help to reduce pilferage rates in the retail store. Also, an analysis of the system of distribution may reveal opportunities for minimising the loss in transit. However, combating these elements may involve higher costs.

Finally, in discussing packaging as an aid to sales and distribution, its role of protection must not be overlooked. It is vital to a product's

---

2 *Retail Business,* December 1972, no.178, p.24.

success that it be of a consistently uniform quality for the sake of repeat purchases. If not, an adverse effect on sales will result, not only of that particular product but of others in the product range.

CONSUMER BEHAVIOUR AND PACKAGE DESIGN

When there is no choice offered in a particular product the consumer's decision is simply whether to make the purchase or not. Where competition exists, each manufacturer must try to influence the consumer's choice, which means that it is necessary to understand the motivations behind that choice and use packaging to appeal to them. Motivations, however, will vary amongst consumers. One person will buy a product/package because it looks cheap or it is all that is required or can be afforded, whilst another might appeal because of prestige. A man will be more attracted to the package that expresses masculinity, and a woman will prefer something more elegant. A young person will respond more favourably to a more exciting pack than an older person who will be happy with something more conservative. Therefore, a package design that tries to appeal to as broad a market as possible will not be as successful as one that is suited to a particular market segment.

A market appraisal will involve identifying the potential users of a product into consumer categories and analysing the benefits they expect from purchase. Potential consumers can be classified by age, sex and socio-economic group. In international marketing, nationality is a further consideration. When the potential market segment has been defined, packaging in conjunction with the other elements of marketing strategy may be manipulated in appealing to the relevant segment.

ELEMENTS OF PACKAGE DESIGN

The appearance of a package can be varied through the use of colour, shape or size, graphic illustration and package copy. It is the combination of these elements which is used to establish the identity of the manufacturer, say what the product is and establish a reason for buying the product. In addition, within a self-service environment, the package must instantly attract attention to itself from amongst the competing products on the shelf. The pack should be pleasing, especially when it remains in the home during the product's use. The last two objectives may sound contradictory but it is a problem that the creativity of the designer must solve.

Colour as a means of attracting the consumer

The colour of a package makes the first and probably the greatest impact on the consumer. The main significance of colour is that it creates certain psychological and physiological reactions, which can be used to advantage in package design. Some of the associations that certain colours have are listed below:

> Blue, coolness/distinction
> Red, heat/excitement
> Purple, gold, royalty/richness
> Orange, warmth/movement
> Green, nature/quiet
> White, purity/cleanliness
> Yellow, sunshine/warmth
> Brown, utility

The different shades of these colours will further effect their association, e.g. green, although reflecting nature in a food product will tend to symbolise decay or poison when darkened. Furthermore, such associations will not necessarily hold for all products.

Orange and red are believed to rank highest in attracting attention. Black and blue are also important, but are not in themselves always the most well-liked. This may be offset by the use of contrasts such as black on yellow or by using a colour that differs from the general trend of competitive products.

Colour as an expression of the product. The colour of a package can indicate characteristics about the product it contains. Pink may be suggestive of a cosmetic product; integrating green on the package of a chocolate bar suggests a mint flavour; a blue and white combination give the impression of cleaning and hygiene, as on a toothpaste pack. Applications of colour on some containers run the danger of 'sameness' with competing products highlighting particular colours. As an alternative the corporate/brand colour may take the primary role whilst the colour that is more akin to the product will play a subordinate role.

Product differentiation. Colour can be an important factor in establishing the identity of a company's range of products. The yellow of Eastman Kodak is one of the best examples. A more common use of colour is that of product differentiation between the varieties of a product line, e.g. shampoos, cleaning agents etc.

Product quality. This may be enhanced through combining the appropriate colours associated with a refined taste. Gold, maroon and purple are prominent in this respect, while for cheap, mass-consumption products, yellow is more appropriate.

Colour and nationality. Colour strategy applied in segmenting the home market in terms of age, sex and socio-economic group will not always be relevant for the export markets. The same colour may have different connotations from one country to another, and this will require research. For example, blue is a masculine colour in Sweden, but feminine in Holland, and those living in hotter climates require brighter colours as opposed to more sober ones.

Shape and size

The size of a package will, to a large extent, be dictated by its contents. One point should be noted. A container should not be so large that it could deceive or mislead the consumer as to the quantity of its contents.

The shape of a package offers more scope in design. A distinctive shape compared to competitors' packs assists instant recognition even when the brand name may have been forgotten. High-speed packaging lines for mass-consumption goods, however, will impose limitations on shape, leaving graphics to dominate the design. Three further aspects of shape should be considered:

1 It is desirable that the shape of a container should invite handling, for once a person has picked up a pack he is halfway to buying it. If he should find that the package is of an inconvenient shape in the hand, a moment's hesitation will cause the pack to be returned to the shelf.

2 Shape, in some cases, conveys the properties of the product;

delicacy or strength denoting a feminine or masculine product.

3 The decided shape and size of the container in the case of foodstuffs or household products must fit into the average size of fridge and cupboard.

GRAPHIC ILLUSTRATION AND PHOTOGRAPHY

These provide the easiest means of establishing the contents of the package, but may be dispensed with where the packaging form affords viewing of the product. A glass bottle, transparent plastic film or window cartons permit faster recognition. Unfortunately, some products are not very attractive in their purchased condition, especially frozen and dehydrated foods. A photograph or illustration will therefore be required to depict the prepared product or the results to be achieved when used, but the portrayal must not exaggerate the product's likely final properties. The illustration in other instances may show a new use for a product, or where the product itself is not particularly attractive (like disinfectant) the ingredients (pine or lavender) may be featured.

The trademark is an easy method of conveying the brand or corporate name as it emphasises a family of products as a unit. The goodwill associated with leading items in a range of products is then transferred to new additions or less important items in the range.

Package copy

The printed copy describes the contents of the pack and how they are used. There is a limit to the amount of information which can be intelligibly incorporated on the average-size consumer pack. Ideally, the copy should be simple, legible and attractively arranged within the overall package design, permitting the other elements in the design to work to full effect. The following points may be observed in the compilation of package copy:

1 Layout: the face of the pack will be read from left to right as the eye moves. The basic information to be presented on the front panel in descending order includes corporate/brand identification, product name and description, any consumer

information or benefits (but not cataloguing) and legal requirements. The back panel of the package can be used more freely.

2 Lettering: copy tends to be less legible in capital letters than in smaller type, and words will be more legible if the space between the words is greater than the thickness of type. The typeface can also help to say something about the product, e.g. a script style can denote a traditional-style product.

3 Legal requirements: ingredients and weights should be in legible colours (not yellow and white on light backgrounds) as consumers must not feel that this information is being concealed in any way.

4 Surface of pack: as not all products have flat display panels, some special considerations are necessary. Identifying copy on cylindrical shapes should cover at least 60 per cent of the circumferences so that it will be visible even if the package is placed badly on the shelf. Frozen food products also present problems. Much jumbling occurs in many refrigerated displays, and this will require identifying copy on all carton panels.

The overall design

The above paragraphs have only been concerned with individual items in the package design for a product, package contents and reasons for buying. What is required is the marshalling of all these items into a homogeneous whole. The package designer – fully briefed on all aspects of the product to be packaged, its distribution, sales conditions and usage – will, armed with samples of competitive packs, present specimens to the marketer, who will then evaluate which is the most suitable for the product.

Various tests are available to measure the consumer's response to a package design in relation to competitive packs. For example, a tachistoscope determines the speed of recognition by a consumer of the package and distance at which the elements of design are recognised. Although the package design may be considered good in itself, it must prove suitable for bulk display. En bloc, some displays can give a monotonous appearance. Ideally, new packaging should be test-marketed, as success at this stage will indicate a high chance of success.

The ultimate success of a package will be determined by the role it plays as an integral part of marketing strategy in the market place. The package design itself is therefore conceived in relation to other marketing communications. Its featuring in press and television advertising, still seen mainly in black and white, must assist recognition at the point of sale. As part of the product the package must provide some definite advantage (unique selling proposition) compared to existing competitive brands. Shape often provides the easiest means of conveying this as illustrated by the chianti wine bottle or the dimple Haig bottle. The value of packaging design as a direct expression of marketing is not to be underestimated. A.C. Nielsen, the market research agency, has found that 67 per cent of new product failures can be traced to the inadequacy of the product package.

PACKAGING MATERIALS AND DESIGN

The selection of materials available to serve a product's packaging requirements is wide. The basic packaging materials of paper and board, tin plate, plastics, aluminium, glass, cellulose film and, to lesser extent, wood, can be manufactured into flexible, semi-rigid or rigid containers. These containers may come in the form of wrapped films, bags, cartons, cans, bottles etc. However, the functional performance of the package will usually dictate the choice of packaging form.

Hazards of transport, suitability for dispensing and reclosing, and suitability for printing and labelling must be taken into account. For food packages, problems of odour, light and heat will need to be considered. The availability of existing filling, closing and labelling machinery will impose limitations on the material used, whilst what the product can afford at a given level of volume will be a further constraint.

The actual choice of material will, in turn, impose certain limitations on the projection of the package as a communications tool. Shape of the package, visibility and the attractiveness of the product will be affected to some extent by the choice of material. At one extreme plastics packages can be produced in a variety of shapes and sizes while metal containers are largely limited to variations in height and diameter. Glass containers have more versatility in shape than those of metal but there are technological limitations. The growing interest in glass containers for packaging fruit give the product a much more appetising and aesthetic appeal in comparison with the traditional tin can. Furthermore, the tin can is being superseded by the rigid plastic container for such items as glue and paint.

Packaging costs

It is difficult to be specific about packaging costs expressed as a unit of the selling price, but an estimate of 50 per cent for the variety of packaged goods may not be far out. For those packages which form an integral part of the product, like aerosols and collapsible metal tubes for toothpastes, the packaging costs will be much higher. The Prices and Incomes Board reported that packaging costs accounted for approximately 10 per cent of the retail selling price for toothpaste and toilet preparations.

It is believed that the use of glass containers as opposed to tin cans will add an extra 1p to costs, but this may be considered worthwhile from the viewpoint of marketing effectiveness. Thus, the important point for marketers is that if a more expensive material is used, lower profit per unit must be more than compensated for by the increase in sales. Ideally, this should represent an amount that provides an acceptable return on the increased investment.

LEGAL REQUIREMENTS

The marketer will need to be familiar with legislation that imposes certain requirements on the content of package design, especially the package copy. Much of the legislation affecting this area is involved with the food and drink industry, but some acts, such as the Weights and Measures Act 1979 and The Trade Descriptions Act 1968 are more generally applicable.

Lack of attention to legal requirements at an early stage in the design process may have disastrous results. In a new product launch the discovery that legal regulations have not been adhered to when the product/packages are being produced will lead to considerable financial loss incurred in redesigning packaging to correct the error, or the exact timing of the launch may be ruined. It may, however, be possible to use the existing container or packaging by the application of a flash panel to eradicate the error, but will still involve extra cost and critical delays. If a mistake is not realised and a prosecution is brought, besides the imposition of a fine, the name and goodwill of the consumer and retailer will be lost and the product may have to be withdrawn from the market. In some cases the retailer and supplier may also be liable to prosecution.

PACKAGING ORGANISATIONS

Brief mention should be made of the organisations which seek to improve performance and standards of packaging. The packaging section of the British Standards Institution issue standards on a national basis which serve as a guide to the functional performance of a package. The code is an important term of reference when considering the packaging of a new product as information is given on factors to be considered when selecting the degree of protection required. The main groups of packaging materials and standard test methods are covered. The Design Council is more concerned with aesthetic aspects of design in relation to packaging. The council itself will, if required, suggest a shortlist of designers who might be compatible with a customer's needs. The Institute of Packaging was formed in 1947 and has been active in promoting education in packaging technology. Membership of the institute by examination requires a certain level of knowledge to be attained in the practical aspects of packaging, packaging materials and packaging economics.

The Research Association for the Paper and Board, Printing and Packaging Industries (PIRA) has a packaging division which carries out a whole range of research projects on the technical problems associated with packaging including those relating to transit and retail packaging. Its information department monitors information on a worldwide basis relating to the technical and market aspects of packaging through its publications, whilst the training department organises courses and seminars on topical subjects of interest in packaging.

CONCLUSION

There are many ways in which packaging can promote a product. It must be remembered, however, that it is only one part of marketing. If a package fails, the product will probably fail, but an effective pack will not guarantee the product's success. Self-service, convenience and unit packaging, plus economy will, in the future, be the main factors that govern packaging development. Development in packaging technology and marketing expertise will continue to work toward these ends.

READING LIST

P. C. Griffin and S. Sacharow, *Principles of Package Development*, AVI Publishing Company, 1972.
E. P. Danger, *Using Colour to Sell*, Gower Press, 1968.
F. A. Paine (ed.) *Fundamentals of Packaging*, Blackie & Son, 1962.
E. A. Leonard, *Introduction to the Economics of Packaging*, McGraw-Hill, 1971.
J. Pilditch, *The Silent Salesman*, Business Publications, 1961.

Journals

Modern Packaging, McGraw-Hill, New York.
Packaging, Tudor Press, London.
Packaging Review, IPC Industrial Press Ltd.
Packaging Abstracts, PIRA.
Packaging Design, R.C. Publications Inc, New York.
Packaging Engineering, Angus J. Ray Publishing Co., Chicago.

17

Pricing as a marketing tool

Professor F. Livesey, Preston Polytechnic, School of Economics and Business Studies

It is a truism that profitability is affected more directly by pricing decisions than by decisions relating to any other marketing variable. It follows from this that the pricing plan should be an integral part of the marketing plan and hence ultimately the corporate plan.

PRICING AND CORPORATE OBJECTIVES

The starting point of the corporate plan is, either implicitly or explicitly, the company's objectives. In some instances these corporate objectives can be translated directly into pricing objectives. For example an objective of short-run profit maximisation implies that a price should be set that would maximise total contribution, or perhaps total cash flow, during the current planning period. (The price that will meet this objective will, of course, depend upon demand and cost conditions.)

In other instances the implications for pricing of a corporate objective may be less clear cut. Consider, for example, an objective of long-run profit maximisation (long run being specified, perhaps, in terms of a given number of years). This might imply that the firm should set either a high initial price which it would subsequently lower in the face of increasing competition, or a low initial price in order to deter potential competitors and establish a high market share. (This distinction between a 'skimming' and a 'penetration' price policy was first made by Joel Dean when analysing the pricing of pioneer products.)[1]

The long-term nature of this decision emphasises the need to integrate pricing objectives within broader corporate objectives. Integration is also required because of the implications of the pricing decision for other aspects of company policy. It will be sufficient to quote three examples. First, although with a skimming price policy the firm would expect to reduce its initial price, it can often delay such reductions by introducing a series of product innovations, i.e. there are important implications for its R & D activity. Second, a penetration price policy frequently leads to losses being made until the firm obtains the volume of sales that justifies the low price. The firm must ensure that it can fund these losses from reserves, from the cash generated by other products or from external finance. Finally the choice between a high (initial) price/low volume and a low price/high volume strategy has clear implications for policies relating to other marketing variables, and in particular advertising and distribution.

IMPLEMENTATION

The need for an integrated approach also applies to the implementation of the corporate plan. This becomes especially important when obstacles to implementation arise. Consider the situation in which a company has the dual objectives of maintaining market share and profit margins, but is unable to achieve both. This might happen because costs have risen more than was anticipated or because a new competitor has entered the market.

An integrated response to this situation would involve a reconsideration of all aspects of company policy. For example if it was decided that priority should be given to maintaining market share, this might require an increase in advertising expenditure, an increase in incentives to the sales force, an acceleration of R & D activity and/or a price reduction. If, on the other hand, it was decided that priority should be given to the maintenance of margins, this might imply

---

1   J. Dean, *Managerial Economics*, Prentice Hall, London 1961; and 'The Pricing of Pioneer Products', *Journal of Industrial Economics 1969*.

maintaining prices and attempting to reduce 'organisational slack' by various means ranging from a reduction in expense accounts to the renegotiation of manning levels.

In the absence of an integrated approach sub-optimal pricing decisions are likely to be taken. In the first instance considered above price may have to bear the full burden of the adjustment required in order to preserve market share. In the second instance prices may be shaded even though the revised company objectives do not require this.

The main reason why price may have to bear an inappropriate share of the burden of adjustment is that it is easier to effect changes in price than in other variables. Eventually, of course, a failure to achieve objectives may also trigger changes in other variables, but only after a considerable lag. If you are in doubt consider within the context of your own company the second situation above, where the most appropriate response was a reduction in organisational slack. Could you say that when such situations have arisen the marketing department has never agreed to shade prices, the shading having continued for quite some time before the introduction of cost-reducing procedures?

THE RELATIONSHIP BETWEEN PRICE AND OTHER ELEMENTS OF THE MARKETING MIX

It was suggested above that pricing decisions should be taken in conjunction with decisions on other elements of the marketing mix. This implies that the company's pricing discretion may thereby be constrained. The classic example of internal constraints on pricing decisions was provided by Oxenfeldt in his analysis of the choices facing U.S. producers of television sets in the early phase of the market's development.[2]

Oxenfeldt compared the situation facing three companies. The Zenith Radio Corporation had extensive experience in the manufacture of car radios. This experience had resulted in the accumulation of substantial production expertise and a healthy liquidity position.

2   A.R. Oxenfeldt, 'A Multi-Stage Approach to Pricing', *Harvard Business Review* 1960/61.

However the company's outstanding resource was probably its wide-spread distribution network, especially important since in this market retailers have considerable influence on customers' decisions. In addition the company had built up a considerable degree of consumer loyalty, reflecting the very high reputation of its radios. This enviable collection of assets gave Zenith a high degree of freedom in its pricing decisions, although it seemed clear that a price towards the upper rather than the lower end of the range would be appropriate. In order to avoid damaging its reputation with both purchasers and stockists of radios, Zenith was obliged to offer a high quality television set, which implied a relatively high cost of production.

The Columbia Broadcasting Corporation had a very different set of assets from Zenith. The company was primarily familiar with the management of entertainers and with the production of television programmes. Its manufacturing facilities were of poor quality and it had no established distribution facilities. However it did have great prestige as a producer of television programmes, and it also had substantial low-cost advertising facilities at its disposal. The mass production of a cheap set was clearly ruled out, so CBC was also guided towards the top end of the market. Indeed rather than enter into head-on competition with Zenith, its best strategy seemed to be to sell, at a price above Zenith, a highly styled product through a limited range of prestige outlets.

Finally, Emerson was one of a number of firms for whom a low price policy seemed most appropriate, because they lacked the financial resources needed to convey a quality image and because their previous experience was with products at the cheaper end of the market. Emerson's chief asset was in fact a very efficient manufacturing organisation, geared to high-volume low-cost production. This allowed the firm to charge the low price that was required, given the absence of any other distinctive marketing advantage.

It can be seen that the limitation of pricing discretion that arises from internal factors does not necessarily imply low prices; indeed in many industries there are firms which are enabled as a result of their marketing activities, to charge premium prices – IBM in the computer market, Gardner in commercial vehicle engines, Lowenbrau in beer and Estée Lauder in cosmetics.

Marketing in Action

PRICE DIFFERENTIALS

The discussion to date has proceeded on the (implicit) assumption that the firm charges the same price to all purchasers. But in many firms this is not so; price differentials are widespread. In such instances a decision has to be made concerning the most appropriate pattern of differentials. Moreover, since differentials are usually expressed in terms of discounts from the basic price, a change in the pattern of differentials may require a change in the basic price in compensation.

Price differentials may relate to the geographical area supplied, the time of supply, the functional role of the customer (manufacturer/ wholesaler/retailer/consumer), the personal characteristics of the purchaser and the quantity supplied. In some instances the differentials may take several of these factors into account, so that a very complex pattern can result. Two basic considerations should underlie any pattern, simple or complex.

First, what are the differentials designed to achieve? There are several possible answers to this question: to influence the pattern of orders and hence lower costs (discounts related to the size of individual orders); to tie customers (discounts related to the quantity purchased over, say, a year); to increase market share while avoiding head-on competition with a dominant supplier in the major market (differentials related to the geographical area supplied); to persuade distributors to undertake additional functions or to open up a new distribution channel (discounts related to the functional role of the customer); to increase capacity utilisation (discounts related to the time of supply).

Second, what costs are involved in supplying a certain purchaser or group of purchasers? The provision of adequate information on costs is, of course, of general importance for pricing decisions, but certain concepts attain greater prominence when the market is divided into submarkets or segments. Under these circumstances it becomes particularly important to be able to identify the incremental cost, i.e. the additional cost that would be incurred in supplying particular customers, and escapable cost, i.e. the cost that would be saved by ceasing to supply.

204

THE PRICE SENSITIVITY OF CONSUMERS

Although a firm's pricing discretion may be limited by internal factors, as demonstrated above, there may remain a range of prices consistent with its marketing mix. The choice of a price from within this range could have the utmost importance for profitability, and it is therefore important that the firm should have information concerning consumers' perception of price and, more specifically, their price sensitivity. Techniques designed to provide information on price sensitivity can be grouped into five broad categories.[3]

The analysis of past data not generated specifically for this purpose in the first instance

The main problem in analysing past data is that of disentangling the effects of changes in price from the remaining changes, in incomes and tastes, for example, that might also have occurred in the period studied. The most common method of trying to overcome this problem is by the application of multiple regression analysis. The potentialities and deficiencies of this technique have been described by Professor Robinson.[4] Robinson, using data from the U.K. National Food Survey for 1956-67, derived an estimate of -0.4 for the elasticity of demand for butter (the elasticity of demand is a precise measure of consumers' price sensitivity). This estimate compares with one of -0.3 for 1960-66 (National Food Survey Committee) and -0.4 for 1921-38 (Professor Stone).

The high measure of agreement among these three estimates probably reflects stable demand conditions for butter. A wider range of estimates has been obtained for other products such as cigarettes and cars. For example, ten estimates of the price elasticity of demand for cars in the U.S. in the post-war period produced figures ranging from -0.6 to -1.4[5]

---

3   Additional examples of the use to which these various techniques have been put are contained in F. Livesey, *Pricing*, Macmillan, London 1976, ch.4.
4   C. Robinson, *Business Forecasting*, Nelson, London 1971, ch.4.
5   C. Griffin, 'When is Pricing Reduction Profitable?', *Harvard Business Review* 1960.

However, even where differences of this magnitude arise, the estimates may provide useful guidance for producers. It has been suggested that given the typical cost structure of U.S. car manufacturers, price reductions would be profitable only if elasticity were -4.5 or above.[6] In other words all the ten estimates would lead to the same conclusion, that prices should not be reduced.

It should be noted that both sets of estimates referred to above refer to the total market. These values can be applied to the individual supplier only if all suppliers change their prices at the same time and to the same extent. To try to get round this difficulty firms sometimes attempt to estimate the elasticity of demand for their own products by analysing internal data on sales and prices. However, since the data was not specifically designed for this purpose, it is not always available in the form or on the scale required. For example, the sales data may refer to larger groups of products than the price data. The methods described below are designed to overcome this problem.

Price experimentation

The manufacturer of a well established product may change the price for a limited period and compare sales in this period with sales in previous and subsequent periods. It is necessary to ensure as far as possible that normal trading conditions prevail during the experimental period. For example, a period should be chosen which minimises any seasonal influences; if the change takes the form of a price reduction it should not be promoted as a 'special offer'.

Unfortunately there are several factors outside the control of the manufacturer which can bias the results of the experiment. First, even if the price reduction is not promoted, consumers may see it as a promotion and hence may increase their purchasing rate above the long-term level. Conversely, when the price rises again, the reduction in sales may be greater in the short than in the long run (partly because of the earlier build up of consumers' stocks).

Second, bias may occur through the responses of distributors. A lower price normally implies a lower absolute margin for distributors. But given that the price reduction was temporary the manufacturer

---

6   C. Griffin, ibid.

might feel obliged to maintain the previous margins to protect goodwill. However, insofar as the margin offered might influence distributors' willingness to promote this product or brand at the expense of competitive products, their behaviour during the experimental period might differ from that where price and margins are permanently reduced.

Finally bias may arise from the activities of competitors. Many markets, in particular for low value consumer products, are characterised by frequent changes in competitive activity: for example, price reductions, advertising campaigns, competitions. If one (or more) of these occurs during the experimental period, the results obtained will be suspect. One way of reducing the possibility of bias from this source is to vary prices on a regional basis. This may give a better indication of consumers' price sensitivity provided that (a) competitors are not differentiating their activity regionally, and (b) consumers in different regions do not differ greatly in their response to price changes.

Hypothetical shopping situations

An alternative approach which avoids some of the problems associated with price experimentation is to establish a hypothetical shopping situation. This involves asking potential consumers whether or not they would be likely to buy a product (or, less frequently, a brand) at various prices. If the product is familiar to the consumer it may simply be named; if not the consumer may be given a verbal or pictorial description or, more rarely, shown the actual product.

This method works best when used with a large (preferably at least 1,000) sample of consumers. In order to apply statistical analysis it is necessary to discover the limits of the price range that is acceptable to the consumer. The simplest way of obtaining the information is to ask each consumer to name her (or his) limits. A more time-consuming, but more realistic and hence more reliable method is to put a number of prices, in turn, to the consumer and ask whether she would buy at that price.

Probably the most interesting finding emerging from the application of this technique is that the volume of sales is likely to *fall* when price falls below a certain point, a response that can be explained by the fact that consumers see the price of a product as an indicator of its quality. It was shown above that the other elements of the marketing mix enable some companies to obtain premium prices. If price is seen as an indicator of the quality of these products it follows that a reduction in price would lead to a reduction in both margins and the volume of sales.

Information on the acceptability to consumers of different prices can be supplemented by information on the price last paid for the product. A comparison of the two sets of figures can indicate whether consumers see the existing price range as correct or whether products are seen as being under or over priced. This information is useful both for a firm considering entering the market and for an existing supplier who is considering whether to move to a new place in the price structure.[7]

Simulated shopping situations

This method is similar in some respects to the hypothetical shopping situation, but here the consumer is presented with a mock-up of a shop (or a department), e.g. a trailer furnished with shelves stocked with groceries. Different prices are set during different 'trading periods' and each shopper is asked to make the 'purchases' that she would have made had she been presented with the choice in practice.

This is a more difficult and expensive method than the hypothetical shopping situation, but has the advantage that the consumers are placed in a situation more closely akin to their actual shopping experience.[8] (It should be noted, however, that in neither situation are consumers asked to make purchases.)

The analysis of data derived from informed opinion

The basic justification for this method is that the cost of collecting information can be reduced if, instead of interviewing a large number of consumers, the manufacturer seeks the views of a smaller number

---

7   This method is discussed at greater length in A. Gabor, *Pricing, Principles and Practices,* Heinemann, London 1977.
8   Results suggesting that the simulated shopping situation gives more reliable results than other methods are presented in R.G. Stout, 'Developing Data to Estimate Price-quantity Relationships', *Journal of Marketing,* 1969.

of people who are in touch with consumers, e.g. distributors or the manufacturer's staff.

The information obtained may be subjected to a simple head-counting exercise. Alternatively, it may be used as the basis of an elaborate model incorporating, for example, Bayesian decision theory. This approach allows the possible outcomes of a series of interconnected events to be explored. For example, a reduction in price may lead to an increase in sales; this may cause rival manufacturers to reduce their prices; these price reductions may cause plans to increase capacity to be modified, etc. Probabilities are attached to alternative outcomes at each stage and so a series of joint probabilities attached to the alternative final outcomes that stem from each initial price are combined to give an expected pay-off from that price. A comparison of these pay-offs indicates which price is likely to be the most profitable.[9]

Professor Oxenfeldt concluded a recent article with the following words: 'The corporate pricing function within a decision-making structure is a very complex process. Many components must be integrated and managed as a unit if the firm is quickly to capitalise on its pricing opportunities.'[10] Although this chapter has not encompassed all the relevant components, it has demonstrated the complexity of the pricing function and the benefit to be derived from a well developed pricing plan.

---

9   For a detailed illustration of this method, see P.E. Green, 'Bayesian Decision Theory in Pricing Strategy,' *Journal of Marketing*, 1963.
10 A.R. Oxenfeldt, 'A Decision-Making Structure for Price Decisions', *Journal of Marketing*, 1973.

18

Advertising

John Hobson, Hon. President, Hobson Bates & Partners Limited

In a modern industrialised society virtually the whole population has some discretionary spending power, i.e. money to spend on goods which are not necessities, like basic foods, shelter and clothing. It has the capacity to buy improved utilities, extra amenities and modest luxuries. Industry responds by making goods and offering services to suit a wide variety of tastes. No one could want or afford them all. People have to choose.

In order to choose, the consumer needs suggestions and information about what is available, what might suit his personal preferences, what could be new and interesting experiences. Before buying goods or services, he wants to hear about the performance or satisfaction which those goods and services will give him. He may see the products on display in shops or supermarkets; the satisfactions he can be informed about through advertising. If one were to say that the totality of advertising as it appears in print, or on television, or by radio is a kind of supermarket of satisfactions, it would not be an unfair definition of the place of advertising in modern society.

Although advertising owes its existence in this way to the service it gives the consumer, it becomes a vital service also to the producer. To him advertising offers the lowest-cost channel of communication for his messages offering the goods or services he has for sale. As a result of low-cost communication to millions of people with considerable frequency, he can achieve economies of scale which enable him to reduce prices. He can influence demand in such a way as to maintain a steady flow, which in turn enables him to maintain a steady flow of production. He can modify seasonal influences on demand with the same advantage, and can assure himself of the rapid pay-off of investment in new production lines and machinery and in research and development. Although advertising is only one element – the communication element – in the marketing mix, it very often can be the critical factor in a marketing decision because it can control the speed at which vital costs can be reimbursed, and new products or improvements to existing products launched.

As a result, advertising has a vital role to play in the economy of the consumer societies of the West. It is one of the most vital tools of competition and innovation which maintain the dynamics and the initiative of industry. It provides the outlet for the results of sound research and development, without which an industrial nation must go into a decline. Advertising helps to maintain employment and the uses of all resources, at a steady pace, without undue swings in supply or demand. It increases the aspirations of the public so that the desires to work harder and earn more money are increased. It improves the quality of material life for the mass of the public. It may be objected that it puts too much emphasis on material aspiration and well-being, but advertising is only responding to social trends, encouraged by the redistribution of wealth over the last century. Advertising does not govern the shape of society; it only reflects the shape that exists.

Advertising is basically communication. There are many kinds of advertising other than in the marketing context: government propaganda, advertising for churches and charities, financial news, advertising to fill jobs and get jobs, and so on. In the rest of this chapter, the word 'advertising' is used in the context of the commercial functions of advertising.

ADVERTISING AS A MARKETING ACTIVITY

The impression the public has of advertising might be that a vast amount of money and effort is being spent on a lot of bright ideas or momentary inspirations. It is a misunderstanding for which even the less well-informed social observers could be pardoned, but it is curiously prevalent also among many people concerned with industry even in the consumer goods fields.

In fact, good advertising is the result of careful planning and research, which lead in almost every case to each advertisement being given its particular content or form, and its direction to a selected audience of potentially interested consumers. The serious sponsors of advertising have no money to waste; for them it is not an art form, or a display of ego or personal interests. When industry spends something over £1000 million on display advertising for consumer goods every year, it not only expects to get, but actually does get what it regards as a proper return for its outlay.

The basic purpose of advertising, then, is to offer goods and services for sale. Each particular advertising campaign for a particular product at a particular time is part of what one may term a deliberate marketing intention on the part of the sponsors, who base their carefully considered strategy and tactics in the first instance on the properties and utilities, shape, packaging and colour of the product, and calculate the latest trends of public behaviour, recreation or outlook, new factors in retail distribution and effect of competition. The marketing intention takes in the method of transport, trade margins, price merchandising, wholesaling and retailing decisions, the role of the sales force, the after-sales service facilities, and a number of similar considerations. It will comprise a careful identification of the best potential market in terms of people, geography, seasons and spending power; and will duly arrive at the advertising message, and the deployment of budget best calculated to carry it. The choice of advertising is virtually the last element to be decided in the marketing complex, and, although it may represent a very large part of the financial outlay and may in the result determine the success or failure of the whole marketing plan, it is in itself very largely governed by the other elements in the plan. Because the advertisements are the main, and certainly most obvious, outward and visible signs of the plan, many people get the impression that the advertising is the only really important element, that it *is* the plan in its own right.

Next, it is worth remarking that virtually no two marketing plans, or their consequent advertising programmes, have identical intentions. There are, of course, certain broad groups of similar circumstances which call for fairly similar treatments; but with each tactical situation, on which each plan is based, there are differing weights of contributory factors which make every case different from any other.

It is not feasible to lay down a kind of blueprint that will fit the needs of a number of marketing or advertising intentions.

ADVERTISING OBJECTIVES AND TECHNIQUES

The two most crucial stages in developing an advertising campaign are *(a)* the strategic decision on objectives and *(b)* the choice of creative treatment. The former is bound up in the total marketing intention; the latter is a matter of advertising techniques.

The considerations leading to decisions of strategy are as wide and various as the field of commerce itself. Nevertheless, it is possible to list five main types of consideration which normally affect the advertising objectives:

1 The range, type and intensity of consumer wants comprising the market for our product, together with estimates of the trends of public outlook or trade development, which may affect those wants in the future.
2 The efficacy of the product itself.
3 The strength of the sponsor's resources for promoting it.
4 The existing disposition of competitor's strength.
5 The type of purchasing occasion arising from the character of distribution for this type of product.

One talks of 'the market' for a type of product, but this apparently straightforward concept of the market conceals a wide variety of types and degrees of want varying by age, geography, outlook, habit, price, occasion of usage, availability and so on. By means of a painstaking assembly of facts through market research, retail contacts, and all other methods of fact finding, the size of the potential sale for our product, associated with each degree of necessity can be calculated, thus setting-up a choice of differing objectives for the advertising. It is axiomatic that no product is ever equally perfect for all sectors of the market.

The first consideration in choosing an objective will probably be the special qualities or performance of a product. The addition or adjustment of qualities would be considered in order to create a better advertising proposition. The decision will also be affected by the areas of strength or weakness of the competition. It is no good tackling an objective head-on where strong competition is entrenched.

A vital factor is the resources which our sponsor can put behind his campaign. Only too often, ambitious sponsors with slender resources attempt an objective too big for them.

The strategic advertising decision will also be greatly influenced by the type of purchasing occasion, e.g. an impulse market, a carefully considered purchase, a product limited by distributive conditions to tied outlets, a cut-price supermarket situation etc.

Finally, one must look forward from the market, the competition and the distribution, as they now exist, to possible developments foreseen as a result of trends in public spending, outlook and living patterns, and position of the product in its market accordingly.

An illustration of the strategic advertising decision might be given in the case in the breakfast cereal market. Here are five products which have been deliberately aimed at five sectors of the market. The market leader uses his dominant resources to promote a broad sense of pleasure and wholesomeness, which can apply to everyone. Another brand with a more rugged product and a lower budget concentrates on youngsters through their sporting interests. A third attacks a limited but specific health area. A fourth goes for the children's market with the appeal of a sense of fantasy and fun, while a fifth tackles the same market with the appeal of premium gifts.

It is probable that this strategic decision overrides even the creative decision in importance. The most sparkling and competent creative execution will be wasted if the policy objectives are not correctly chosen. It happens only too often. At the same time, within the right strategic decision there is wide scope for success or failure, brilliance or dullness, competence or incompetence, in the creative execution.

There are three main considerations likely to influence the approach to the creative decision, (a) the tactical objective of the particular phase of advertising, (b) the choice of main and secondary selling arguments, and (c) the manner or atmosphere of the presentation of those selling arguments.

TACTICS

There are an infinite variety of tactical situations. To name a few – we may be launching a new product with new utilities which need pro-

claiming and explaining. A dramatic piece of news like a price reduction or a new model may be announced, or the memory of an
established brand name may be merely sustained with a fresh render-
ing of its well-known claim. The virtues and the responsibility of a
serious industrial concern may be expounded to an audience of
managers, or the objective may be to give a company in the popular
consumer goods field a favourable image against which its goods will
sell automatically. A race for our brand against a very similar brand of
some other firm to gain a larger share of the market may occupy much
of our time, or it may be that greater concern is felt for widening the
total market for a class of goods because, if the market widens, our
brand must automatically gain the lion's share.

There are probably three main elements in the tactical use of
advertising – to penetrate, remind and create favourable associations.
The relative importance of each element in the plan of the particular
campaign will tend to determine which type of media or campaign
approach will be used. For example, television and large spaces in the
press and magazines are ideal outlets for telling a story in depth, while
posters and smaller spaces in the press and short television flashes
(little more than moving posters) are good for repetition which, as Dr
Kelvin points out in *Advertising and the Human Memory,* not only
prevents us forgetting but serves as the means of progressive assimila-
tion of the advertising message.

Then the question of the selling arguments arises. It might seem as
if the choice were obvious, determined simply by the properties of the
product. This, however, is unlikely to be so in the majority of cases. It
will be true at a moment when a product has clear and simply
expressed product advantages over its competitors; but this situation
will not hold good for long because it will only be a matter of time
before the competition is forced to include those same advantages.
Look around the whole field of consumer goods and you will find very
few markets in which there is not a handful of equally good competitive brands. If one has edged ahead in product quality, the others
have caught up. Indeed, this continuous competitive improvement is
one of the great merits of the system of which advertising is a part. In
this situation advertising has to find some aspect of a brand on which
to focus, an aspect on which the competition has not focused. Nor is
this limitation of the scope of the product claim to a single aspect a
disadvantage; indeed quite the reverse. The consumer finds it far

easier to identify, and therefore to remember at time of purchase, a product which has one single claim associated with it. So, however many good points a product may have, it is wise for the purposes of advertising to focus on one only, and allow the other values to emerge in course of use. Naturally, that one point must be an important one capable of influencing a sizeable part of the market.

ADVERTISING AND MARKET RESEARCH

What are the techniques for assessing the best choice of product claim? First, there is the obvious selection of an objective built-in utility superior to that of competition, but this is usually a short-lived advantage. Next, there is the historic flair and inspiration of the salesman for judging what the public wants most in the area of this product, and for concentrating on this aspect of the brand's properties. This competence, whether rational or intuitive, is one of the chief qualities of a great industrialist or a great salesman.

But in the intensive competition of today, and where the stakes are high and the penalities great, the hit-or-miss risks of intuition are not always acceptable. Market research, and especially depth research, are employed more and more to help in defining those areas to which the product's copy claims can best be directed. Market research covers all types of consumer investigation, but is generally associated with research designed to establish a pattern of behaviour. From the patterns of behaviour by people of various descriptions the motives of that behaviour are deduced. Depth research, or motivation study as it is called, consists of interviews directly designed to establish attitudes, motives and feelings about products and their usage, without the risks of deducing them from behaviour patterns.

A lot has been written and spoken about 'hidden persuaders' since Vance Packard's book was written. Certainly, the book overdramatised what is a very natural and sensible process. Let us be clear that in buying, as in many aspects of life, the number of decisions that can be taken on strictly rational grounds is very few; not only because it is seldom possible to assemble all the facts, but also because rational decisions involve a painful and complicated mental process which only a few people are either capable of or willing to undertake. Therefore, the majority of decisions are made out of feelings, habits, instincts and impulses. It is commonsense, therefore, to try to chart those feelings, habits and impulses which surround the purchase of goods being sold.

The purpose of any such research, as indeed of the alternative – flair and intuition – is to establish that aspect of the product's claims which interests a large enough market, which has been neglected by competitors, and with which therefore this particular brand can become associated with major selling effect. Sometimes, of course, the need for being different leads to an exaggerated or partly untenable vision of a claim, even among well-intentioned salesmen. The public's safeguard in this case is that, since the success of any product depends on repeat purchases, not merely on a single purchase, and since nothing makes the public react against a product more than disappointment in an advertised claim, it is bad commercial policy as well as undesirable ethically to fall into the trap of exaggerated or dishonest claims.

DEVELOPING IMAGE AND SUBJECTIVE VALUES

The third main area of consideration in the approach to the creative decision is the associations with which the advertising can endow the product. This is something quite apart from the substance of the claims one makes for the product, yet it is of very real significance in the selling situation. It is the same subjective element which, when applied to corporations, is sometimes called the 'image'. It arises from the fact that when people make a purchase, they do not only buy something having objective values, but they buy satisfaction which includes subjective values also. The most obvious case is a woman buying a hat. She does not only buy a head-covering or a piece of coloured felt, she buys a satisfaction that includes such subjective values as fashionableness, a feeling of style, a sense of daring or renewed youth or whatever. But while this is an obvious case, the same principle applies just as readily to purchases of everyday things. With petrol you buy a sense of power or the feeling of a wise bargain. With beer you may buy a sense of manliness, or a sense of fun or a sense of healthfulness. With chocolate biscuits you may buy a feeling of gaiety, and with a car you certainly do not only buy a means of transport, but also a feel of dashingness, of luxury, of importance, of smartness, or whatever attribute has been added to the machinery by the advertising, the line of the bonnet, or the number of marginal gadgets.

There is plenty of evidence to show that these subjective values represent a very real increase of satisfaction in the purchase and use of the product; and the improved product commands a definite preference, and often a higher price, from the buyer than the same product not so improved. In the advertising aspect of their creation (and it is one of the most potent effects of advertising) the method is usually that of building up certain deliberate associations by the type of verbal or visual treatment, the use of colour and the associated pictures or personalities. It is as if a pattern of subjective associations is integrated with the substance of the product and becomes a real part of it. In an economy where the public could afford to pay for nothing except objective values this situation could hardly arise, but in an affluent society where almost everyone has a spending power in excess of physical needs, scope is widening for following one's whims into the area of subjective satisfactions.

Techniques of advertising presentation are a subject of endless fascination. They embrace all the most intricate aspects of perception, communication and persuasiveness. They cover everything in verbal and visual techniques from journalism to poetry, from realism to impressionism, from the *News of the World* to *Vogue*. One can only hope to touch on a few of the main points.

The first is to recognise the different audiences to whom the advertising must be addressed: top management or the housewife in the Durham back streets; children or the fashion-conscious women of society; bank managers or miners. The tone, the contents and the treatment will vary according to the audience. But certain factors will remain reasonably constant.

The first need for any advertisement is to gain attention. By and large, people do not aim to read advertisements – though in fact the advertisement section of a woman's magazine has a high readership in its own right. However, even here one is wise to start with the assumption that people will not want to read a particular advertisement. In the newspapers advertisements have to capture attention. On television, there is much talk of a captive audience, but this can be misleading. The audience may be captive, but its attention is not necessarily so; it may be talking or knitting or reading.

TECHNIQUES OF ADVERTISING

Here is a first axiom for getting attention: that it is the interest of the message that attracts attention – not its size, visual impact or its violence. The eye and mind work so fast that they shrug off instinctively a first impact of size or surprise or violence in an advertisement, before they have even assimilated what it is about, unless subconsciously there is an awakening of genuine interest. Clearly, interest in a product message is not universal; it will always limit itself to some section of the total public. For example, even a little advertisement headed 'Indigestion' will be noticed by the 3 or 4 per cent of people who at that moment are conscious of having a problem of indigestion. One of the reasons why advertising gets a bad name for being excessive or boring is that far more people every year are being exposed to far more messages than can be of interest to them personally. Men particularly become irritated with all the household advertisements which have no interest for them. In newspapers one can select those advertisements on which, because they say something of personal interest, one wants to focus, and ignore the rest. On television it is not so easy to ignore those of no personal interest, and this is why television tends to get a worse name in the context of intrusion that the press does.

Since the attention of an advertisement is gained by the first awakening of interest, it is vital that the attention-getting element should signal the sector of interest the advertisement aims to attract. Otherwise, one may only attract interest than cannot lead to sales. Humour, so beloved of many superficial observers of advertising, is a dangerous weapon for this reason, because (although it can add a certain cheerfulness to the image of the product) it too often attracts the attention of masses of people who are not potential buyers, and it may obscure or even damage the serious appeal to those who are.

The second key factor is the essential need to offer a benefit to those forming the potential market. People neither buy, nor want to think about buying, something that does not promise them a benefit for their money. It may sound a self-evident truth, but it is surprising how often it gets overlooked in the intricate and elaborate process of advertisement creation. Ideally, the benefit should be clearly conveyed in the attention-getting element in the advertisement. Sometimes the sponsors of advertisements, or their creators, are so shy about their whole function of selling they will go to great lengths to avoid seeming to intrude anything so blatant as a selling-point in the advertisement. But really the function of advertising is not to amuse, not to educate; not to decorate the hoardings or enliven the newspapers, but to sell; and only when an assured commitment emerges can it afford to do the others things as well.

The third element worthy of focus as important is that of giving a 'reason why', i.e. the reason why this product can offer such and such a benefit. More is often achieved through an appeal to the emotions than to the mind (because people are lazy about using their minds); but people are both mind and emotion, and their emotions react more easily if they are offered some concession to their logical process as well. It is wiser therefore to say, 'X is better because . . .' than just, 'X is better'.

The final element in a good advertisement is a bold display of the brand name. Once again this may seem obvious. After all, the function of an advertisement is to get the public to ask for a product or at least to recall its name in the shops. But there are some people who believe that a prominent display of a brand name will make people pass on from your advertisement because they believe they know what you are going to say about that product. This is a risk which must be taken, and be counteracted by the other elements in your advertisement. There are advertisers who believe that their advertisements are so well-liked and recognised that it is a good idea to leave the name out altogether. This is treating advertising as some kind of parlour game, not the expensive, productive and important process it really is.

THE UNIQUE SELLING PROPOSITION

Ideally the benefit should be one which the product alone can offer: it may be desirable to go back to the product formula and build-in some unique added benefit that its competitors do not comprise. It may only be possible to seek a unique way to express the benefit, or a unique aspect of the benefit to stress. Most products can offer a whole spectrum of benefits ranging from solid factors such as the price and performance, to elaborate subjective benefits derived from the manner of presenting either the product or the advertising. Somewhere at some point of this spectrum the advertising can be coloured with a unique shade, giving it a separate identity from its competitors. It is vital to end up by leaving in the public's mind a clear identity for your product – a uniqueness in an important selling area; what has been termed by one great American expert, Rosser Reeves, a Unique Selling Proposition.

This positive proposition of a benefit can then be enhanced by any one of a wide range of subjective associations which, providing they are relevant to the purchase of the product, can add to its total attraction. Such associations may be gay or fanciful or fashionable; they may offer a sense of a bargain, youthfulness, or keeping up with the Joneses. These are well-tried examples; there are many others. From these elements the total advertising presentation is built up to do its job of making a potential market interested in trying this product through the promise of a satisfaction which is part objective and part subjective.

THE ADVERTISING CAMPAIGN

A campaign concerns the total effect and sequence of the advertisements for a product. This technique was crystallised by Sir William Crawford, one of the great advertising technicians of the early days, in the three-word precept, 'concentration, domination, repetition'. It is still, and must always be, the clearest reflection of the processes which go to make-up mass selling.

Concentration

This is the selection of one shade in the spectrum of possible appeals for the product and the avoidance of diversity of appeal and dispersal of resources. It implies, of course, the careful selection of the appeal best calculated to gain a response from a sector of the market, which in turn is calculated to offer the best sales potential, having regard to the particular attributes of the product, the state of competitive activity and the resources available for promotion. It would be useless to select an area of product appeal which brought head-on collision with a competitor of much greater resources, or to comprise a sector of wants to which the available budget was insufficient to do justice.

It implies also the virtues of simplicity and single-mindedness in execution.

Domination

Domination is the gathering of the available forces of money and presentation techniques in such a way as to create a dominant impact on the minds of the chosen public. It will comprise an element of size at the initial stages of the campaign so as to gain attention and outweigh competitive claims. It will ensure that in the selected area of consumer needs, the name of the product will come out top of the alternatives in the memory of the potential customers. Given a budget insufficient to cover all areas, classes or segments of the public, domination will necessitate a concentration of effort in terms of geography or choice of media or some other means so that in that area of concentration the product can outweigh all rivals.

Repetition

Repetition is an essential part of the techniques of all advertising. With most consumer goods it is the repeated purchase that makes the selling investment pay off. The product drops only too easily out of mind and memory, and is supplanted by some lively newcomer unless the satisfied customers are reminded. Then it must be remembered that virtually no first impact of advertising reaches everybody; what appears to be repetition is very often merely a continuation of first impact on groups of customers not previously reached with the message. Every week of every year a new group of potential customers grows into the market. The advertising campaign therefore needs to be continued over a period of time, and a disposition of available resources must be made accordingly.

THE STRATEGIC FRAMEWORK OF ADVERTISING

The above are the salient factors which go to the strategic framework of an advertising campaign. There are executive processes which have then to be considered.

First and foremost comes the creative execution. To some people the creative element appears to be the most important, and certainly it is usually the most noticeable. A campaign tends to be judged superficially on its creative impact; in fact, unless the marketing conception is right, the creative impact can increase and intensify the misdirection of the expenditure and effort. Creative execution can only be considered after the strategic conception. It is usually a wise plan to present the strategy as a document for agreement by all concerned before going to the next stage of writing or visualising the actual advertisements.

Clearly, there must be vitality, craftsmanship, humanity and, hopefully, a touch of creative inspiration, to turn a campaign plan into warm, sparkling communication. The agreed campaign message can be given vividness and brilliance, but it is wise to remember that vividness and brilliance have their own glamour and can divert the critical instinct from the fact that the basic message may be the wrong one. Both in the creative process and in the initial selection of the creative executive, those concerned must keep their eyes firmly on the ball.

It is of little value to try to define the right ingredients for creative quality. Too many experts would give different answers. Tastes change from year to year. Different media require different treatment. If an advertisement is to be as helpful as possible to the consumer in making a choice, it needs to portray a realistic situation with which that consumer, usually a woman, can identify. In that situation her need is defined, and the usefulness of the product or service in satisfying that need realistically presented. The creative quality will emerge in the vividness, the impression, the humanity, in which the need and its satisfaction are pictured. Television is of course an ideal medium for this kind of treatment, because realism and demonstration are a natural part of it. The essence of creative ability then becomes the capacity to stand in the very shoes of the people you are appealing to, understand their needs, sensitivities and feelings, so that the process of identification comes most cogently to them.

A good deal of advertising creativity concerns itself wrongly with over-emphasis on technique, and the intrusion of the creator's own ego and feelings. A typical case is the use of sex interest or symbols into irrelevant contexts, simply because the creator is interested in these symbols. Many advertisements appealing to women portray sex interests which are clearly male because the creator is a man. A certain amount of advertising also betrays the creator's desire for applause for his own cleverness among his own confrères, rather like the centre forward who has just scored a goal, lifting up his arms and waiting to be embraced by his colleagues. And other advertising betrays a misuse of techniques admired and copied from more relevant contexts, which in a wrong context become just plain silly.

The right creative execution is a vital part of the marketing concept of the campaign because clearly the more effectively and cogently the advertisement can communicate with the maximum number of potential buyers, the quicker the budget cost of the advertising will pay off, to the profit and success of the advertiser.

MEDIA PLANNING

The next step in the executive process will be the choice of media. Indeed, it may need to be considered at an early stage because it may govern both the economics and the creative execution of the whole campaign. The choice of media is a whole subject in its own right. Suffice it to say here that the essence of the choice is to reach the maximum number of the clearly defined target audience, in the right atmosphere for the particular message, at the lowest cost. Since target audiences for a particular product seldom identify themselves, in the consumer goods area, exactly with media readership, the problem very often comes down to choosing the media with the minimum wastage. Again, however, television which may involve maximum wastage may nevertheless be the best choice simply because it offers the best medium for the message. The available media statistics, whether sifted by computer or other techniques, can offer extensive guidance to relate coverage of a particular audience to cost, but there still remains an imponderable element of choosing the best media to suit the character of the product or the particular type of message.

The only other aspect of running an advertising campaign that this chapter will cover is the function of the advertising agency in this context. The basic contribution of the agency must be its expertise in particular services – top creative ability, experienced media men for selecting and buying media, good technicians in the printing and blockmaking and other mechanical processes, and competent coordination, at executive level, of all the many details of a campaign. It is possible for an advertiser to buy many of these services from specialists outside the service agency, but, in this country at least, there is no real sign that advertisers prefer to take on the job of coordinating such outside services themselves. The agency package is still the most convenient method.

THE AGENCY RELATIONSHIP

There is, however, one other great value in the agency arrangement. The manufacturer tends to look at his marketing proposition from the boardroom downwards. He relates it to his manufacturing, profits, raw materials, distribution and the like. It is, to many manufacturers, an enormous advantage to have the compensating service of people who look at the same proposition from the market upwards. This is the special competence of the good agency. The manufacturer's personnel, even if they have the ability and training to take a consumer's view may, in certain circumstances, not have the independence to prevail on the board to make essential changes. The agency is an independent body and will be listened to more readily by the board. Finally, the manufacturer, being concerned with his own type of business and immersed in it, may not have had the useful experience of outside industries, of successes and failures in other related or unrelated fields, which an agency with many clients can gather together. The manufacturer values someone competent to trade ideas with as a means of measuring his own interests against outside criticism.

ETHICS

Much has been written about the ethics of advertising. Essentially, since advertising is a communication process, the ethics of advertising are the ethics of those who utter the communication. The advertising of bad products or services is bad ethics. Sometimes, also, the urgent search for additional sales may lead an advertiser into promoting his product for purposes outside its normal range, for which it is of dubious value. But good marketing, which is offering products which clearly have a true and well calculated market, does not need 'sell at all costs' advertising.

Within the limits of advertising itself there are two aspects of ethics which may be considered. The first is the honesty and truthfulness of the satisfactions offered and the information given. This requirement is now well controlled by the combination of the Advertising Standards Authority (operating through the Code of Advertising Practice Committee) in relation to print and other non-broadcast media, and the control committee of the Independent Broadcasting Authority, in relation to television and radio. This sensibly operated control system, run by people who understand the problems of advertising, has given the UK the most acceptable standards of advertising practice in the world.

The second is a much more subjective area of advertising, what may be called the helpfulness of the advertisement to the consumer in making his or her choice. Questions of relevance, good taste, sufficient information, and other factors which cannot be controlled by a rule-of-thumb system as easily as truth and honesty can be, are inevitably left to the good sense and sensitivity of those, whether advertisers or agencies, who are practising advertising. At the same time, self interest works to encourage the advertiser to make his advertisements helpful, because they will improve the long-term goodwill of his business, and the confidence of the public in his advertising. Social sense and business expediency combine, and in the long run the factor of consumer acceptance will be paramount.

19

Public relations

Norman Hart, Director, Communication Advertising and Marketing Education Foundation Limited

Public relations is concerned with maintaining good communications between an organisation and its various 'publics'. Each organisation is usually involved with a number of publics and the importance of these will vary from company to company and from time to time. Figure 19.1 shows a typical group of publics for a trading company.

In marketing, the primary consideration is for customers, and here it is important to consider the position of public relations as against advertising and selling. In very general terms, selling is concerned with clinching a sale following the creation, by advertising, of a desire to purchase; and all of this carried out within a favourable two way atmosphere built up by good public relations. The favourable climate of opinion created in the mind of a buyer will make him more amenable to pay regard to a company's advertising, and in turn more likely to wish to conduct business. This, then, is the role of public relations in the marketing mix, and it will be apparent directly that there are many ways of achieving this end.

The image of a company or a product can be influenced by any of the following factors. These are not intended to be exhaustive but merely indicative of the wide-ranging items to which consideration must be given:

(a) letterheadings and correspondence;
(b) telephone service and switchboard manner;
(c) personal appearance of salesmen;
(d) packaging of products;

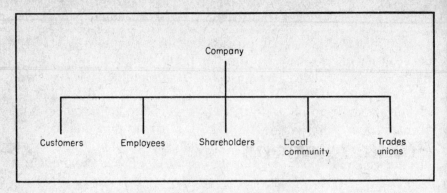

Figure 19:1   A typical group of publics for a trading company

 (e) advertising – press, television, posters;
 (f) editorial publicity;
 (g) displays and exhibitions;
 (h) publications and sales leaflets, and
 (i) films and photography.

It should be noted that press relations enters into the field of public relations only in so far as it is of value in achieving good editorial coverage. Equally, press relations can lead to new product mentions securing sales leads. In this role it is closer to the promotion function (including advertising) than public relations. Before turning to media, or channels of communication, it is important to consider briefly the nature of the publics it is necessary to influence.

PUBLICS

In consumer marketing, the primary target audience is usually a simple one comprising all, or specific segments of, the general public where the buying decision is made by one person. This might be a housewife (in the use of foodstuffs) a child (in the case of ice cream) or the man of the house (with a beer brand). Within a family unit the purchasing decision may be influenced by more than one person. Also to be considered are the intermediaries in the distribution process, the wholesalers and retailers. The purchasing pattern then follows the path from

Supplier ⟶ distributor ⟶ consumer

In the industrial marketing process the first difference is that the decision-making process is often far more complex. Whilst there might not be distributors to consider, it is often impossible to define with whom a purchasing decision rests. Very often there will be technical and scientific staff involved; production management may be concerned, purchasing officers have a part to play and so often does the board of directors. There may well be a couple of dozen who at some stage can exert an influence on what and where to purchase. Simplified, this can be expressed as follows:

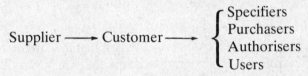

Time-scale is another factor which needs to be considered since industrial purchases are traditionally considered to have a long gestation period of a year or two. This surmise should be examined, however, since a position to the contrary may easily apply as in the case of a vacuum cleaner for a housewife, and a gross of paper clips for an industrial company. The gestation period is often a consequence of the relative value of the investment involved.

The setting of objectives is dealt with later in this chapter, but it is useful to look at what might be considered typical public relations goals in marketing terms:

1 To position a company as being amongst the top 10 (or 5 or 3) suppliers of children's toys in the UK.
2 To secure a reputation for a company's products as being good value for money (or safe, strong or accurate).
3 To make known a new brand name such that 1 in 2 buyers automatically associate it with the right product and company.
4 To ensure that 80 per cent of potential buyers relate the company name to lawnmowers (or any other specific product group).
5 To cause all buyers to form an opinion that a company is honest, fair, ethical, and generally one with which they would like to do business.

6 To exert influence on the government to give tax concessions on one's own group of products.

7 To bring to the government's attention and exert public pressure to prohibit 'dumping' of products which are directly competitive.

8 To enhance the reputation of one's own staff amongst journalists, opinion-formers and customers so as to build up confidence in the company itself.

THE PUBLIC RELATIONS MIX

To achieve any public relations objective, the chances are that more than one medium can and should be used. First, it is necessary to consider each channel of communication, and the impact it is likely to have on a customer, and then to evaluate the usefulness of each within the context of the desired effect and the available budget. Figure 19.2 indicates the kind of forces which can be brought to bear.

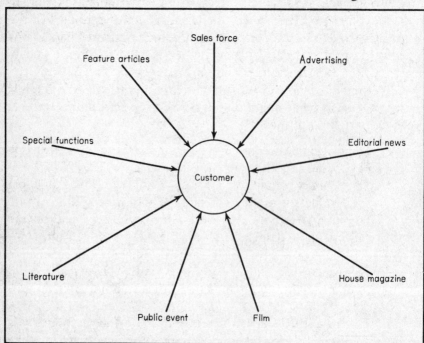

Figure 19:2 The forces which can be brought to bear

It is intended here to examine the principal media which are available. It is not possible to look at the detail involved in utilising these since this must devolve on to the expert. It is necessary, however, for the reader to be able to make a judgement on how best his communications channels should be deployed.

Company publications

A valuable feature of publications in public relations is that they are of a more permanent nature than other forms of communication. This is especially true of brochures intended to put across, say, the nature of a manufacturing process or the care which is put into manufacturing a product, or into research and development, or the way in which a product contributes to the welfare of the community. The presentation of publication must, of course, reflect the image of the organisation, and for this reason the temptation to economise falsely must be resisted. Savings can be made by avoiding a wastage in re-writes and redesigns, and by setting about the whole production process in a methodical manner.

The objectives need to be defined and an outline produced before starting to write the copy. A designer should be brought in only after the copy has been agreed, and then a tight briefing is necessary so that the objectives and constraints are known in advance. High quality can be achieved without high expense, by restricting the use of colour, avoiding complex artwork, and by giving detailed attention to the type mark-up. A long production run can do much to reduce the unit cost of a publication. It is sometimes acceptable to use even electric typewriting in place of the more expensive typesetting, in fact multicoloured glossy brochures can sometimes back-fire in public relations terms. They can be indicative of a company with rather more money than sense as against a simple workmanlike publication which, if professionally produced can create a favourable, and certainly acceptable, impression. External house magazines often have an important role to play in marketing, particularly with industrial products where there tends to be a good deal of innovation and the number of potential buyers is small. This also applies in consumer marketing where they can forge a valuable link with distributors. The editorial content needs careful consideration in order to ensure that it is directly relevant to the interests of customers. As regards production, the temptation to follow commercial magazines must be avoided if budgets are to be kept down. Many very successful company periodicals are no more than what might be described as duplicated broadsheets, yet they do a first-class job.

Customers are usually far more interested in content than in presentation, and the overriding factor is to put across the points clearly, without elaboration. The annual report is a useful opportunity for correctly positioning a company in the eyes of its customers, for it is certainly read by a wider audience than shareholders. Annual reports have changed from the stark financial document required by law, into a publication having useful statistics, some facts about the company's progress, for instance, and the interesting developments in products and distribution.

Editorial publicity

Publicity in the editorial columns of the press (and in television and radio) is often regarded as the mainstay of public relations. While this is not necessarily so, the fact is that such publicity can be of considerable value in its own right, whilst in comparison with other means of communications it has special advantages. Editorial matter is read by a higher proportion of readers than advertisements; also, the message which appears has an implied support from the publication and is not therefore regarded as being partisan or biased. Editorial publicity is not a cheap alternative to advertising. The company concerned has no control over what appears, if indeed anything is printed at all. Also, an item will be published only once, and even then the timing is a matter for the editorial staff alone. As regards costs, it is happily true that no payment is made to a journalist for writing a piece about a company or product and, whilst the preparation of material for the press involves a tangible expense, in the form of press conferences for instance, this is not usually of the same order as the cost of inserting advertisements. Basically the press is interested in securing news items or features.

For news, publications rely heavily on press releases from organisations about people, products, contracts, re-equipment, innovations, achievements, exports, research work, as well as set-backs, disasters and disputes, and so on. The preparation and distribution of press releases are specialist functions and no attempt is made here to deal with them in any detail.

Attention must be paid to certain basic criteria, however, which are ignored time after time. First, a release must contain news of consequence, not to the company, but to the ultimate readers. In this respect, an outside public relations consultant can be helpful in that he is likely to be more objective and to have sufficient independence to make his point known. A further requirement is that the news should be relevant to the readers of a particular publication and, since there might be hundreds of periodicals to be considered, this presents no small task to the supplier of news. A single press release sent to all publication outlets is rarely adequate and, consequently, tends to miss valuable opportunities and build up ill will amongst journalists.

Where a particular news story is of sufficient importance, or where it is anticipated that questions are likely to be stimulated, a press conference is of value. Here, journalists will be devoting their attention to the subject exclusively as against just a quick glance at a press release. Further, the discussions which take place both formally and behind the scenes can result in greater cover than would otherwise be obtained. Press visits to factories or supermarkets etc. are similar subjects of interest.

A feature article is a different matter and provides the opportunity to look at a subject in depth. It is important here to have a good relationship with the press. Features rarely arise out of a journalist's mind in isolation. They come about from an interchange of views with a variety of people ranging across a wide spectrum of subjects. Such personal contacts may result in a good story, but only if this is judged to be so in terms of the readers' interests. It is as well to realise from the outset that the result might be a story which the originator regards as highly unfavourable, but that is a risk incurred in seeking out this form of publicity. A point which should be made is that it is rare to find a journalist who will break a confidence and, by and large, a company can expect to get a fair hearing.

A further source of supply of feature material is in the form of the contributed article for which a fee is payable; also a personal interview presented in the form of a conversation. This latter is one of the most common forms of publicity on radio and television. In these media the greatest hurdle to overcome is that interviews are unscripted and are likely to be subject to nervous reactions on the part of the person being interviewed resulting in less than adequate replies being given. It may be encouraging to know that the inter-

viewer is also subject to nervous tensions and is rarely as knowledgeable about the particular subject as the interviewee.

Advertising

A common misunderstanding is that advertising and public relations
are two different functions – one concerned with selling goods, the
other with building up a reputation or an image. This is not so.
Advertising is a channel of persuasive communications which
happens to be particularly effective in many areas of 'sales promotion'. In certain circumstances it can be most relevant in achieving
public relations goals. Equally, there are numerous instances of 'sales
promotion' activities not involving advertising at all, and sometimes
relying largely upon, say, editorial publicity to secure sales leads.

In the examples given earlier of typical public relations objectives,
there are instances where traditional public relations techniques, like
editorials and special events will not come easily, maybe because the
product is fundamentally uninteresting. Press or television advertising may then be necessary even though the cost will be high.

Prestige advertising, as it is sometimes known, has earned the poor
reputation of being wasteful. This may have been so, but there is no
longer justification for it to involve more wastage than any other form
of marketing activity. After all, a sales call can turn out to be wasted
time. The essence of using advertising efficiently for public relations
purposes is in 'before-and-after' research. This applies even more so
than in some promotional advertising where at least there are other
indicators such as sales figures, retail audits, representative reports
and the like. Advertising should be beamed at a well-defined target
audience, and the effects carefully measured. Advertising can also be
used to support the publicity leading up to a major event which itself
is concerned with public relations, e.g. a conference or a seminar. It
need hardly be said that every advertisement, as with every exposure
of the company to the public eye, is automatically contributing to a
company's image. This applies also to letterheads, vehicles, outdoor
signs, salesmen's suits, company vehicles and switchboard operators
as well as to traditional sales promotional media like advertising,
posters, point-of-sale display and packaging.

Exhibitions and display

Exhibitions have an important role to play in public relations as well as in securing direct sales leads. Their cost need not be excessive. True, with many large public exhibitions the impressive stands are expensive, and often rightly so, but the lavish presentation is frequently noticed more by the exhibitors concerned than by the visiting public. Agricultural shows, trade association conferences, local company sponsored events all offer important public relations opportunities.

With many exhibitions, shell schemes are available furnished with display boards which are reuseable on other occasions. Indeed, the very furnishings can be owned by the company and used for one show after another. Many trade shows are more concerned with public relations than direct selling. Here, firms set up a centre which is concerned largely with providing an opportunity for meeting with customers and entertaining them with a view to strengthening contacts. It is important to ensure that the maximum use is made of any exhibition. Many firms fall down by concentrating their energies into putting on their particular show and passively waiting for the visitors to stream in. Much better to take these as an added bonus and to set to work ensuring that all the people who are considered to be of importance are invited to come, and with some attractive reason given for their sparing the time to do so.

Audio-visual techniques

Audio-visual techniques are fast developing and in doing so are providing new opportunities, sometimes at very low cost, for communication with both small and large audiences.

The conventionally sponsored film continues to require a high investment if done properly, and professionalism is necessary here, since viewers will tend automatically to relate the quality of presentation with what they see in cinemas and on television. Film strips, colour slides, records, tapes and cassettes can all be produced well at a much lower cost and can be used with impact for audiences of half a dozen or so, or can be posted to large numbers of individuals or groups of people to whom both the method of presentation and perhaps the novelty will ensure a good return for the money spent.

Audio-visual aids have the merit of either enlivening a personal presentation, or indeed, supplanting it. The new generation of video equipment is starting to provide exciting opportunities for sales and public relations presentations.

ORGANISING FOR PUBLIC RELATIONS

In a small firm it is often the chief executive who directs the public relations function. It is important to remember though that every employee has a public relations role to play and this should be encouraged. In larger companies the public relations function fits in most often as part of the marketing operation even though it may become involved in other aspects of the business: there may be a marketing or publicity manager, and here the public relations officer may be on an equal level or possibly a member of their staff. Alternatively, the public relations officer may report directly to the chief executive. Whatever organisational basis is used, it is important that the public relations function is positioned close to top management with access to policy makers and with authority to promote the development of initiative.

There are three basic ways of organising for public relations: to handle it entirely within the company, put it out to a public relations consultancy, or a combination of each. There is some evidence to suggest that the latter solution is proving to be to most effective. The company man is obviously very close to the needs of the business and also to the necessary sources of information. He suffers, however, from company constraints and it is not always in the best position to view matters objectively: neither is his advice necessarily regarded as highly as that from someone outside. His staff is also limited in terms of numbers which may put limitations on staging certain large special events.

Public relations consultancies are expensive, but can often be engaged at less than the cost of setting up a complete in-company operation. The consultancy suffers from the lack of personal contact and detailed knowledge of the business, but has the advantage of being able to call upon a wide range of experience, and to give impartial advice which sometimes is found to be more readily acceptable.

A compromise solution is often to designate the public relations function to an existing member of staff and to use a consultancy on a carefully restricted basis. The advantage is obviously to keep expense to a minimum, and to have ready access to detailed information, whilst being able to call upon professionals when needed. In a business world where communications are becoming more and more vital and techniques more sophisticated, the need for professional advice is growing and should be discounted only as a last resort.

Evidence of professionalism is not hard to find since growing numbers of practitioners are members of the Institute of Public Relations, and consultancies are fast developing standards in conjunction with the Public Relations Consultancy Association. There is now a nationally recognised qualification in public relations, namely the Communication Advertising and Marketing (CAM) certificate and the CAM diploma.

SELECTING A PUBLIC RELATIONS CONSULTANCY

Public relations consultancies are available to perform various tasks. Some are prepared to do business on a purely *ad hoc* basis, just to supplement one's own staff for a special occasion. More often, however, they will be retained on a permanent basis for which a fee is payable at regular intervals. In this instance they are available continuously to act as consultants and give broad advice on matters of policy. This can be most useful since their range of expertise is often widespread and there is also the benefit of the outside view being both more objective and sometimes more acceptable to company management than advice from a staff man who would have a more restricted field of reference.

In the main, consultancies perform a dual role of offering advice and carrying out much of the executive work. Here, they can be regarded as an extension of a company's own publicity department.

The selection of a consultancy is a difficult task since the usual 'criteria' of scientific assessment do not apply. The approach must therefore be methodical and based upon a careful enumeration of the specific requirements and objectives of the public relations function. List first the publics which are to be influenced, and then check whether the executives concerned have a familiarity with these. If not, do they seem able to adjust themselves to the new circumstances which will face them? Influencing housewives can be quite a different matter to that of influencing members of parliament or local councillors, trade unionists, teachers or students. Similarly, are the executives familiar with your type of organisation – its size, scope and type of product? There is the size of budget to be considered. Will the company be small in relation to others using the same consultancy or will it be so large as to be beyond the capacity of the consultancy to handle?

In order to do the job well the executives handling the account must really get inside the firm in spirit as well as in person. Relationships are going to have to be built up between a large number of people and a feeling of mutual confidence is essential. There needs to be an audit of strengths and weaknesses in which a subjective assessment can be made against every specific requirement. This not only helps the company to make a final judgement but also facilitates comparison of contenders on a shortlist. The question of whether or not to ask for a public relations plan before making a choice is a matter of deciding whether the facilities and information which must be made available, and the time taken, is worthwhile. It will also be necessary to make a payment for any such work done.

APPOINTING A PUBLIC RELATIONS EXECUTIVE

Clearly, the usual practice of personnel selection is as applicable here as for any other appointment. A job specification is needed followed by a man profile and a comprehensive interviewing system. But what is one looking for? It would be difficult to set down in detail the basic requirements a prospective public relations officer would have to meet that would be equally valid for every reader of this book, but there are two fundamental guidelines. In the first place, it is important for the executive to have a thorough familiarity with the marketing function, since here the concern is with fitting the public relations operation to the needs of marketing. Second, when the stage has been reached in which to perform in public relations satisfactorily, there must be an extensive knowledge and experience of each of the major channels of communication likely to be required. Many of today's public relations personnel have entered the business from journalism, and learned the hard way about all the many other facets of the business. That, now, is not enough. As has been shown earlier, public relations will often call for the use of exhibitions, displays, advertising, design and so on. The executive responsible here must have an adequate knowledge of all these elements.

SETTING OBJECTIVES

The key to achieving good results and, therefore, good value for money is in setting up a system whereby results can be measured. This is not a difficult task providing it is accepted that the degree of accuracy will sometimes be low without becoming involved in prohibitive expense. A prerequisite of any meaningful measurement is to set objectives and to quantify these, no matter how approximately. Take, for example, the simplest form of press operation, the opening of a major new plant. One objective might be to secure a good editorial mention in each of the nine important trade magazines, to get coverage on television, radio and in the 'management dailies' and to persuade the 50 leading potential customers to visit the plant. Against such a goal can be placed a budget which top management can see in advance and determine whether the likely results are worth the expense. At the end of the exercise, the public relations staff are able to examine the deficiencies and pinpoint reasons for success or failure.

Another very simple objective might be to secure, in the course of a year, 20 feature articles in national (or international) magazines. The point of setting what after all is a purely arbitrary goal is that, unless a plan is made to make contact with the right journalists and brief them as to a particular purpose, and then commission writers on a programmed series of subjects, the chances are that the job will never be done.

The operation becomes a little more sophisticated when the objective is expressed more in marketing terms. Take as an example the launch of a new product. The public relations objectives may be set as positioning the product such that 80 per cent of potential buyers have heard of the brand name after a period of three months, and can correctly associate it with the product and the company producing it. This calls for a classical name association test which can be carried out just as well by postal research as by personal interview. Fortunately, with a new product the initial benchmark is known to be zero, and there it may be necessary to be involved in only one research programme. In this situation the campaign necessary is drawn up together with a budget, and again the cost effectiveness of the exercise can be measured and shortcomings investigated.

In just the same way most public relations operations can be monitored. Customers' attitudes, buying motives, company awareness, advertisement effectiveness, reader response to editorials are some examples of activities that are well within the range of any well-established research organisation. And for every piece of sophisticated research there will be found on investigation some quite elementary techniques which can be applied with some noticeable benefit to a company. In the case of exhibitions, for example, the value for money both in absolute terms and in comparison with other shows can be considered by such simple data as the number of pieces of literature distributed (and under what conditions), the number of visitors to sign the book (or put a foot on to the plinth) or take a drink in the bar, the number of inquiries recorded, people spoken to, the number of passers-by. The latter also gives useful information on corridor traffic which may help in determining the position of the stand. The same simple techniques can be applied to film shows, house magazines, column inches, facility visits, talks, exposure to posters and so on.

In developing the discipline of measuring results there may be an understandable reluctance based upon the fear that failures will be exposed. But only by doing so will failures be turned into successes and the public relations function grow to its rightful place in business operations.

20

Direct marketing

Bill Livingstone, Senior writer, Primary Contact Ltd.

Direct marketing is simply a marketing operation where the sale is made direct to the customer, without resort to normal retail outlets. It is wider in scope than direct response or direct mail, although it uses the techniques of both these disciplines.

Direct marketing includes operations employing door-to-door selling and the traditional mail order catalogues distributed through commission agents (Littlewoods is an example). However, the scope of this chapter is limited to cover direct selling off-the-page and through the post.

At the time of writing there is an apparent gloom over the direct marketing operators owing to a number of factors. The long-promised recession seems to have arrived in earnest, and direct marketing is no more immune to its effects than any other form of selling. The casualties and withdrawals are in a particular field of direct marketing which was a victim of its own success: off-the-page selling in the colour supplements. The pioneers in this field broke new ground by proving that it was possible to sell off-the-page to the ABC1 readers of the supplements; others saw their success and followed suit. The peak was reached in autumn 1979. The growing body of direct marketing companies were clamouring for space in a reduced number of colour supplements (the *Sunday Times* was not printing). The problem was aggravated by the absence due to strike action by ITV and the *TV Times*, with refugee advertisers looking for somewhere to spend their budgets.

In short, the market was getting overcrowded, and a clear-out was

241

inevitable, recession or no recession. Very few, if any, of the major off-the-page companies expect to make a profit from their colour supplement advertising. Such advertising is increasingly regarded as a self-liquidating method of freshening their direct mail lists and perhaps familiarising the public with their corporate identity. Profits come from large-scale direct mail operations using computer-held lists.

OPERATING REQUIREMENTS

To enter this particular area of direct marketing requires rather stringent qualifications: a lot of money (allow around £25,000 for each ad – space, production and product cost – with no real hope of making substantial profits); a lot of time (building up a list of mail order buyers could take years); access to a list of credit card holders (makes paying easier); and links with a retail chain (as an outlet for the inevitable leftover products).

Luckily, there are more modest ways of making money through direct marketing. These will be examined later, but first let us look at the basic requirements for a profitable direct selling operation. Yeck & Maguire in *Planning and Creating Better Direct Mail* quote the 'Cullinan formula for growth in direct mail profits'. In order of importance the eight requirements are:

> the right product
> at the right price,
> to the right list,
> at the right selling cost,
> with the right method of buying,
> at the right time,
> in the right market,
> with the right creative selling techniques.

'The right product' tops the list. What is the right product? In their booklet 'Entering the mail order market' the Post Office list 13 advantages for mail order products:

> new in concept,
> unique,
> exclusive to you,

lightweight and compact for ease of transport,
looks good in presentation and is exciting to write about,
has a high margin,
has a reliable source of supply,
can be given a price advantage over competition,
good value for money,
strong to obviate breakages in carriage,
can be added to,
easy to use, and
has a definable and accessible market.

Products to be wary of:

those that can be sold only to a small and indefinable market,
failed retail products,
products that need demonstration,
low unit price.

To the list of advantages could be added 'a well known brand name' as a requirement, although this conflicts somewhat with other requirements (such as 'exclusive to you' and 'has a high margin').

Where price is concerned, to some extent your product will be priced for you. What are competitors charging for similar type and quality of product? You cannot go too much above that, unless you are offering something special in terms of service, availability etc. If your product is unique, or exclusive to you, it is a matter of what you think the market will bear.

Cost price includes not just product cost, but selling costs (which can be as much as one-third of the selling price), transport, storage and overheads. It's the relationship between selling cost and buying price which determines the viability of a product for direct selling. A very rough rule of thumb is that the selling price should be three times the product cost.

The Cullinan formula is intended, of course, to be applied to direct mail, hence the importance of the list. There are in fact a number of alternative media available to the direct marketing operator. The large off-the-page specialists tend to restrict themselves to the colour supplements, backed up by a direct mail catalogue operation. Using the colour supplements exclusively has always appeared to be a very risky business. Of course, they offer colour, allowing the product to be shown in the best light, they have a high quality readership and are provenly effective. Even so, £10,000 seems to be a lot to spend on an untested product (as, believe it or not, frequently happens).

Far too little use is made of 'postal bargains' pages and limited run direct mail, for dual testing/selling purposes. 'Postal bargains' pages tend to be thought of as exclusively the province of corn cutter and patent truss merchants, but this is not the whole truth. A sample 'postal bargains' page (admittedly in the *Sunday Times*) offers a photocopier for £59.95 and Design Centre-approved chairs for up to £267. Apart perhaps from the New Garden Dog Loo ('1,000s sold worldwide') there is very little in the corncutter class.

But direct mail should be regarded as an essential part of any direct marketing operation. Even if your off-the-page operation is satisfactorily profitable on its own, if you do not use mail you will be neglecting a valuable resource – the names and addresses of your customers, all of them provenly receptive to mail order offers. The use of direct mail can build up a profitable long-term relationship. Equally important, direct mail allows you to engage in low-cost testing, and testing is essential for long-term efficiency and profitability. Test the offer, of course, but also other factors such as reply device (e.g. Freepost, business reply, telephone) letter length, printed matter etc.

The basis of successful selling by direct mail is a good list. How do you obtain a list? The ideal method would be to get hold of a successful direct marketing company's list. However, such companies are understandably reluctant to allow such access. Lists may be rented from list brokers or mailing houses, though this costs money and you have no guarantee of how 'clean' (i.e. up to date) the list is. Respondents to press advertising can form the basis of your list, and names can be obtained from such sources as telephone directories and voters' lists. (It is useful to have some knowledge of which addresses are in well-to-do neighbourhoods.) Once you have your list, it can be held on a computer. This not only simplifies the physical process of addressing, it also makes list maintenance and classification much easier.

Whether using press or direct mail, the reply mechanism is important. It should be prominent and simple to use. Freepost (in press advertising) or reply-paid cards (in direct mail) generally improve response. Allowing respondents to pay by credit cards has been shown to improve response by as much as 40 per cent, although you must allow for card companies' commission of up to 10 per cent in your pricing.

In the Cullinan order of priorities, 'creative techniques' come eighth and last. It can be put a little higher. It's certainly true that even the best creative work will not sell the wrong product or overcome the handicap of a poor list, but poor creative treatment can cripple a direct-selling operation. The most common problem in direct-selling creative work is trying to be too clever and obscuring the message.

The creative rules are simple: always keep in mind a picture of the person you are selling to; make the product the star; include a benefit in the headline; make headline and illustration work together; use words like 'new' and 'exclusive' where possible; give all the information required to close the sale; tell the prospect what you want him or her to do; break up long copy with sub-heads and illustration; give a reason or incentive for acting quickly.

THE FUTURE

Although there may be hiccups in the growth of direct marketing, the general trend seems to be in its favour. The increasing number of working wives means that 'shopping' as a skill has declined in status; convenience is more important now – and buying by mail is very convenient. Mail order business now totals well over £2,000 million a year, and is taking an increasing share of total retail trade. The percentage of non-food retail trade carried out through mail order has increased from 7.1 per cent in 1971 to close to 9 per cent today. Another indicator of increasing direct mail activity is the number of business reply/freepost items handled by the Post Office: up from 96.9 million in 1971 to an estimated 305 million by 1980. Information systems such as Prestel Viewdata will make 'homeshopping' even easier, especially if linked with interactive home computer terminals.

Of course, a chapter of this length can do no more than sketch in the broad picture. Anyone considering entering the direct marketing field would need much more detailed advice and help.

The Post Office is, not unnaturally, keen to see direct marketing activity expand and offers a number of useful services and incentives to operators in the field, especially newcomers. It also produces a series of free booklets giving practical advice on direct mail and direct marketing. Contact your Post Office representative through your local head or district Post Office.

The British Direct Marketing Association, at 1 New Burlington Street, London W1X 1FD, can also direct you to specialist agencies operating in this field.

21

Sales Promotion

Alan Toop, Chairman, The Sales Machine

> Arguably, sales promotion is the most important marketing tool in use today; firstly, because promotional activities, especially price-cutting, have a direct and considerable effect on the fortunes (literally) of most mass-manufacturing and mass-retailing companies; secondly, because monies spent on sales promotion, as far as they can be estimated, are greater than the expenditure on any other marketing function.

So starts Chris Petersen's book, *Sales Promotion in Action*[1]. And he continues with a definition of sales promotion which we have adopted at The School of Sales Promotion which we both run: sales promotion involves –

> a featured offer
> of tangible advantages not inherent in the
>   product or service promoted
> for the achievement of marketing objectives.

'A featured offer' is one that is not just a normal and unremarked and taken-for-granted aspect of trade in the product or service being promoted. 'Of tangible advantages not inherent in a product or service' means that the offer must be of a tangible, physically quantifiable nature, not just an appeal to the emotions or intellect, as is often the case with classic media advertising. And the offer needs to be of something which is not *essential* to what is being promoted to make it fit for its purpose. For example, the offer of fuel injection as a superior alternative to carburettors, at no extra charge, might form a sales promotional offer for a car; a free engine would not.

---

1   Associated Business Press, 1979.

'The achievement of marketing objectives' can mean a whole variety of possible objectives, as is illustrated by the following list of examples of sales promotions:

1   '2p off', which has as its objective the selling of more product to the consumer.
2   'Half-price this week only!' is aimed at selling a lot more, very quickly.
3   'We won't invoice you for 90 days' is intended to persuade the trade to take delivery now when you have delivery capability to spare, even though the consumer buying season does not start for another two months or more.
4   'A free case to you the wholesaler, for every 10 cases you sell to your retail customers' aims to motivate someone else to sell more.
5   'Your first month's stock free!' may persuade a retailer to stock your product.
6   'You could win this gold bar if you're displaying our Gold Seal when Miss Goldilocks visits your store' may persuade retailers to erect displays.
7   'Try this sample, then take this 10p coupon to your nearest . . .' prompts trial of a new product.
8   '30p a case discount, enabling you to offer it to your customers at only 22p a packet' should encourage the retailer to feature this low price in his own major advertising campaign.
9   'Free colour licence when you rent this TV' overcomes the barrier formed by the cost of the licence fee when renting colour television.
10 'Send six proofs of purchase to obtain this tea towel free' has as its objective to retain repeat purchase loyalty over six purchases.
11 'Save for your old age as you smoke Filter X' is intended to retain repeat purchase loyalty forever.
12 '£25 off these language tuition tapes when you book your holiday with us', communicates the fact that we specialise in holidays for the intellectually curious.

Is sales promotion really so very different from advertising, then, if its objectives can include communicating the character of holidays? The answer must be yes, even though the differences are not necessarily those implied in the old distinction between 'theme' advertising and 'scheme' promotions; the classic dividing of support activities 'above' or 'below-the-line'; the distinction between long-term, strategic, media advertising and short-term tactical sales promotion.

One difference has been already noted. This is the more tangible, physical, character of many sales promotions, appealing through the tactile qualities of three-dimensional physical objects as much as through the senses of sight or sound which are more the province of television commercials or press advertisements.

Indeed sales promotion has media of its own which have just this dimension of physical immediacy:

> door-to-door distribution of, for example, a sample of a new product and a coupon worth 10p when taken to the shop and redeemed against a full-size first purchase of the new product; promotional teams of in-store demonstrators, or display checkers (e.g. Miss Goldilocks, above), or promotion announcers, or sample or coupon distributors in-store;
> the promoted product's pack, in which promotional premiums can be packed.

Of course sales promotion does also make use on occasion of classic media such as press advertisements, to help communicate an offer.

Much sales promotion activity is short-term, concerned with the here and now. It is designed to produce a quick and numerically measurable result: more sales to the trade; or more housewives buying this month than last; or more agents handling the service than ever before; or 1,500 grocers displaying pre-packed display units.

But sales promotion is not *necessarily* short-term. There are many case histories to prove the contrary. The annual Miss Pears Competition is still going strong, having been originated in its present form in 1957, and dating back to 1932 in an earlier version. Similarly the British co-operative movement has been offering dividends as a loyalty bonus, a classic sales promotional technique, since 1844 (rather longer than most current advertising campaigns have been running). Of course, not everybody noticed the dividend was a sales promotion until co-op societies started offering instant dividends in the form of co-op dividend stamps, in the '60s.

Similarly, much sales promotional work is concerned with offering incentives: 'Buy this and I'll give you that', or 'do this and I'll make it worth your while'. Co-op dividend stamps illustrate this approach, but incentive is a very inadequate description of many other sales promotions. The annual Miss Pears Competitions, for example, generate a number of entries which though high compared with many other competitions is low compared with the total number of purchases of Pears Transparent Soap made during the year. The competitions are therefore offering a direct incentive to buy to only a rather small minority of all the users that Pears needs to sell to to reach its sales targets. The rationale of this promotion, the reason why Pears have persevered with it over the years, must clearly lie elsewhere. We can safely conclude it is because the competition communicates a message about the brand, associating it with skin of girlish freshness.

ADVERTISING OR PROMOTION?

So when does one use advertising, and when sales promotion, to achieve given marketing objectives? As in so many areas of marketing, there are few hard and fast rules. It is essentially a case of 'horses for courses', of one technique being more likely to succeed than another in a given set of circumstances.

Budgets are important in this context, the amount of money available to finance sales promotion and/or advertising. Your advertising agency will tell you that it is not worth spending below a certain minimum level in the various classic media, and that below this level your brand or service's 'voice' will be drowned in the hubbub of other advertisers shouting their wares. And this minimum level is likely to be higher the higher your immediate competitor's spending.

Among British manufacturers of packaged goods more and more advertisers have been dropping down to and below this minimum level of media budget over the past decade. This is not least because such manufacturers have channelled more and more money into sales promotion, including price cutting, under pressure from the ever more powerful retail trade on whom they rely for the final distribution of their goods to the end consumer.

Sales promotion is such a great rag-bag of methods and media, of techniques and tactics, of possibilities and opportunities, that more often than not some sort of cost-effective promotional scheme can be created on budgets significantly lower than those required to sustain a classic advertising campaign. Indeed, as I wrote in my book:[2]

> 'The very lack of clearly defined boundaries to sales promotion activity represents its constant potential for original solutions to marketing problems. The very lack of well-established traditions in sales promotion encourages innovation, encourages radical answers to fresh challenges as they arise.
>
> In no other part of the whole spectrum of marketing activities is there more call for imagination and inventiveness; for lateral as well as logical thinking; for understanding of what will not just gain attention but will also maintain an audience's interest. In no other marketing activity is there greater scope for creativity; and in no other can creativity produce commercial dividends so cheaply.

Budgets are not of course the whole story. Some marketing tasks have become almost the preserve of sales promotion, since sales promotion techniques have proven so effective in accomplishing them. For example, sampling new products, where the letterbox distribution of small-size samples and/or high-value coupons can produce a widescale trial by consumers quicker and probably in greater depth than waiting for media advertising to persuade them to go in search of the product in the shops. Again, a series of in-store demonstrations of the new product will create a level of consumer purchases that will convince the retail chain that the new product is worth stocking and assigning shelf space.

The competitive situation cannot be ignored either. Some markets have become so heavily promoted that an unpromoted product or service has become well nigh unsaleable. And it is not just competition with outsiders that counts: some large food manufacturers, for example, often formed from a series of takeovers or mergers in recent years, ask their sales forces to handle so many different products that to get the sales force to redirect the necessary attention to any one of these products requires the product to carry a new promotion. This may or may not be an appropriate way to get the company's employees to do what it wants, but that is often the way it is.

---

2   Alan Toop, *Only £3.95?! – The Creative Element in Sales Promotion*, The Sales Machine, London, 1978.

WHO IS RESPONSIBLE?

This brings us to the who and how of sales promotion. Who should be responsible for sales promotion in a promoting company, and how should they organise the creation and implementation of sales promotion? The topic is important. As suggested at the beginning of this chapter, expenditure on sales promotion now probably exceeds that on almost any other marketing function. In many companies in which the division of total support budgets between advertising and sales promotion ten years ago was typically advertising 60 per cent, sales promotion 40 per cent, these proportions are today reversed. The first observation about who does what in sales promotion is that few companies as yet involve their senior management in sales promotion as fully as their huge and growing spending on sales promotion would seem to justify.

Most commonly sales promotional activity is regarded as a marketing department responsibility, in which the initiator of any single promotion is most likely to be a senior brand manager. The marketing manager, to whom this senior brand manager reports, may or may not get closely involved in approving of the promotion proposed. It is quite likely to depend on his personal taste, rather than on any clearly defined responsibility written into his job specification. The marketing director is unlikely to be involved, except in the most general terms of approving annual promotion budgets and broad promotional strategies. He is much more likely to be closeted in meetings with his company's advertising agencies, deciding on the next television commercial, even though the money to be spent on it may be modest in relation to the sales promotional fortune being spent by his subordinates. Below-the-line can mean out-of-sight.

The management structure of some companies is even worse adapted to the realities and needs of sales promotion in another respect: that is, by far the fastest growing part of sales promotion spending over the past decade has been on trade bonusing, trade discounting, 'special allowances' and on price-cutting activities of all sorts. A large part of this expenditure is channelled through the hands of sales managers, who in practice take decisions as to how precisely it is used.

These sales managers have a variety of titles, including 'national accounts manager', but they all have in common the fact that they report to the sales director; they are not part of the marketing department, and they are not profit responsible. Much of the price-cutting budget is therefore used to gain sales, and the cost of these sales, and their profitability or otherwise, is only rarely the responsibility of the sales personnel spending the money. Not surprisingly, therefore, the promotional cost of these sales – in a situation where competitors respond to '20p a case' with '22p a case' and to '2p off' with '3p off' – rises steadily. Thus the sums of money available for other forms of brand support, notably advertising, are steadily eroded.

Thus, the growth of retailer power, about which we have all heard so much in recent years, has in part resulted from the weakness of manufacturers' management structures: their slowness to adapt to the realities of promotional spending.

Be that as it may, the promotions need creating and need implementing. Price promotions, almost more than any others, need a touch of imagination, a spark of creativity, an element of the new, the different, the surprising, to transform them from pedestrian, take-it-or-leave-it offers into offers that cannot be missed and probably will not be refused. So how does that senior brand manager (or whoever it is that is responsible) set about the task?

ORGANISATION OF PROMOTIONS

Firstly, at the risk of stating the obvious, he (or she) needs to know something about sales promotion. Such is the comparative youth of sales promotion in its modern form, and on its contemporary scale, that knowledge and experience of sales promotion and expertise in its use are less widely diffused than is the case with other marketing functions such as media advertising, market research or new product development.

If there is any doubt about the understanding of sales promotion of whoever is going to be responsible for it, it should be improved. He should buy a book or two on the subject (see the reading list at the end of this chapter); attend a training course on sales promotion (there is a small but growing number); study the code of practice issued by the Institute of Sales Promotion; read any reports he can find on the results of previous sales promotions carried out by the company;

persuade one of the better sales promotional consultancies (more of them in a moment) to arrange a two-day visit to observe sales promotions being created and implemented.

Much depends on the human resources the company does or does not have. Some, for example, handle all sales promotional work in house. Such companies typically have a sales promotion manager running a department which may well include a premiums buyer, a print buyer and an executive controlling the handling and clearing operations of internal departments responsible for redeeming coupons channelled back from the distributive trade; fulfilling applications from the public for mail-in offers of premiums and cash refunds; and judging entries for prize promotions such as competitions and draws. How the starting ideas or concepts for such promotions are originated in these in-house operations is less clear (though none the worse for that), and certainly some such companies have careful methods and techniques for evaluating and developing at least those concepts, perhaps the more orthodox, which lend themselves to, for example, consumer panel pre-testing.

SALES PROMOTION CONSULTANCIES

At the far end of the spectrum other promoting companies buy-in or contract-out their promotional work. At its simplest, this consists of appointing a sales promotion consultancy (one that can demonstrate its facilities for implementing as well as creating promotions) to look after the total sales promotion operation. They do so in much the same way as a full service advertising agency creates the advertisements, commissions film production companies or finished artwork studios to produce them, selects the media, negotiates price with the media, books the media, and commissions the research required to check these decisions, at both pre and post stages. In sales promotion terms this full service includes:

> creating the ideas for the promotions;
> producing designs and writing copy for all forms of communication of the promotions in sales promotional media, such as pack, point-of-sale display, in-store leaflets, sales presenters etc.;
> commissioning finished artwork for these sales promotional media;
> briefing, seeking competitive quotations for and then commis-

sioning the manufacture of any premiums required by the promotions;

briefing, seeking competitive quotations for and then commissioning all print material required by the promotions;

briefing, seeking competitive quotations for and then commissioning companies specialising in these fields to handle postal applications or entries from the public, to redeem coupons returned from the trade, to distribute promotional material door-to-door, to send promotional teams into stores to demonstrate, to distribute coupons or samples, or to erect or check displays;

commissioning whatever research may be appropriate to check the correctness of decisions both pre and post the running of promotions.

As with advertising agencies, the key contribution is the creative function. Well managed implementation is vital, but should be taken for granted in any first class sales promotion consultancy. But good administration alone will not justify the substantial fees such consultancies earn; good ideas will. They will provide the means of cutting through the ever-increasing promotional clutter that disfigures so many markets today.

Between the exclusively in-house and entirely bought-in extremes there are many gradations and variations. Most promoting companies cluster round the mid-point of this spectrum of possibilities: probably employing consultants to create the concepts either on ad hoc/one-off commissions, or (more and more commonly nowadays) on a retained basis; possibly buying print through the company's print buyer when his quotations are more attractive than the consultancy's; perhaps leaving the consultancy to buy any premiums that need creating, but contracting direct with premium manufacturers when the premiums are available off-the-shelf, and so on. Thus a division of responsibilities and functions is arrived at which best suits the needs and resources and, indeed, the management philosophy of the promoting company.

The first-time user of sales promotion can apply to the secretary-general of the Institute of Sales Promotion[3] to obtain further details

---

3   Institute of Sales Promotion, 548 Chiswick High Road, London W4, tel
    01-995 4686.

of the growing number of sales promotional consultancies, as well as details of companies offering specialist services in fields such as coupon clearing, postal application handling, prize promotion judging, in-store demonstrations and merchandising.

Any company using or proposing to use any outside services such as these can be sure that Britain is as developed and sophisticated in terms of skills in all these sales promotional functions as any other country with which this author is familiar, including the US. Indeed, it is measurably in advance of many other countries, including most in Western Europe.

READING LIST

Hans Ferree (ed. 1973–5) and Christian Petersen (ed. 1976–7), *The Handbook of Consumer Sales Promotion*, Kluwer-Harrap, Brentford, Bound (revised) as *The Digest of the Handbook of Sales Promotion*, 1979.
S. Gentry and L. Rodger, *How British Industry Promotes*, Industrial Market Research Limited, 1978.
Christian Petersen, *Sales Promotion in Action*, Associated Business Press, London 1979.
Julia Piper, (ed.), *Managing Sales Promotion*, Gower, Farnborough 1980.
Alan Toop, *Choosing the Right Sales Promotion*, Crosby Lockwood and Son, London 1966. In paperback by The Sales Machine, London 1978.
Alan Toop, *Only £3.95?! — The Creative Element in Sales Promotion*, The Sales Machine, London 1978.

22

Sales management

David Senton, General Manager, Marketing Improvements Limited

The advent of conceptual and practical marketing, was seen by many managers as an attack on the pre-eminence of the sales force. Many painful and wasteful battles have been fought between 'them', the marketing staff and 'us', the workers in the sales field. Some writers have even predicted the gradual disappearance of the sales force. But as the dust settles, one can see clearly that selling is not separate from marketing but one of its arms, and in many companies the most important.

Many managers seemed to expect that, once the transition had been made from sales to marketing orientation, the old stability of action would return. However, in most industries the same changes which forced a reconsideration of the total marketing effort are still active. There are major changes occurring in the environment, the economy, in markets and individual sales territories year by year. The five main factors affecting the sales force, common to most industries are:

1   A tendency towards fewer customers, each growing in size and dominating a greater percentage of the market.
2   The larger companies which are arrogating greater powers of negotiation to themselves.
3   Smaller customers and accounts which are becoming uneconomic to service by traditional means giving rise to a need to search for other methods of servicing, e.g. telephone selling and franchise distribution.
4   Some of the manufacturers' traditional functions which are

being taken over by distribution networks in many industries, e.g. the growth of branding, not only in the food industry but also in such areas as insurance and pensions.

5 Increasing competition between manufacturers especially with the accelerated growth of multinational trading blocs.

These changes will not necessarily mean that the basic function of the sales force changes, but it will undoubtedly become increasingly refined in several ways. The traditional Jack-of-all-trades approach to the definition of the sales job must give way to a clearer identification of fewer specific tasks for the salesmen to perform, so fewer salesmen will be needed both because of the reduction in roles but particularly because of the reduction in numbers of accounts. Moreover, the sales forces that remain must be of higher status, better qualified, and more professional in their approach, able to utilise not only their own skills, but also the available support from the rest of the company. Furthermore, this support may well emerge as it has done in some companies as sales teams headed by the territory salesman, backed by customer service personnel in the sales office, and having available technical expertise from a service section. Thus, the sales organisation in total must be far better geared to the needs of the market place and the uses, if it is to compete successfully.

THE CHANGING ROLE OF THE SALES SUPERVISOR

These factors must mean that the role of the field sales manager also changes. It is too simple to say that the sales manager's job is to gain results through other people; this is true of any manager in business. We must recognise peculiar difficulties which the sales manager faces.

The sales force is normally geographically spread and so cannot be supervised as closely as many other departments, causing particular problems of motivation, communication and control for the manager and feelings of isolation for the salesman. Second, the sales force spends the vast majority of its time with people other than company employees – usually, of course, with customers. This will cause attrition whereby the salesman's attitudes and skills are worn down by the constant contact with opposing views. Furthermore, the kind of people who choose this isolated and wearing life are often those least capable of coping with it. Men who choose selling as a career are normally outgoing, gregarious individuals, yet the structure of their job ensures that they spend a minimal amount of time with their colleagues.

Because of these particular difficulties, the field sales manager must provide strong leadership and training to overcome them. Indeed, although he will be engaged in many other facets of his job, the prime function of the first-line sales manager should be seen as the continuous refurbishing and development of his men's attitudes and skills.

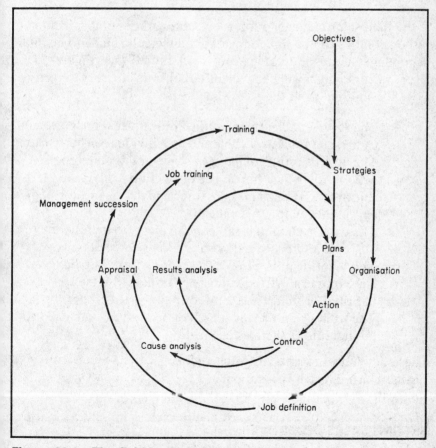

Figure 22.2   The fields sales manager's job

With these key tasks, it is clear that the job of management is radically different from that of the salesman. Simply viewing the sales management position as a natural promotional goal for the best salesman, has led to problems in many companies.

Obviously, the sales manager must know how to sell; indeed, with increasing customer demand he will probably be an above average salesman, but, since the majority of his results will be gained from his own sales force, his key ability must be the ability to develop others and gain sales results through their efforts.

THE JOB OF THE FIELD SALES MANAGER

If the field sales manager's job is examined, the way in which main responsibilities can be linked together, and can be made to be inter-dependent upon one another can be identified (see Figure 22.1). Every sales manager will be involved either in an advisory capacity or as a decision maker in the following areas:

1   The setting of clearly quantified objectives for achievement by his sales force as a whole and by individuals in particular.
2   The identification of precise strategies – main courses of action – by which his objectives will be achieved.
3   The organisation of his sales force and the disposition of men and money within his control.
4   The construction of clear, concise plans, to identify the timing, cost and coordination of all sales force actions.
5   The identification of precise controls including budgets.
6   The appraisal of individual performance, regularly on an informal or field basis, and formally at least once a year.
7   The training and development of his staff to enable plans to be met and objectives achieved.

These activities are critical to the success of the selling effort and further consideration is justified.

SETTING SALES OBJECTIVES

It is incredible how many companies still see the setting of objectives either as a fashionable requirement of an MBO system or as a need to repeat undefined general management ambition. These are of no use either to the manager or his sales force. Objectives are essential to define the success of the sales force, for assessment of systems of decisions and of people, to identify the resources which are necessary in terms of people and money, to enable sequential strategies to be set and integrate the sales force activities with other marketing activities. Besides which, objectives are the basis for the sale manager's operation. They are necessary to:

1   Define success, e.g. to know that business in a particular market segment has been increased by 75 per cent is meaningless unless it was stated at the outset what target was intended.
2   Permit assessment of decisions made, the systems set up and the people who activate them. Without specific objectives it cannot be assessed whether the systems were effective.
3   Estimate resources of men and money which will be needed to achieve objectives. Until objectives are defined the size of sales force needed cannot be defined.
4   Permit sequential logical strategies to be set. Too often the sales manager will decide upon a course of action, and then pause to calculate the outcome and the result, which then becomes the objective. The logical order must surely run:
    (a) What achievement is it that is being attempted? (objectives).
    (b) Which courses of action will produce that result? (strategies).
5   Integrate the sales effort with other marketing actions.

It is important that the different stages of objectives setting are also identified. Most sales managers will be given, with or without consultation, certain overall financial objectives in terms of revenue or contribution to be gained. The sales manager has usually to restate these in terms of the market and the product lines he is selling, the market share which must be gained, or the average order size to be achieved.

Clearly, the objective selected must be precise and specific in quantity, timed, measurable, capable of achievement (realistic) and written down, or they will be overlooked or distorted.

THE CONSTRUCTION AND SELECTION OF SALES STRATEGIES

Strategies are the major courses of action open to the sales manager which will achieve his stated objectives. In considering his objectives the sales manager should always have a range of alternatives open. He must ask himself two key questions: 'What are all the actions we might take to achieve our objectives?', and 'What must be done differently next year to ensure the different results we require?'

Some examples of strategies are shown in Table 22.1.

These examples merely identify three strategies. In most situations there will be many more. The most important creative contribution made by the sales manager in planning is in the exercise of his judgement in selecting strategies against the criteria of risk, cost and time involved and against the level of effectiveness specified.

FORECASTING AND THE SALES PLAN

The process of forecasting does not rightfully belong in a chapter on sales management since the development of the sales forecast is becoming, more and more, a marketing function, in many companies based on sophisticated computer models or advanced statistical techniques. However, sales and sales management must provide certain inputs of market intelligence and, of course, are heavily dependent upon the end-result.

The majority of operating forecasts used by companies today, are based upon two factors:

(a) The assessment of present trends from historical sales information and the projection of such trends into the future;

(b) the application or judgement to those projections on how variables both inside the company and outside (in the market) are likely to affect the predictive level.

However, in many companies the common initial input in forecasting is the sales force composite, i.e. the collation of the estimates of the sales force in their individual territories and particularly in their major accounts. The possible sources of error here are obvious: the bias of the individual salesman, the inability of individuals contacted

Table 22.1
Examples of sales strategies

Objectives	Strategies
Consumer:	
To increase market share from x to y% by 30 June.	1 Concentration of sales effort on major outlets over £100,000 potential, to secure 5 conquests per man.
	2 Increase average off-take in all medium outlets to 10 case minimum drop.
	3 Establish formal displays in all cash-and-carries by 1 April.
Service:	
To increase pensions business written to £20 million by end of 1980.	1 Run series of evening seminars for company accountants with follow-up by individual salesmen.
	2 Review all existing pension schemes and increase cover.
	3 Identify all professional companies with 10+ employees without pensions cover and two schemes per salesman.
Industrial:	
To maintain present tractor sales at 1,000 per annum in a declining market per region.	1 To increase distributors' winter stocking to 40% of annual off-take.
	2 To support distributor sales staff in arranging competitive demonstrations.
	3 To initiate drive to purchase competitive 3-year old trade-ins at economic rates.

in customer companies to predict their own product requirements and technical inability to estimate changing market structure or competitive action. However, if the sales manager structures this input with care it will be one of his most reliable sources of information.

In some companies targeting is seen as a process separate from forecasting. Once the forecast has been set an arbitrary increase or figure is laid in order to 'give the sales force something to aim at'. It is doubtful whether this provides a positive motivation since the sales force will normally be aware that the management will be satisfied with less than the target achievement. In a production company it is little short of disastrous to increase a forecast by an arbitrary percentage, since in the event of the sales force all achieving that target, a pronounced product shortage will occur. Indeed, in one company where a commission was being paid on achievement of target this created a difficult situation. Targets must represent that part of the forecast for which the salesman is individually responsible.

Having set sales forecasts and targets the sales manager must now consider how they will be achieved. Considerable thought will have already been given to the outline of the plan in setting objectives and formulating strategies, but in planning the details of action the manager must consider five main points: what is to be sold?, to whom?, at what price?, by what methods?, and at what cost? In some of these areas, particularly the product range and the price structure, he may well have limited influence since they are often controlled by the marketing planning department, though undoubtedly he should give his advice as a consultant member of the marketing team.

One particularly useful aid is a matrix of markets and products. A simple example is given in Table 22.2. A construction equipment company has broken down its trade situation in terms of three product lines and three major markets. Each market segment/product cell shows the potential and actual sales, thus identifying which are the significant portions of the market to be aimed at and what penetration is now being achieved. At the end of each column is entered the trend of that particular product line or market segment, so that management is aware of future possibilities. For example, it might be that a high penetration has been achieved in the loader/local authority market, but the market as a whole is declining and therefore future growth must be sought elsewhere. The degree of detail that the

Table 22.2   Customer strategy form

Salesman _____ Date _____

Name and address _____

Current contacts _____
(names and positions)

Product/market matrix this year

		Markets				
		(a)	(b)	(c)	Trend	Total
P R O D U C T S	A	Potential Actual				
	B	P A				
	C	P A				
	D	P A				
Trend						
Total		P A				

Competitive activity _____

Targets next year

		Markets			
		(a)	(b)	(c)	Total
P R O D U C T S	A				
	B				
	C				
	D				
Total					

Action

Contacts to be made _____

Call frequency _____

Objectives of calls _____

Support required _____

sales manager will identify on such a matrix will obviously vary considerably from industry to industry. Clearly, each cell identified here could be expanded considerably, if management found this of use, to include last year's results, this year's, the forecast for next year, percentage changes over the previous year and figures for the market as a whole.

INVOLVING THE SALES FORCE IN PLANNING

The quality of the plan and the likelihood of its achievement will be enhanced if the salesmen are involved. Not only do salesmen often have particular local customer and territorial knowledge which is useful to the manager in planning, but also the very involvement of the sales force will aid commitment when the plan is put into operation. Strangely, it is usually discovered that a sales force is over-

Table 22.3 Markets

	Markets				
Products	Government	Local authority	Industry	Trend	Total
Bulldozers	Potential				
	Actual				
Scrapers			800 pa	Sales up 20%	
			500 pa	Market up 30%	
Loaders		1000 pa			
		800 pa			
Trend		Market declining			
Total					

optimistic when estimating likely future trends. To avoid excesses, the manager must attempt to structure his sales force's input and force them to consider the facts.

Naturally, this is very important when dealing with the estimates of sale to major clients and accounts. The systematic way to plan at this level is to develop customer strategies as shown in Table 22.3. The process begins with a matrix analysis similar to the global tabulations made earlier by the manager. However, the markets referred to here related to the client's market and these may be expressed geographically or by type of business, by nature of the client's customer or even by the client's production processes. The aim is simply to identify not only how much of the product is being sold to this client, but also where it is being used and, hopefully, where products could, but are not, being used. Targets are then set sector by sector in the client's business. The salesman identifies who is to be called upon within the customer's company, how frequently and what is to be done during those visits. Further refinements can be added by identifying the support needed by costing the strategies, thus leading to an identification of the profitability of the account. Such strategies have the added advantage of controlling the salesman's performance on a continuous basis in those accounts which are keys to the company's success as a whole.

THE STRUCTURE OF THE SALES PLAN

Having completed this work the sales manager must bring together his decisions in the form of a written plan. Such a plan will usually contain the following elements:

(a) a statement of the company's overall objectives for the planning period;

(b) a brief summary of the market situation, likely economic change, and competitive activity;

(c) a clear statement and tabulation of all forecasts and individual targets broken down by salesmen, value and product;

(d) the method of organisation of the sales force identifying any territory change;

(e)   sales force action to be taken during the year including recruitment, training, any special incentive schemes, etc;
(f)   a statement of the marketing support which will be available to the sales force in advertising, promotion and merchandising terms, and
(g)   the controls which will be used including budgets.

There seems little reason why such a plan, once printed, should not be circulated to the entire sales force, thus ensuring full commitment to the plan and clear identification of what everyone's contribution will be.

ORGANISATION OF THE SALES FORCE

In many companies, the organisation of the sales force remains static, changing only when forced to do so by movement of company personnel, or pressure from the market. In deciding the way in which manpower resources should be organised, the manager's first consideration must be the type of contact and service necessary to satisfy the market's needs.

Changes in the structure of markets, growth of certain major accounts, demand for specialist advice, need for a particular service such as merchandising and the requirement to negotiate major contracts at high level all force more stringent examination of how the field force should be disposed. There are several major options open.

Geographic

This is by far the most common method of organisation. It has the advantage of diminishing travel cost and of allowing the salesman to build up considerable local knowledge in a confined area.

Division by customer market

As the salesman becomes more involved in his customer's problems some companies have found more logic in concentrating a salesman's activity within a single market. Although extending geographic coverage, this allows the salesman to build up his expertise in the client's operation and to gain great acceptance by virtue of his creative input.

Division by sales function

For certain companies there is a clear distinction between pioneering and servicing, e.g. trading stamps, or between the specifier and purchaser, e.g. the building and pharmaceutical industries. In such situations the different types of approach may warrant separate sales forces.

Division by size of account

In situations where sizes of contract vary widely some companies have divided their sales forces between negotiation with national accounts, selling to medium-sized outlets with the traditional sales force, and telephone sales and order-taking for all small accounts.

Division by product type

Where the technical aspects of the product are crucial, specialists in particular products are required. If possible, this should be avoided in view of the waste of effort in having the same major customer contacted by several salesmen from the same company.

By customer service team

Some companies have even developed their organisation structure to match the organisations of their major clients, so that the customer is contacted at all levels by members of a sales team often consisting of salesman, manager, inside sales support and technical adviser.

Having decided the most appropriate form of contact the manager can calculate the numbers of salesmen he will need to perform the job. He must identify the numbers of accounts, who should be contacted, the frequency of contact necessary for each client, the average daily call rate and the number of days in the year spent selling in the field. The equation will run:

$$\frac{\text{Number of actual \& potential customers} \times \text{annual call frequency}}{\text{Average daily call rate} \times \text{Number of selling days per year per man}}$$
$$= \text{Number of salesmen required}$$

For example, a sales manager of a company selling industrial cleaning goods has identified 1,000 accounts which must be serviced. 50 major wholesalers and cash and carries require 50 calls per year each; 250

medium-sized accounts (£3,000 to £15,000) require 25 calls per year; 300 accounts (£500 to £3,000) require 12 calls per year; 400 accounts must be visited 6 times per year. The average daily call rate is 8 calls per day. The number of selling days per man/year is 215.

$$\frac{\begin{array}{r} 50 \times 50 \\ +250 \times 25 \\ +300 \times 12 \\ +400 \times 6 \end{array}}{8 \times 215} = \frac{14,750}{1,720} = 8.6$$

Thus, to service that work-load the manager will require 8 to 9 salesmen, if this can be done cost-effectively.

STAFFING THE ORGANISATION

It is not intended to identify recommended recruitment procedures in this chapter. However, there are certain particular problems inherent in the staffing of the sales force which should be mentioned. Although the sales manager is often able to delegate recruitment to a personnel department he must first identify both the job to be done and the profile of the ideal candidate. So much recruitment is dependent upon a hunch, 'feel' and subjective judgement it is essential that, before seeing anyone, the sales manager sets down who it is he is seeking and for what purpose. Secondly, when the applications have been received, processed and references have been checked, the final decision as to whether a man should be hired or not should rest with the manager since he will be responsible for the man's performance after he has accepted a position. Thus, for staffing purposes a sales manager must be skilled in two areas; the writing of clear and specific job specifications and in conducting recruitment interviews.

CONTROL OF SALES ACTIVITY

In planning organisation and staffing the process of control will be facilitated by clearly defined targets laid down and agreed between the salesmen and the sales manager during the planning process. It is essential, of course, that any control process by the sales manager is intended to control not only the results achieved, but also the actions of the salesman causing those results. The results themselves can be caused by a multiplicity of activities – by market, competition, production supply, or the economy at large, as well as by the salesman himself. It is most important that the sales manager should isolate those activities for which the salesman can be held responsible, and through which an improvement can be expected in sales results.

Thus, the controls exercised by the manager and the salesman will include not only such flexible standards as unit targets and value in the various product groups, but also diagnostic standards, based on those quantitative and qualitative activities which influence the salesman's success. These are:

1   Who is called upon (defined by a client list, a prospect list and/or a customer profile).
2   How many people are called upon (which can be based upon a standard call rate or prospecting rate).
3   How often should such accounts be called upon (which will be reflected in an annual call frequency for all major types of account).
4   Most importantly, what is done when the salesman is face to face with the client or customer to whom he wishes to sell.

APPRAISAL TRAINING AND DEVELOPMENT

With the controls shown in Table 22.4 it can be seen that the sales manager's appraisal of a salesman should consider the question of the developmental needs of the individuals in his sales force, rather than simply to conduct an annual salary review, or even to apportion congratulation and criticism on the results of the year's efforts. Unless an appraisal of performance is followed by an agreed plan for the skills and knowledge to be exercised by the sales force, the appraisal as such is meaningless.

The process is very simple. Although there will be differences in frequency of accompaniment between new and experienced representatives, a day spent with the man in the field will commonly follow a simple six-step process. This process will take time and one will conserve it for those specially selected calls where it is necessary

Table 22.4 An example of a key analysis

Description of task	Level of performance				Controls used to measure results
		1st qtr	2nd qtr	3rd qtr	4th qtr	
Achieve sales targets	*New machines*					Review of sales with manager on monthly basis, at sales meeting of all significant shortfalls
	Tractors	£140,000	£70,000	£10,000	£80,000	
	Combines	90,000	30,000	30,000	—	
	Balers	7,500	—	15,000	—	
	Ploughs	3,000	3,000	5,000	8,000	
	General machines	10,000	15,000	6,000	5,000	
	Barn machines	10,000	10,000	20,000	2,000	
	Total new machines	£265,000	£128,000	£86,000	£95,000	
	Used					
	Tractors	£ 10,000	£50,000	£20,000	£50,000	
	Combines	—	20,000	30,000	—	
	Others	5,000	2,500	2,500	5,000	
	Total used machines	£ 15,000	£72,500	£52,500	£55,000	
Gain new customers	35 new customers yielding minimum of £70,000 by end of 12-month period (particular machines may also be specified) e.g. minimum 4 new baler conquests					Review prospect cards weekly Review conversion rates monthly Review monthly sales records Identify major prospects and agree customer strategy
Plan to make more profitable use of time	Daily call rate average 8 calls, at least 2 prospect calls Daily plan formulated and carried out Average daily mileage 125					Daily submission of report Submission of plans on field visits Journey plans Individual call plans

Make sales propositions which are up to the required standard	Sales interview conducted in line with predetermined plan according to general principles of the selling cycle as taught on company courses Product information accurate Arrangements for follow-up clearly agreed with customer	Monthly observations by sales manager
Maximise profitability	Keep to discount limits set by manager (define limits per machine group) Evaluation of used machinery to show on average % accuracy- $\pm$ 7½% Achievement of used machinery sales targets	Review of new machinery sales record Review of prices paid for used machinery Review of sales of used machinery
Maintain and make full use of equipment and sales aids	Car in good order and appearance Catalogue up-to-date Literature stock up-to-date and kept in presentable condition Record cards readily available and up-to-date	Observation and inspection by sales manager on field visits
Maintain control over credit and ensure prompt payment of accounts	Keep to agreed predetermined limits (Specify limits for each category of client; record on card.)	Monthly review of outstanding accounts

to bring about the maximum impact and improvement. It might be used to prepare a call where one has wanted to open an account for a long time, or where the call objective is to gain acceptance to those items of product range, not so far accepted by the customer. The manager will meet with his salesman, on an agreed day and they will discuss the structure of the day, how it has been planned, routed and organised. Before the first call is made this six-step process commences with:

1 An analysis of the customer's record, discussing when the last call was made, what objections were raised, which products the customer concentrates upon, what kind of business he is in and in which markets he is attempting to develop.

2 The manager will listen to the representative's plan for the call and if necessary, help him to prepare for it. He must identify the prime objectives of the call, decide whether or not these are specific and whether they can be measured. He will also discuss the representative's intended handling of the call and the structure he intends to adopt.

3 The manager will ensure that the representative understands the agreed plan. If necessary he will discuss in some detail how a particular objection is to be answered and could even, with the new representative, rehearse this answer.

4 The manager will define the role he will take during the call. Since it is a training call he will simply act as an observer. If, however, he is intending to make a contribution on the call, his part must be precisely defined and also what the representative should do at that stage.

5 Having commenced the call, the main function of the manager is to watch and listen. The difference between this, a training call, and a joint selling exercise cannot be over stressed. So many sales managers, having been salesmen themselves in the past, are tempted as soon as an interview starts to slip away or move from the subject in hand, to step in and attempt to put the interview 'back on track' again. Whilst this is exactly what one would do if one was selling, in a training exercise it will produce no effect in improving the representative's performance in other calls.

During a month, a representative may make 150 calls of which the manager sees half a dozen. The training intent is to

improve the other 144. An attempt to simply solve the
problems arising from the present call will not help the
representative when his manager will not be present. Therefore, as far as possible, within the bounds of courtesy, the
manager should merely observe whether the representative
follows the plan agreed and what techniques of persuasion
are used in order to help the client to buy.

6   When the manager and the salesman have returned to the
car they will analyse the call together. The manager's job is
primarily to help the salesman to identify what could have
been done better, or in a shorter time, and to discuss in detail
how these particular problems affect the overall performance of the representative in his territory. This will normally be the part of the process which the manager will
dislike most at first. Just as in appraisal we are happy to
express the good news but reluctant to talk of the bad news,
so in training and appraisal in the field the manager will often
not question closely enough why particular problems arise,
nor how the representative should solve these problems.

In attempting to solve this difficulty many managers have found
following predetermined routine useful. In order to set the tone for
the interview the manager should first begin with an appreciation of
things well done and praise for selling skills well used. Secondly the
manager should question the representative in order to obtain his
own view of his performance and where he himself felt that the
interview could have been improved and which weaknesses he realises occurred. It is much better for the salesman to recognise his
shortcomings than for the manager to have to tell him what they are
with all the accompanying problems of acceptance which that entails.

Naturally, if he cannot or will not acknowledge that there were any
faults the manager will have to tell him what they were. He will also
then, of course, have to gain agreement that the faults occurred and
were serious.

Finally, the manager should discuss how the problem is to be
overcome. Again, the process is a two-way discussion rather than a
lecture, and must include examples and a practice run of the technique, with a new representative if necessary.

It is most important that at this stage the manager concentrates his
attention on the faults of technique and not of personality. It is

important that he discuss specifics giving precise examples of what occurred, and avoid giving general advice or counsel. It has been shown clearly that giving general advice in unlikely to improve a representative's performance since he will perceive that an improvement is required of him but not understand precisely how to make that improvement. Such a process can only lead to frustration and a decline in sales performance.

The manager completes the process of training with an agreement on the necessary follow-up and sets specific times for the checking and discussion of improvement. Ideally, this will be recorded on a simple field appraisal form, which both the manager and the representative hold and which will be discussed at the start of the next field training exercise.

CONCLUSION

The nature of sales management has changed radically in many industries in the last few years. Basically, since his job is to gain results through other people, the manager must consider how he can achieve those results through the actions of his staff. His main function, therefore, must be seen as one of development.

ACKNOWLEDGEMENT

The matrix analyses on planning used in this chapter are reproduced by permission of M.T. Wilson from: *Managing a Sales Force*, Gower, 1970.

23

The art of negotiation*

John B.J. Lidstone, Deputy Managing Director, Marketing Improvements
Ltd.

Many supplier/buyer situations which have been traditionally viewed
as 'selling' relationships have changed significantly over the last
10–15 years. During that time a large number of major customers
have developed their own expertise and their own commercial
strategies, and are just as sophisticated as the major manufacturers.
Some of them, perhaps, are even more advanced. Certainly some are
more powerful. Recently there has been a considerable and growing
concentration of buying power into a few hands, in the retail food
business, for example.

These two developments have meant that there is an increased
amount of interdependence between suppliers and customers.
Although the two sides still occasionally make independent warlike
noises, there is a large amount of tacit agreement that both sides need
each other if they are to achieve their individual objectives. Occasionally local situations change this balance of need: the manufacturer's need to supply often rises at the end of profit accounting
periods; and sometimes a buyer has a heightened need to purchase
from a supplier to combat competitive activity, or to meet seasonal
objectives.

But for most buyers and sellers most of the time, the need to buy
and the need to sell are more or less equal. This is turn means less and
less emphasis on 'selling' and more and more on negotiation. To

---

* This chapter is based on material prepared by John Lidstone to accompany the
Video Arts film *Negotiating Profitable Sales*.

understand the difference between the two techniques let us start by looking at selling, and then go on to examine the important ways in which negotiating differs from it.

Some of the more simple and routine approaches to the structuring of sales techniques tell us about the salesperson's needs, for example:

> opening statements;
> presentation of features and benefits;
> overcoming objections, and
> closing the sale.

Some approaches tell us more about the customer's needs, for example:

> 'I am important and want to be respected';
> 'consider my needs';
> 'will your ideas help me?';
> 'what are the facts?';
> 'what are the problems?';
> 'what shall I do?', and
> 'I approve'.

Whatever the approach, the objective (in terms of the desired end result) is to raise the customer's perceived need for the product or service to a level where, to satisfy that need, he makes the decision to buy.

If we examine the movement of the two parties (seller and buyer), we can see that, in selling, the salesperson does not move his position. He induces the buyer to move towards his position by heightening the buyer's perception of his need for the product or service. Thus, sales objectives, in the perception of the salesperson, can often be expressed as being to obtain an order, of a given volume or revenue within a certain time.

Successful sales technique is not negotiation, but it produces the basis for negotiation. By sales techniques the customer is moved to a position where, in order to satisfy his now heightened perception of his need, he has to consider the purchase decision. He then turns his attention to the *terms and conditions* surrounding sale and purchase. Having been satisfied in the selling process that he can actively consider purchasing, he will now be seeking the best possible deal in a number of detailed areas. For example, where price is concerned, he will be pursuing discounts and other reductions in the form of bon-uses, help with financing, credit etc. He will ask at what price he will have to buy to satisfy his criteria; what the resultant saving/loss will be and when he will have to pay and in what currency.

As far as the product is concerned, the buyers will be considering factors like the precise specification and the type of packaging. Then, of course, there are the service aspects, such as when and where the product can be delivered and at what rate; what technical support there will be and what after-sales service can be negotiated.

Based, therefore, on the platform of a common need to buy and supply created by the sales process, negotiation is the give and take process whereby the final, detailed terms and conditions surrounding the purchase/supply decision are agreed. In this negotiation phase the supplier is tailoring the detail of the marketing mix (product, price, presentation) to fit the local, immediate needs of one particular customer. Because of this, both the supplier and the purchaser are involved in controlled *compromise*. This element of controlled com-promise (which is recognised by experienced negotiators) often clashes with the essentially uncompromising nature of the sales process.

A vital aspect of negotiation is the arithmetic, what the deal adds up to. The ability to understand the financial position of the buyer's company is essential, as is the ability to calculate the financial implica-tions of any changes made to the 'package' during the negotiation. A good sales negotiator must understand balance sheets, profit and loss accounts and cash flow forecasts.

Given the underlying mutual needs, the strategy of negotiation is concerned with the actual and stated magnitude of those needs on both sides. At the start of a negotiation there will usually be a gap of terms and conditions between what the buyer says he wants and what the supplier says he is prepared to offer. The major strategic task of the sales negotiator is to measure accurately the actual gap that exists between himself and the buyer, and to distinguish between the *actual* gap and the *stated* gap. And the major initial strategic ploy in negotia-tion is for both sides to *exaggerate* the distance between them.

Sometimes (not always) a buyer will open up a negotiation by deliberately (or automatically) exaggerating his stance. For example:

'Before we start, if you're thinking of offering me a deal on product X, forget it, because your competitors have already agreed the next supply contract with us.'

'There's no point in talking to me about increased availability. We do not have any increase in demand this quarter.'

Alternatively, the buyer may attempt to suggest that he is not likely to come to an agreement because of other negative factors which he raises at the beginning of the interview. If, as is often the case, this is a strategic ploy, he will, if you allow him to save face while doing so, move from this initial stance to an actual stance quite quickly and with a little encouragement. We must be clear about the reasons for this initial stance. It is done purely to pull the supplier out of position.

Thus, the first task is to establish by discussion the *actual* gap that exists between supplier and buyer. This is invariably achieved by an examination of the needs and covering benefits on both sides, but the supplier must ensure that *he* restricts the loss of position that this manoeuvring entails for both parties. (The supplier is usually more anxious to sell than the buyer to buy.) Usually the parties will take up their actual stances with ritualistic face-saving comments, which are important if the fabric is to be preserved.

These factors suggest that two research activities should be carried out in advance of any negotiation. First, the supplier must have information on the buyer, his situation, his applications, availability of funds, limits of authority. Second he must have clear, up-to-date information on the competition, the relative technical, financial, delivery, and pricing action they can take: the need they have for this order – the business and marketing success they are experiencing elsewhere – and the restraints present in their production facilities.

The supplier should ask major questions about markets, company and competition.

QUESTIONS ABOUT MARKETS

1 What proportion of existing and prospective customers expect to negotiate the conditions of purchase?
2 What proportion of different categories of customer expect to negotiate?
3 What percentage of present sales volume do they represent?

4   What percentage of present profits is produced by sales to these customers?
5   What proportion of cases involves:
     (a)   a group decision?
     (b)   a decision made by one man alone or with the advice of others?
     (c)   informed professional purchasing?
     (d)   first time purchase or re-purchase?
6   How strong are the buyers – what is the strength of their need to buy relative to our need to sell?
7   What proportion of negotiations involve contractual agreements?
8   How can a planned and skilled negotiation strategy help to service the market?

QUESTIONS ABOUT THE SUPPLYING COMPANY'S OWN OBJECTIVES

1   How does existing negotiated business aid or conflict with these?
2   What strengths and weaknesses are highlighted?
3   Are any changes necessary in the ways in which we negotiate business? Looking at past cases honestly, on which sides of the points of need balance did we conclude business?
4   Who is currently responsible for selling to whom and at what levels? Is too much or too little responsibility being given/ taken? How is it being used? Does the level of contact meet the real needs of the market?
5   What levels of negotiating skills and authority are needed, and what levels exist?
6   What commercial and marketing benefits could result from better negotiation, or from applying negotiation skills to a wider level of sales activities? Are we satisfied with present margins from negotiated business? Are we sure that we are obtaining the optimum share of volume?
7   How can a planned and skilled negotiation strategy help the company?

QUESTIONS ABOUT THE COMPETITION

1 Do we know how well our competitors perform in negotiating business?
2 What are their apparent strengths and weaknesses in negotiation? Look at, for example, speed of decision, range of authority (e.g. in respect of price), product range, promotions, service, distribution, prices, capacity, cost, volume.
3 To what extent do they appear to strengthen or weaken the market?
4 What relationship can be perceived between the answer to 3 and correlation of their volume to their profitability?
5 What are their main concessions?
6 How do our plans compare with theirs?
7 How can we minimise their impact when we are negotiating with the buyer?

There are two basic negotiating strategies which can be adopted if we want to gain the order – the quick kill (or final offer first), or the holdback. If we are indifferent to the result then we may wish to adopt strategies which enhance any future negotiation and weaken competition.

We must determine, from our research into the client, whether we have a dominant or subordinate position to him, in relation to single supply sourcing, technical merit, delivery capability. In terms of technical merit, the client *must* perceive the advantage. In many negotiations the client negotiating team may initially have insufficient knowledge or concern for technical performance. In other situations the supplier overestimates the technical advantage.

If we are in the process of tendering to a buyer not known to indulge in post-tender negotiations we can adopt only a quick kill strategy. However, when we know some discussion and bargaining is expected we can submit an offer which includes a defined negotiating margin, either in the main pricing, or in non-specific reservations on terms and conditions. We are then able to adopt a strategy which gives time to establish more clearly the negotiating position.

In dealing for the first time with a known 'bargainer', beware of the common delusion that he will recognise a 'fair' competitive offer and deal with it as such. Part of the satisfaction in the deal may well come from his enjoyment of the negotiation process itself.

THE TACTICS OF NEGOTIATION

We are now concerned with reaching, from the actual points of difference between the parties, a mutually acceptable agreement. We can see in this stage that the essence of negotiation is *compromise*, actual or apparent. The discussion proceeds in a highly structured way, each side reducing the gap by a series of mutual concessions.

At this stage the skilful negotiator trades a concession which in fact costs him little, but which has a real or implied value which brings him a relatively more valuable concession from the other party. A great deal of skill is required on the part of the supplier in raising the apparent cost to him and value to the buyer of a concession he is trading. Remember that if there is no apparent cost to you then you are really conceding nothing.

With these concessions we must credibly raise the value to the buyer of the concession we are offering by applying the benefits of the concession to his needs. We can reinforce this value by stressing credibly the high cost of the concession to us. For example: 'You will understand that guaranteeing the special stock support is not something I could agree to easily, considering the cost and the existing commitments of my limited budget'. Similarly the buyer will magnify the cost to him and the value to us of his concessions. You must attempt to minimise the value to you of his concessions.

Concessions must be traded carefully. That is to say, you must not take your hands off your concession until the buyer has agreed on what he will do in return. ('I will do this if you do that'.) If you continually talk about your concessions alone, the buyer will accept them without reciprocation.

In many respects, negotiation is a vital game played for real consequences. Any unduly early attempt by either side to 'dig in their heels' by being genuinely inflexible will be met by reciprocal inflexibility from the other side, and the negotiation will break down. Certainly the conclusion of the negotiation may be that both sides agree that they cannot reasonably bridge the gap between them at this stage, or in this instance. That conclusion leaves open the possibility of further negotiation on the same subject, or new negotiations in another area. A breakdown in negotiation caused by the *unreasonable* inflexibility of one party will not leave those possibilities so open for the future.

At all times, even when we have reached a point beyond which we are not prepared to go, we must appear to be reasonable. Remember that you are playing a ritual game which is firmly based in hard financial reality, and that for many buyers much of their sense of achievement comes from 'playing the game well'.

There is also a point in a negotiation when the amount of time invested makes the deal harder to call off. In other words, if the buyer declares stalemate, or that he has reached the point of no return, and you have been negotiating for several hours, you will both be losing a considerable 'time' investment in the deal, apart from other considerations. At this stage it is worth pointing this out and suggesting another look through all the aspects of the proposed deal before admitting defeat. Equally, it is important to bear in mind, and perhaps make use of the fact, that the pressure to come to an agreement rises as the negotiation proceeds, as a consequence of increased time investment.

The definition of a successful negotiation from the supplier's side is one which ends on his side of the point of need balance, but where the buyer believes that the deal favours him.

The steps and methods to be used in achieving a successful outcome are as follows:

1 Allow the buyer to do most of the talking in the early stages. Try to get him to declare all the points he wants to discuss before dealing with any of them, but do not frustrate him by refusing to answer his questions, for example:

   Johnson (buyer): Well, for one, finance. Take the recommended parts stock you've got down here. Now I understand why it's higher in volume and value than for a standard machine, but so far as we're concerned it still represents a higher financial commitment than we're prepared to accept. So I think we should start by discussing ways and means of reducing that commitment.

   Edmonds (sales negotiator): Yes, we can certainly talk about that.

   Johnson: Never mind them for the moment. I'd like your suggestions on the recommended parts stock. After all, you were the one who brought up the importance of coming to a decision today. Let's get the parts stock recommendation out of the way and we can steam ahead.

Edmonds: All right, Mr. Johnson, if that's what you insist on.

2   Move the discussion from opening stances to a clear statement of actual stances, taking care to restrict the losses on both sides. It is your responsibility to 'save face' for the buyer.

(a)   If the buyer first presents his stance, you can
accept it and persuade him that the negatives are greater than the positives;
accept it and go back to the initial problem with alternatives;
ignore it and take your own stance;
take the opposite stance;
accept it and use the 'suppose' technique.

(b)   If you present your stance first, you can
take an exaggerated view;
take an actual stance, when strong;
'give' the buyer his stance, by seeming to accept his initial position;
place both stances in the current environment, in other words, a summary of both positions.

An example of the buyer's opening stance and the seller's counter:

Johnson: Oh, I see no reason at all why we shouldn't reach agreement today, Mr. Edmonds. All you and I have to talk over are a few points concerning the total package. Matters like getting the machines in, developing the staff and so on. The areas, in other words where your company – I'll say frankly – is a little weak as compared to some competitive quotes.

Edmonds: You needn't tell me, Mr. Johnson. We know how worried our competitors are!

3   Avoid taking a premature stance on any point which might result in reaching a point of no return too early in the negotiation. Remember it is easier for the buyer to walk away than for you in most circumstances.

4   Make a trial close on a clear statement of the actual gaps between you, e.g.:
So what you're saying, Mr X, is that assuming we can resolve these points (give details) we have a deal?

5   Trade any concessions one at a time ensuring that you raise the value of your concessions to him above their cost to you. Make a small move on your part seem large to him.

6   Devalue the cost to the buyer, and therefore downgrade the value to you of any concessions that he offers, for instance:
treat it as given (assumption) that there is no real concession;
competitors always expect it (or more);
there is benefit to the buyer in agreeing;
'we've got the benefits anyway';
'we don't want the benefit';
'you'd incur the cost anyway';

7   Upgrade the value and cost of any concessions that you give to the buyer.
Imply that we cannot really give it, e.g.:

Edmonds: Mr. Johnson, what you're asking me to agree to is . . . well it's a serious policy question. So serious I'd really have to take advice on it from our machine scheduling people.
Refer to major problems that will be solved by the concession.
Refer to savings gained by the buyer e.g.:

Johnson: Now, in order to pay them that kind of money, I imagine you'd be quite prepared to make some form of reduction in the course fee per head?

Edmonds: I know what. Instead of bringing them in on Saturday and Sunday, let's make it Friday and Saturday. That reduces your overtime costs by half, and the overtime it does leave you paying we could discount by knocking 20 per cent off the training fees.

Calculate the financial results of the concession, e.g.:

Johnson: How would that help me? I'd be just cutting down your costs.

Edmonds: Not necessarily. Suppose, for instance, that you collected the 787s; in that case we could completely remove the delivery charge from our quote. I think that's about 0.7 per cent, but it could be as much as 1 per cent.

Refer to loss if concession not given.
Refer to past gains from similar concessions.
Imply loss that we shall incur by giving concession, e.g.:

Johnson: Twenty per cent? Hardly seems enough.

Edmonds: I think it is if you remember that we also wouldn't be passing on to you the extra costs we'd incur by having *our* staff in on a Saturday.

Build up notional cost or opportunity cost of giving the concession.
Start by implying we are going to give a small concession then give a large one or enlarge the small concession.
Not normal practice: 'competitors don't do it'.

8 Be positive and not defensive when the buyer asks for a concession you cannot give, by:

building cost of giving the concession;
minimising the importance to the buyer of the concession;
'persuading' the buyer that the benefits of the deal without the concession still justify acceptance;
offering an alternative concession;
summarising the problem area and offering alternative concessions, or a choice of solutions;
showing the concession would put the buyer at a disadvantage.

9 Have facts and figures fluently to hand (but not 'pat' or 'glib' ones).

10 avoid emotional reactions, but satisfy the buyer's emotional needs. The good buyer/negotiator will try to put you under emotional pressure, e.g.:

Johnson: 'Obviously I'm disappointed you find yourself unable to offer me the facility of a buy back guarantee, but equally obviously, that is something it might be unfair to expect you to commit yourselves to.

11 Allow the buyer to save face in giving you a concession.

12 Ensure that the buyer is given the 'value satisfaction' he needs, and that you confirm it.

SUMMARY

Negotiation relies on accurately identifying at the preparation stage:

the buyer's needs;
our needs;
the point of balance;
the value of our concessions to the buyer;
the benefits to the buyer of our concessions, which will increase their value;
the concessions he will give, and how their 'cost' to him can be minimised;
the buyer's likely initial stance;
how we can move the buyer from his initial stance to the point of balance.

We are then in a position to meet the buyer without fear of conceding points for no reason. We will be able to reach a point of balance where the buyer is satisfied, and we have achieved our objectives. Finally, never forget the four negotiating commandments:

1 Aim high.
2 Get the other fellow's shopping list before you start arguing.
3 Keep the whole package in mind all the time.
4 Keep searching for variables.

24

Exhibitions

Harry McDermott, Director of Surveys, Exhibition Surveys Ltd

An exhibition is a complex means of communicating with the market place and can help companies achieve a wide range of objectives. Yet because effectiveness is not always easy to measure, exhibitions are often misunderstood, misused, or not used at all.

The common perception of an exhibition is as a display, a presentation to view, or a showing off, but the main and underlying purpose is to enable the exhibitor to meet people of value to his business; not just to have these people see the exhibition stand but to meet and talk with them. Upon this rock of meeting useful contacts the other many and different reasons for exhibiting are built, as is an ability to define measurable objectives. Lose sight of either of these factors and cost-effective exhibiting goes out of the window.

The vast variety of exhibitions can be bewildering. There are trade or technical exhibitions, public exhibitions, international, national and local events, exhibitions in the UK and overseas, in established exhibition halls, in hotels, in a field under the sky or under canvas, in caravans, buses, trains, or aircraft. The bewilderment is only momentary, however, if you know where you are, in a marketing sense, and know exactly where you want to go.

Unfortunately many exhibitors do not have clear objectives, and far too many marketing people do not have a clear-cut idea of what an objective is. Many of the common feelings of disappointment and frustration with exhibitions and the experience that they are expensive and wasteful come from lack of adequately defined exhibiting objectives. It is also a fact that carelessly planned, or unplanned, participation in an exhibition is one of the quickest ways to waste a great deal of a company's promotional budget.

THE PLACE OF EXHIBITIONS IN THE MARKETING COMMUNICATIONS MIX

Wherever marketing communications need the ingredient of meeting people of specific value to the company within sight, sound, smell and touch of the product, an exhibition can contribute usefully.

Some of the more important uses of exhibiting are:

1 To meet and identify many potential buyers (purchasing influences) in a relatively short space of time on neutral ground.
2 To give a practical demonstration of equipment to a large number of people. Exhibitions are especially important for demonstrating heavy capital equipment which it is impossible to take to the customer.
3 To introduce *new* products, companies and concepts.
4 To maintain or develop a company's image in the market; to increase awareness of the company and its products.
5 To sell.
6 To protect your market by preventing competitors making undue inroads, and to keep an eye on the competition.
7 To find new agents or distributors.
8 To research into products and markets.

HOW TO DECIDE WHERE TO EXHIBIT

Exhibiting is obviously only part of the marketing effort. Its role must be thought through clearly in advance and it is important that specific objectives are created and written down. The discipline of writing down objectives on paper is worth money in the bank. It also makes easier the decision on where to exhibit, because the exhibition's characteristics can be compared with the criteria written into the objectives. The objectives must include a specific reference to the number and type of persons to be met on your stand.

Decisions on whether or not to exhibit should be made by senior executives capable of assessing the media. To evaluate shows there must be an adequate supply of unbiased facts and figures from the organiser or from independent research organisations. You need to know whether or not the exhibition is capable of producing an adequate number of visitors of the right quality for your company's needs, that is, to match your objectives. The important exhibitions in your industry are probably already known to you.

If you are not sure which events to consider, then a good starting point is the monthly publication *Exhibition Bulletin*. This is a list of events arranged chronologically by town within country with subject/industry cross references. It lists the names of the exhibitions, their dates and venues, plus the exhibition organisers' names, addresses and telephone numbers. Two other worthwhile sources are the Association of Exhibition Organisers (AEO) and the Incorporated Society of British Advertising (ISBA). Not all exhibition organisers are members of the AEO. ISBA guards the interests of exhibitors and publishes some valuable pamphlets about exhibitions and exhibiting.

Organisers of successful, well managed exhibitions usually have available all the information needed to enable a potential exhibitor to decide whether or not to participate. This includes an independent and detailed assessment of the numbers, quality and post-show reactions. The detail is essential; if you market a highly specialised type of air compressor it is of relatively little value to know how many visitors are interested in some general 'dustbin' heading of 'Hydraulic and Pneumatic Equipment'. Some organisers have an immense amount of useful information available for the asking. Organisers of less successful, less well managed exhibitions sometimes try to conceal the facts, have less adequate information available, and have no truly independent assessment of visitor numbers or quality.

Ask the organiser of the events in which you are interested for the information contained in the Exhibition Data Form (EDF) published by the Audit Bureau of Circulations and available from those organisers that use the ABC vetting system: the ABC system is helpful, but the amount and type of information supplied is limited and insufficient for many marketing purposes. Ask the organiser also for independent survey information giving audience quality plus post-show reactions and opinions. If the information is not available, ask why not. Also ask the exhibition organiser for his estimate of the attendance and visitor quality at the *next* exhibition and how he will verify these estimates.

Beware if an exhibition organiser is unable to provide you with *verified* facts to enable you to judge whether or not your company should exhibit. Such organisers are sometimes not very marketing oriented, and if they fail to market their own product properly they may not possess the marketing skills to develop a first-class exhibition for their exhibitors.

Another independent information source is Exhibition Surveys, a company which for over a decade has conducted major surveys of several hundred exhibitions and conducted several thousand surveys of individual exhibitors' cost effectiveness.

Is there sufficient verified evidence that the exhibition being considered attracts enough of the visitors you need to meet to make exhibiting worthwhile? Here is one way of looking at the problem: Let us say that the information you have shows that about 10,000 people visit the exhibition and that, of these, about 3,000 are interested in your specific product areas. You are unlikely to meet all 3,000 on your exhibition stand: experience shows that about 40 per cent of the 3,000 (1,200 people) is usually possible. In other words, this 1,200 is your potential audience.

The figure of 40 per cent is based on several thousand studies of exhibitors' performance of medium to large companies at trade/technical exhibitions during the past ten years. It is an average, of course, and varies with the type of exhibition and stand. Nevertheless, 40 per cent is a very good guide to potential audience, that is, the number of people likely to visit the stand *if the stand is 100 per cent effective*.

Next we need to estimate the number of people who will actually visit the stand. To calculate the probable achievement, let us assume that the exhibition stand will be 76 per cent efficient (the current average efficiency) in contacting its potential visitors. This means that you are likely to meet about 900 visitors (1,200 × 0.76) on your stand and have useful sales talks.

A sales call is probably the nearest equivalent to meeting a useful contact on an exhibition stand and, in technical fields, the current cost per sales call is around £30 plus overheads. So those 900 sales talks at the exhibition are equivalent to spending £27,000 on outside sales calls. Can you exhibit properly for this sum? If you can, then your decision should be to exhibit. Although, on this basis, the expenditure of £27,000 is justified it does not, of course, follow that you need to spend anything like this sum. As a general rule of thumb, you should be able to make useful contacts at less than half the cost per sales call.

If you cannot afford the cost of meeting *all* potential visitors you should consider scaling down the size of your exhibiting operation to fit the funds available. If you have £15,000 available you would have to meet and have reasonable sales talks with about 500 visitors to justify the expenditure. Knowing the number of likely visitors is also invaluable when calculating the size of stand and the number of sales staff needed.

DECIDING ON THE EXHIBITION BUDGET

There must be a dozen common and fairly obvious ways of arriving at how much to spend on exhibiting. The trouble with most of these methods is that they ignore the need (if exhibiting is not to be very wasteful) to relate expenditure to potential. It is clearly foolish to spend a lot of money at an event where there is only a small potential. It is equally unwise to spend little where there is a lot to be gained.

Overspending and underspending are both prime causes of wasting a lot of money, resulting in exceedingly high cost per useful contact. Underspending has this effect because the size, effort and interest of the presentation attracts only a tiny part of its potential visitors with a consequently high cost per contact – just as though one had heavily overspent.

If you knew the average cost per contact of the best performers at a specific exhibition (a best performer is considered to be an exhibiting company that meets at least 70 per cent of its potential visitors) you could use this amount as a basis for calculating your budget, so as to avoid over- or under-spending. Based on some 25 recent major technical exhibitions, the current (1980) cost per contact of these best performers is £6.84.[1] Naturally some exhibitions/industries are above this average and some below. Nevertheless £6.84 is a good starting point. If your potential number of visitors was 1,200 then you

---

1   Direct costs only. It excludes all personnel costs (the cost of personnel time, overheads, hotels, travel, expenses etc.) and pre-show promotional costs.

could justify spending £6.84 × 1,200 = £8,200. This rather less obvious method of fixing the budget greatly increases the odds against making expensive mistakes and is a valuable cross-check on the budget arrived at by your company's own method.

PRE-SHOW AND IN-SHOW ACTIVITIES

Successful exhibition organisers spend heavily to attract a large volume of good-quality visitors, but at the most successful events attracting visitors is a two-way affair, a combination of exhibitors' and organisers' efforts.

To make it easier for exhibitors to publicise exhibitions, most organisers provide publicity aids such as stickers for correspondence and cars, posters, visitor information leaflets and complimentary tickets. Much of this is free. You actually pay for it in the space rental fee, so you might as well use it. Research at trade/technical events shows that at least one-quarter of the visitors hear about the exhibition via exhibitors.

Organisers also have press relations departments, a key factor in attracting visitors, which bombard the press with interesting facts and figures. Keep the organiser informed of what you plan to do at the exhibition, particularly of new products and demonstrations. If you have something rather special you can be sure the organisers will be interested. The power of the press is apparent when it is realised that at most technical or trade exhibitions at least four out of ten visitors hear of the event through the press.

At the exhibition the organiser has a press office to which members of the press go on arrival. It costs nothing to have your literature displayed in the press office, yet nine in ten exhibitors do not bother to do so. The presence of information on your company's products or services could influence the press to seek out your stand in preference to others. Make sure during every day of the exhibition that your literature supplies are topped up. The press office is another service that is free or, rather, included in the space rental fee.

Any exhibitor who can devise an appropriate incentive to persuade known purchasing influencers to visit the exhibition *and to call at his stand* is certain of a successful show. *It is well worth the time of senior executives to ponder what appropriate incentive could be used to attract known purchasing influencers.*

In addition to the known purchasing influencers there will be other people at the exhibition you would wish to meet. If left to chance alone, these people would have to see your stand (out of perhaps 300 other exhibitors) and be persuaded by what they saw to come on to it. When you know that on average, a visitor to a trade/technical show stays five to six hours and calls on about 15 stands (28 at consumer public events) it is evident that the odds of chance visits are low. You must do something about this yourself. It cannot be left to the exhibition organiser.

A variety of in-show promotional activities can increase the odds of success. Here are a few ideas: posters that the visitor will see if he arrives by car, by train, by air or on foot; posters in the exibition halls; billboard men or girls walking in or near the exhibition; your staff with interesting messages printed on their clothes (T-shirts); the ubiquitous plastic bag for visitors' literature becomes a mobile placard; beer coasters and messages in packs of sandwiches sold by the self-service restaurant; paper napkins in the restaurant; messages on other (non-competitive) stands, especially if yours is a product used by other exhibitors; advertisements in the exhibition catalogue.

Girls, gimmicks and games are potential crowd pullers. They sometimes work well, but more often attract a low quality audience more interested in the action than your product. However, a dynamic well-thought-out demonstration *closely associated with your products* can attract a large number of high quality visitors, particularly if the demonstration shows how to solve a problem.

Try to have a *continuous* demonstration rather than every hour or so. People usually have not the time to come back later. Continuous demonstrations make far more contacts than those at set times. Extract the most from your demonstration by strategically positioning some of your sales staff in the aisles among the crowd that develops. As your staff hear comments such as 'That looks interesting' they can give out literature or collect names and addresses for later contact by salesmen. But one warning: your activities could inconvenience adjacent exhibitors. Make a point of talking with them beforehand because you will need their goodwill.

A final point about demonstrations: use professional actors, not your own staff. Actors add an air of smooth confidence to the presentation that one's own staff can rarely give. Actors are used to memorising scripts and can handle technical jargon; they are well worth their cost.

ORGANISING AND STAFFING A STAND

The best exhibition organisers are as concerned as you are that your exhibiting is effective and free from traumatic experiences. They know most of the problems, how to overcome them, and are happy to give you the benefit of their experience.

As soon as your exhibition space is booked appoint one of your staff as exhibition manager. He or she will have to be non-flappable, calm, easy to get on with, a clear thinker able to give meticulous attention to detail and be physically robust. The exhibition manager's job is to coordinate the activities of everyone and anything connected with your exhibition stand; the exhibition organiser, your marketing team, your sales staff, the stand designer, the contractor, the unions and site staff.

Usually the organiser provides the exhibitor with a guide book containing step-by-step instructions to enable the exhibitor's stand to be ready on time. Part of the book comprises duplicate forms to be completed and returned by specific dates to ensure each step is taken and executed in the right order.

Undoubtedly the employment of a professional stand designer can save his fee many times over. He knows the regulations governing the halls and the exhibition in detail. He knows how to achieve the effect you want, using the right materials at the lowest cost. He knows the capabilities of stand contractors and if they are likely to be stretched by taking on too much work at a particular exhibition.

To highlight the problems of building and organising a stand the exhibition manager would do well to show the Video Arts film *It'll be Okay on the Day* to his colleagues connected with the presentation. It is an educational film but exceedingly funny.

Consider seriously the modular stand-building systems currently available. Most are simple yet some can also be sophisticated and lend themselves to excellently designed good-looking stands. The cost savings over custom-made stands can be great and there need be little or no loss in appearance.

Good stand discipline is essential. One person should be appointed as stand manager in complete charge of the stand during the exhibition and everyone should be aware of this. Often the person with the right quality is the exhibition manager but to expect him to manage the stand for a week after supervising its erection is asking a lot. When the chairman, a director or any company employee sets foot on the stand, or is about to leave it, he should report to the stand manager and advise him of his movements. One of those slide 'in' and 'out' indicator boards is a great help in controlling staff movement.

Put your best people on the stand, salesmen, engineers and technicians and identify them. Dress them smartly in some sort of uniform to enable the visitor to pick out your staff quickly from other visitors. The uniform could be a jacket or even just a distinctive tie. Everyone should also wear an identity badge.

Organise everything on the stand to give the visitor a pleasant, interesting and, above all, memorable visit. Otherwise the visitor is quite likely to forget calling and much of your efforts and money will be wasted. You must be in control of events. The techniques of selling from an exhibition stand are rather different from most other selling situations. Arrange a showing to your sales staff of another Video Arts film *How not to exhibit yourself.* This delightfully funny film makes a host of important points in a memorable fashion. A fundamental feature of the salesman's approach to a visitor should, for example, never be to ask 'Can I help you?' because it invites a negative reply 'No, I'm only looking'. Far better to approach a visitor who is looking at the product and say 'That's rather interesting/effective/colourful etc. Isn't it? Did you know that . . . ' And then into the selling tack.

Adequate preparation is essential to enable the stand to work properly on the day. A feature of the best organised exhibitors is an exhibition briefing document. This should be given to all staff booked into hotels for the exhibition and to any others who need to know. *This document will prevent a host of small and not-so-small problems occurring.* The details it should cover are shown below.

Exhibition briefing document

The exhibition. Location, dates, hours, tickets: attach a pass to the briefing and advise those who arrive at the exhibition without a pass or ticket how much it will cost them to enter.

The company's stand. Stand number and hall number; the names or companies represented on the stand; the overall theme and the thinking behind its design; details of demonstrations on the stand; details of new products; specific mention of any items that are to be shown to customers but which the company does not want competitors crawling all over.

Company literature. Say where it will be located on the stand and identify the main items of literature. If some is for restricted circulation, say which.

Competitors. Give their names, hall and stand numbers.

Entertainment suite. If you have one, give its location and say whether or not entry is by invitation only. Say if tea and coffee only are available on the stand and give the opening times of the bar in the entertainment suite. State the luncheon arrangements.

Stand rota. A rota is essential but, despite a rota, problems can arise at lunch time. Advise anyone who has to leave the stand that he must keep reception informed and must come back quickly. Use the entertainment suite for entertaining customers and keep reception informed.

Company visitors. Ask members of staff who are not on duty to avoid visiting the stand at the busy period between 11 am and 1.30 pm.

Hotel and transport. Advise the name and location of the hotel and that bed and English breakfast have been paid in advance. Staff should settle extras themselves and claim on expenses. State the method of travel from hotel to the exhibition and the cost of parking at the exhibition.

Services – Receptionists. Number of agency girls on stand; names of people (own staff) who will supervise the stand.

Telephones. Identify location and number of telephones for incoming calls and also those for outgoing calls.

In-and-out board. Ask all staff to use the cards on the board as they enter or leave the stand.

Visitor's book. Use one with loose-leaf binder pages that can be easily sorted or photo-copied. Ask staff to record full names and addresses with care. Do not invite visitors to write their own names otherwise incomplete information will result: 'J.K. Smith of Aberdeen' etc.

Coats and luggage. Ask staff to leave the cloakrooms on the stand free for visitors; identify locations of other cloakrooms and ask staff to keep to a minimum any luggage or briefcases.

Name badges. Must be worn at all times while on duty. Badges will be supplied by the receptionist on the stand.

FOLLOW-UP

In a crude sense what one achieves by exhibiting at a technical event is
a fist full of enquiries at the end of the show. At a consumer event one
would hope to have made some sales. Despite the fact that the
acknowledged purpose of exhibiting is to make useful contacts, many
exhibitors fail to install and use an adequate follow-up system. The
real value of exhibiting therefore slips through their fingers. The bulk
of their budget is wasted. *If you are to exhibit effectively, a follow-up
system is not optional, it is essential.* It need not require much
administration or cost a great deal, but it does need some thought and
persistence to make it work properly.

The follow-up systems can give you a great deal of feedback
information about the visitor:

1   Is the enquirer an existing customer or a new prospect?
2   Is he a purchasing influence?
3   Is he planning to buy your types of product?
4   Were you too late and did the competition sell him first, or
    did your company make the sale?
5   Is he a real prospect and to be retained on the mailing list?
6   Was he familiar with your products/company prior to visit-
    ing the exhibition?

A simple and tested system is to use pads of enquiry forms (in
triplicate) and to ensure at the start of each day that every exhibition
salesman has a pad from which completed forms are collected at the
end of the day. One copy is retained by the publicity department and
the two remaining copies are sent to the local salesman for the
territory. He should be required to report on his visit/telephone call
within seven days. To stress the importance of the follow-up, in some
companies the report is sent by the salesman to the sales director who
passes on the forms to the publicity department.

In these days of high-powered marketing techniques it is still
possible to create an impact and an air of efficiency by writing
promptly to people who visited your stand, thanking them for doing
so and enclosing requested literature. If an exhibition visitor has
asked several competitive companies for information the first one to
respond has the edge. Make certain that your company is fast to

respond. You could have one of your staff on the stand type pre-printed or word-processed letters daily to visitors who have just called.

ASSESSING RESULTS

Evaluating performance starts before the exhibition, not after it, and the early development of measurable objectives is essential. At consumer events, where sales are made directly off the stand, evaluating exhibiting performance is easy: the costs of exhibiting are known, as is the profit on the items sold. But at technical exhibitions quite often the last thing one expects is a direct sale from the stand: this is not surprising because the products may be custom made after years of development and negotiation. In such cases there are two important features to measure:

(a)   the efficiency of the stand in reaching its potential audience, and

(b)   the cost per useful contact achieved on the stand.

If a stand attracts 200 useful contacts out of a potential of 2,000 then it could be thought of as 10 per cent efficient (or 90 per cent inefficient). This type of measurement is possible using a post-show survey of exhibiting performance. It is surprising how many otherwise professional exhibitors are satisfied with inefficient performances through lack of the right kind of information with which to exploit exhibitions better.

The accepted cost of making useful contacts is a company's cost per sales call: the cost per useful contact achieved on the stand is a valuable comparative guide. Related to the efficiency of the stand it enables decisions to be taken that will improve future cost effectiveness. For example, let us say that the stand is 10 per cent efficient, that the cost per contact is £60 and the cost per sales call is £30. From this one could argue that the total budget could remain the same at the next show and that the real concentration on improvement should be in increasing the stand's efficiency in contacting potential visitors. By concentrating on improved efficiency the cost per contact will automatically fall to an acceptable level.

If the stand were, say, 100 per cent efficient, the cost per contact

£60, and the cost per sales call £30, one could argue that the overall budget should be cut. These are rather oversimplified examples, but the principle is sound and well-developed in commercial surveys of exhibiting performance.

It costs money to measure exhibiting performance, but if one's performance is inefficient then a lot of money is going down the drain and no measurements could be very expensive indeed.

25

Distribution channels

Jack Wheatley, Moore's Modern Methods

The process of distribution is not merely concerned with physically getting goods from a manufacturer to his eventual customer. Distribution strategy covers the following basic activities: the choice of available channels, whether or not to confine distribution to one channel or several; whether to go direct to the customer or deal through intermediaries; how much expenditure to allocate for distribution and whether to take a complete or partial financial interest in the available channels.

What might seem the best or only channels available at the start of a marketing campaign may prove to be inadequate or too restrictive for subsequent development of sales, so a manufacturer who opts to distribute entirely through wholesalers may regret his lack of contact with retail outlets when he needs extra sales or when he realises that his wholesaler is also promoting a competitor's output, perhaps to the exclusion of his products.

The choice of distribution channels is therefore one requiring careful thought and a full consideration of the available alternatives.

PLANNING FOR DISTRIBUTION

In arriving at a final decision on which channel or combination of channels should be used many points have to be taken into account. The choice depends not only on costs in relation to funds available, but also on the location of the consumer, the places where he is most likely to see the product and the extent to which it is desirable and/or necessary to maintain direct contact with the consumer. It also depends on the bulkiness of the product, anticipated average order value, credit risks involved in the alternative methods available and the risks entailed in placing all distribution in the hands of an outside and independent agent or wholesaler.

With a new product and particularly if the market is a new one to the manufacturer it still takes great courage to try and by-pass traditional channels. The patterns of distribution and demand are now changing, however, as the ranges of choice open to consumers widen.

Not so long ago, nobody would have considered garages as an outlet for confectionery and soft drinks, newsagents for pop records, chemists for wines and spirits or food supermarkets for clothing and furniture, but all these changes have taken place to the advantage of the retailing outlets and the manufacturers.

Distribution itself cannot be considered in isolation from other aspects of the marketing plan because it is usually up to the manufacturer to promote his products to the eventual consumer and to stimulate demand that will materialise into a decision to buy at the chosen point of distribution.

New methods of large-scale distribution such as hypermarkets and cash and carries are attractive in that they facilitate bulk distribution to a limited number of outlets but, in opting for this method as a sole means of distribution, the manufacturer is vulnerable in the sense that changes in the buying policies of one or two of the outlets can have a significantly adverse impact on his sales volume. The ultimate decision on which distributive channels to use must depend on the costs involved and the estimated net profit contribution available within the various alternatives.

What might seem the best short-term solutions are not necessarily in the long-term interests of the manufacturer and therefore extreme care must be taken before placing all distribution in the hands of an outside body be it a wholesaler, agent or merchant.

The ideal is to have full control over all aspects of distribution, but this may well involve the manufacturer in direct selling costs that the product could not carry in the light of the anticipated sales forecast.

THE WHOLESALER

Traditionally the wholesaler has been one the oldest links in the distribution chain but, while still popular, this method is losing some of its appeal with manufacturers beginning to develop their own images to their consumers. Even so, the wholesaler still offers the cheapest form of distribution as he takes responsibility for storing in bulk and delivering in small quantities to the consumer. This relieves the manufacturer of the major part of delivery costs for he is only concerned with making the more economical bulk deliveries to the wholesaler's warehouses. The wholesaler takes all the small credit risks and absorbs direct selling costs, but very rarely will he avoid selling a competitive product.

Because of the nature of their business, wholesalers carry wide brand ranges and their salesmen become initially 'order takers' with no specific selling emphasis on any particular brand. They tend, therefore, to reflect consumer demand rather than create it.

Although wholesalers can handle all distribution it is advisable for a manufacturer to employ at least a small sales force calling on ultimate outlets to persuade them to place orders for his products from the designated local wholesaler. Orders can be taken and passed to the wholesaler as a gesture of good faith but also as a positive encouragement to stock the manufacturer's product.

Some companies have set up their own wholesaling operations. The speedy, prompt, delivery (SPD) organisation set up by Unilever is an example, and in this case the wholesaling/distribution company stores and distributes for other organisations on a proper commercial basis. In the main, it is better to regard wholesaling as a specialist function and to set up an in-company operation only if it can be done properly and expertly. Few organisations have the required range to do that.

A combination of direct distribution and wholesaling is preferable as the sales contacts that the wholesalers have built up over the years are very useful, but if wholesaling is used it is important to remember that the eventual consumer will need to be exposed to product promotion from the manufacturer. The wholesaler cannot be expected to create the demand for he has too many competing interests.

To avoid conflict with a wholesaler's selling policy a manufacturer can give a different brand name to his product sold through the wholesaler. This technique is used successfully with such products as stationery, clothing and certain foodstuffs.

THE RETAIL TRADES

The structure of the retail trades has altered considerably since Napoleon referred to Britain as 'a nation of shopkeepers'. Many smaller shops have been forced out of business but many that have changed their style of management to compete with the larger, and often impersonal multiples and supermarkets, have survived. Often location has proved to be the prime factor.

Independent retailers

Independent retailers provide an efficient local service at higher prices than the larger chains and multiples and they often provide extended credit and/or free delivery for their customers. As outlets, they tend to sell the products for which there is an established demand, but are often very responsive to good sales promotion of new products and can be more easily persuaded to try new lines than wholesalers.

Voluntary groups

To combat the threat posed by multiple chains and supermarkets, independent retailers have banded together into voluntary groups which started as central buying groups but have now developed into highly efficient retail outlets following common policies extending to product ranges, stock control, accounting, store layout and store promotions. Examples are VG and Mace. Other groups have been formed by large wholesalers to guarantee outlets for the lines they sell and this, in turn, has led wholesalers to develop their own label brands for distribution via the retailers in their group.

Multiple stores

The advantage of using this channel of distribution is that the buying points can be covered by a very small sales force as most items are bought centrally from head offices. Store managers work to central promotional and stocking policies and, providing a manufacturer can persuade the central buyer to stock his product, he is assured that the necessary efforts will be made at store level. Because of the need to achieve fast turnover on what are often narrow margins, multiple stores will not persist with slow moving lines and so the manufacturer needs to back up the stores with adequate promotion to consumers. Multiples have developed from being the outlets set up by food manufacturers who wished to extend vertically into retailing, but some have taken the opposite path backwards into manufacturing; this is what has stimulated the growth of 'own label' brands.

Alternatively, some multiples have arranged own label production by outside manufacturers. This is useful to the independent producer as a channel of distribution but he has to be assured of long-term contracts if he uses this channel as a sole outlet for distribution.

Retail chains

Again, store managers follow centrally laid-down policies but there is usually more flexibility allowed according to local conditions. Stores often trade under different names, but the manufacturer is usually offered multiple outlet distribution and, consequently, a wider coverage.

Local chain store managers are usually very responsive to store promotions backed up by press and television advertising. The combination of a television spot naming a particular retail chain as a stockist of a product and a display of that product with a card saying, 'As seen on television' is very successful.

Department stores

Department stores carry a wide variety of merchandise under one roof with specific departments under their own separate buying and selling management. Each department is organised to sell particular product ranges.

The standard of personal service is often very high. Some of the larger stores have almost become institutions to the criterion of good service and are respected as such all over the world. Buyers are usually very high skilled professionals who anticipate fashion trends and buy accordingly. Manufacturers using this channel can obtain extremely useful market research information by maintaining contact with store buyers. This channel is also used by companies setting up their own boutiques or 'shops within shops', a method particularly suitable for such products as jewellery, cosmetics and clothing. Exporters would find this a useful means of getting established in a new overseas market. Travel agencies are another example.

Cooperative societies

These are becoming combinations of multiples, department stores and supermarkets with the apparent aim of selling their own manufactured products. This is the complete evolutionary cycle, for the first cooperative societies in the middle of the last century were manufacturers setting up as manufacturers and retailers.

Private brands, however, still account for a significant proportion of total turnover and the use of this channel offers the possibilities of large scale distribution from a limited number of outlets.

Supermarkets

These are a natural development of multiples and self-service outlets and now account for a significant proportion of total retail trade. Product ranges have extended from food into a wide variety of non-food items operating under very tight control and measuring efficiency in terms of profit per square foot of floor space instead of as a percentage of sales.

Because of their vast buying power, supermarkets are able to extract hard bargains from manufacturers and lay down very strict conditions of delivery times, quantities, packaging, etc. Manufacturers are offered economic distribution in that delivery points are far fewer than for independent retailers; buying, however, is in the hands of an equally small number of head offices. A manufacturer who opts for supermarkets as his only outlets is subject to sudden changes of buying policy.

Supermarkets are becoming increasingly concerned with multiple product ranges to such an extent that specialist supermarkets dealing solely in product ranges, such as carpets, radio and television, are appearing to attract the customers who are becoming somewhat disenchanted with the lack of choice in the non-food departments of supermarkets.

Hypermarkets

Regarded as the ultimate in retailing, this type of outlet is now well established in the UK. The principle is to provide 'one-stop shopping' for a wide variety of products in an out-of-town location where space is available at lower rents than in town centres. These outlets are very attractive to manufacturers as access and egress is usually easier because of geographical location.

Cash and carry

These outlets have been developed by wholesalers and voluntary groups whereby retailers select the goods they are going to sell from the wide range displayed and collect, pay and transport them back to the shops. This method tends to be used by the smaller retailers, e.g. restaurants, canteens and newsagents. The cash and carry outlets usually maintain regular promotional mailing to their retail customers and run special offer campaigns, but otherwise provide a minimum of service.

As a channel of distribution the manufacturer can make good use of cash and carry outlets to deal with the problems of small deliveries provided he can create a demand by promotion to the eventual outlet and consumer. However, as cash and carries are retailers' supermarkets, good packaging and presentation can be very helpful in persuading retailers to pick products off the shelves and to try selling them in their own stores.

Discount stores

A comparatively recent innovation to the retail scene is the discount store which provides cut-price products with the minimum customer service. This channel is particularly useful for sales of consumer durables and toiletries. Chemists' lines are being increasingly distributed in this manner. Discount trading became increasingly evident following the banning of resale price maintenance.

Mobile retailers

To strengthen the personal service there has been a growth in the number of retailers taking their products direct to the housewife. Grocers, greengrocers, bakers and butchers are using this method and yet dairies who, by tradition have made deliveries of milk direct to the consumer, are trying to cut down on the number of deliveries to reduce costs. Prices charged do not reflect the service provided. Dairies are adding soft drinks and confectionery to the range carried by their milk floats in order to increase sales per journey.

Ready-cooked foods like fish and chips, hamburgers, meat pies and chickens are now sold from mobiles as well as the normal tea, coffee and light refreshments.

Van selling

Van selling is used by manufacturers of perishable foods, particularly bread and meat products, and allows complete control of the distribution operation. Cost per order can be high, particularly in large items where so much time can be lost in finding a suitable parking place or waiting in traffic jams, but total distribution costs can be lower than would be incurred with a separate delivery fleet and a sales force.

Door-to-door selling

A very expensive method of distribution, yet apart from a few highly successful exceptions, door-to-door selling is not widely practised. Government legislation was formulated to prevent the worst excesses of this type of selling whereby housewives were persuaded by unscrupulous salesmen to buy products that would not work or that they did not need or could not afford. It is often used in combination with a national or local advertising campaign. The regular wider promotion gives an air of respectability to the sales staff who follow up and call from door-to-door.

Considerable success has been achieved by companies selling cosmetics, but to be effective the use of this channel for such products requires a very large sales force as the average unit of sale is very low in value. Double glazing, central heating and encyclopedias are more applicable to this type of distribution as the average unit of sale tends to be much higher than with the smaller products.

Garages

Apart from selling petrol and oil, garages are now retailing wide ranges of motor accessories and food lines. The appeal is largely geared to impulse buying because consumers do not normally go to garages just to buy the ancillary items. As channels of distribution, however, garages are becoming increasingly important.

THE COMMODITY MARKET

Perishables are usually distributed through the commodity markets in the UK, but many of them have become so heavily congested that producers are tending to fix up long-term contracts with outlets and deliver direct. Such contracts can be beneficial to the producer in so far as his selling prices are stabilised, but they have to be fixed in the light of a very accurate assessment of future supply and demand which the commodity markets reflect on a daily basis. Other commodities such as rubber, copper, tin, tea and gold are still bought and sold through the traditional markets in London.

Franchising

This is a method of distribution used mainly to further the sales of an idea or a process rather than a product itself. Successful exploitation of this method has been achieved with a wide variety of products including fried chickens, hamburgers, instant printing, drain cleaning, tyre and exhaust fitting, ice-cream, steaks and Chinese food. Financial assistance is provided to the franchisee to set up his business, with the manufacturer taking a share of the resulting profits and providing training in business management. Common standards and common forms of presentation are very important and are enshrined in agreements between the franchisor and franchisee.

Party plan selling

Under this method a manufacturer appoints agents – usually women – who hold sponsored parties in their homes and invite their friends to see the products. Orders are taken and more agents are recruited and so the operation develops. This channel is useful for selling kitchen and other domestic ware, clothing, jewellery and cosmetics but is difficult to use in conjunction with distribution through traditional retail outlets for these do not take kindly to this type of sponsored competition from their suppliers.

Mail order

This has become a popular channel for a very wide range of products and services. Large department stores and mail order houses are investing large sums in postage, printing and distribution of catalogues direct to the public. At the other end of the scale, rare books, classical records and even collections of specially-minted coins and medals are promoted and distributed via direct mail to a specialist public. The big attraction of this method is the direct promotion to the consumer to the complete exclusion of any intermediaries. But perhaps the most spectacular growth in recent years has been direct selling through couponed advertisements in newspapers and magazines – through the Sunday supplements in particular. The method has also spread to television.

Direct selling costs are negligible, but advertising costs are extremely high; however, companies successful in this field continue to use this channel and are clearly satisfied with the returns obtained. Some distributors have extended their operation by setting up their own stores selling nothing but the products advertised by their direct mailing, thus relieving them of small distribution costs. This combination of previously separate channels is typical of what often happens as a marketing operation develops.

AGENTS, BROKERS AND MERCHANTS

The advantage of all of these channels is the personal contact and knowledge they have of a particular market. Agencies are established on an exclusive and semi-exclusive basis and can be very helpful to the supplier entering a completely new market or to one who does not want to employ his own sales force. The agent should act as a member of the manufacturer's sales team as distinct from the wholesaler who is more concerned with the burden of the physical distribution.

Clearly, the granting of a sole agency is a step not to be taken lightly because, if the wrong agent is appointed, considerable harm can be done to the principal's image and development plans before such an agent can be replaced.

Brokers act as intermediaries working on very fine profit margins but, as with agents, they often have very useful contacts. A danger with the broker is that he can depress the market price by selling at cut rates sufficient for him to earn a minimal margin, particularly on volume sales.

Merchants generally operate as a mixture of agents and wholesalers and usually have a good standing in the market place. Care has to be taken in passing them sole selling rights because they tend to carry a wide range of lines and are sometimes unable to put significant emphasis behind any one product.

EXPORTING

Selection of the proper channels of distribution for overseas markets is even more important than in the UK markets where the lines of communication are shorter and mistakes can be more speedily rectified. It is essential that proper account be taken of local customs and practices, attitudes and patterns of demand. For entry into an overseas market the best method of distribution is probably through an export agent. Selection of the agent is clearly very important and the Chamber of Commerce, the Department of Trade and Industry and trade associations can all offer good advice on where to find agents.

Direct representation in large department stores is another successfully used method of distribution because, as in the UK, leading stores are barometers of current demand and can usually place sizeable orders offering economies of scale to distributors.

With some countries, particularly those of the eastern bloc, the distribution has to be through large buying offices in the UK and often there is no direct contact between the manufacturer and his ultimate consumer.

INDUSTRIAL DISTRIBUTION

Techniques of good marketing are being applied increasingly in the industrial field. As far as channels of distribution are concerned the choice is almost as wide as that available for consumer goods.

Industrial products tend to be of a more technical nature so consideration has to be given to after-sales service irrespective of the chosen channel of distribution. Very often a manufacturer will deal with his customer via an agent on all matters of sale and supply, but will deal direct on servicing and maintenance.

Package deals involving products from within a large group of companies can be offered to one common outlet; similarly, a manufacturer may well find many captive outlets within his own group. This opportunity is often missed or just not pursued.

Licensing is a method often used in the engineering industry, e.g. with motor cars and aero-engines. Under these arrangements, the licensee undertakes to produce and sell goods to the licensee's specification for a consideration of the resultant profits. This method enables the manufacturer to expand his revenue without a corresponding increase in investment.

Heavy engineering industries make use of consortia to distribute their products. This applies to such projects as off-shore drilling equipment, building and civil engineering contracts, power station supplies, shipbuilding, etc.

CONCLUSION

Inevitably, the final decision on which channels to use must be a compromise, but it is the purpose of this chapter to provide an outline of the range of possibilities, and even if no more than a stimulation of more detailed and rational thinking on this vital aspect of marketing occurs it will have served its purpose.

26

Physical distribution

Philip Winrow, Principal, L. Phillip Winrow & Associates, Industrial and Management Consultants

Physical distribution has only assumed its importance, within the manufacturer's corporate strategy, during the past 10 years or so. Previously, a definition of physical distribution would have concentrated on vehicles, vehicle loads, warehousing location, number of delivery drops, distance between drops and so on, if it had come from the production-oriented managers. The market-oriented manager would have been concerned with distribution channels, field sales forces, brokerage deals and devices for securing the maximum effective representation of the company's product to the consumer. Although the components of a physical distribution definition are still the same, there is now greater recognition of the fact that an effective physical distribution system is a critical device for maximising the company's marketing effort.

The effective system bridges the gap between production and consumption. This gap has been forced wider over the years by discriminating purchasers using their greater purchasing power, inventory control systems demanding greater utilisation of inventory capital and sophisticated production methods requiring more economic use of expensive and capital intensive production processes. The situation looks like becoming more intensive over the next few years, and an effective distribution system is needed to take the heat off both production and inventories. Rather than becoming a world full of standardised consumers demanding standardised products, the range of consumer choice and demand gets wider every year. The manufacturer will be continually faced with extending his product range, without increasing investment in inventories, at the same time providing an increasingly higher level of service in order to retain a market share.

The physical distributor has to live with two great pressures. First, the retailer or wholesaler is increasingly cutting down on inventories and demanding that an improved level of service insures against stock-out problems. Second, the manufacturer, when reducing stocks of finished goods or field warehouse stocks, is also pushed up against production control problems together with demands to reduce the cost of physical distribution. He then, tight up against production deadlines with little or no finished stocks to fall back on, unloads on to the physical distributor the stock-out problem. The retailer/whole-saler also with reduced stock investment, but needing to satisfy the insistent buyer, also pushes his stock-out problem on to the physical distributor. So with the increasing level of retail prices, the value of an out-of-stock situation can be significant. Figure 26.1 illustrates the total problem.

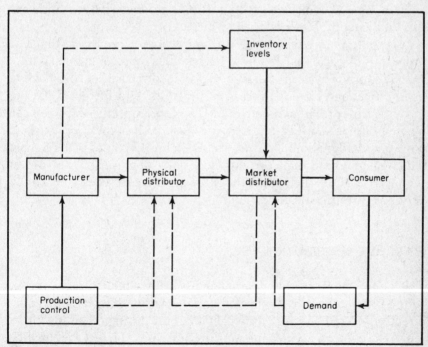

Figure 26.1 Chain of distribution and demand

The solid lines denote the formal relationship between the manufacturer, distributor, retailer and the consumer. The broken lines denote the feed-back of pressures between all three. For the sake of simplicity the intermediate wholesaler has been left out, but one can easily visualise the added complexity sandwiched between the two massive pressures of production and production control on the one hand, and increasingly discriminating market demand and inventory control on the other. It is hardly surprising that the transport manager rarely wins. Although he tries to run a system in which exceptions are rare, in practice rush orders and the exceptions have become the rule.

The physical distribution system has to improve and become more and more effective, not only to withstand the pressures referred to above, but to be able to contribute to the economic efficiency of the company from a corporate production/inventory/market share standpoint. Rather than a marketing or production problem, physical distribution has now become a corporate strategy problem. An efficient distribution system ensures that the company's products achieve and maintain a superior position in the retailers' and consumers' view of competing and substitute products, while optimising the total cost of distribution.

It is quite common to meet the following example of what is a disastrous physical distribution system. Sales representatives make a 10-day journey cycle. It takes 3 days to feed the sales order back to head office, and have it processed. It also takes a further 5 days to have the order filled and delivered. The representative can then call again a day or so after the customer has had his stock replenished. Now the retailer should logically allow in his thinking for the 8 days' lead time, but how many do? All the retailer thinks is that his shelves are now full. Can one expect the representative to receive an intelligent and enthusiastic reception?

EFFECTIVE DISTRIBUTION

The manufacturer has a fundamental problem of how to get a product to the ultimate user with the minimum cost but with the maximum effectiveness. His competitor will be thinking through the same problem. If he comes up with a more efficient system, the fact that the first management has a better product will only be of marginal value.

Despite the constantly changing nature of the market, many companies just do not examine and critically audit their distribution system. The initial setting up of the network would be an enormous and costly task, and many managers prefer to live with the old system fearing conversion costs and possible physical upheavals. With an out-of-date distribution system losses in the market can far outweigh any conversion costs. Moreover, it is surprising how many manufacturers do not know their distribution costs, or believe them to be ridiculously low.

The essentials of a physical distribution problem are (a) the required level of service to the stock keeping of retail outlets and (b) the total cost of the system. Figure 26.2 shows that the cost of the system grows exponentially, rather than in a linear fashion, as the level of service improves.

It is obvious that these two components of the problem are interrelated. The methods used to distribute from the originating point to consuming points have differing levels of efficiency. This may require greater stocks to be kept at strategic points, but there is also a resulting total systems cost. A more efficient method may cost more but may also eliminate strategic stock keeping, which could mean an overall reduced total systems cost. The physical distribution system must then be examined from the following angles:

(a) distribution audit and the total systems cost angle;
(b) optimal level of service;

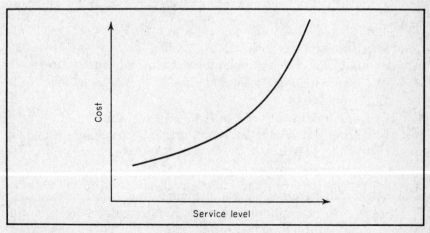

Figure 26.2 The cost of the system grows exponentially

(c) inventory control problems;
(d) transport options;
(e) vehicle and delivery control; and
(f) financial options – buy, hire or lease.

Distribution audit and the total systems cost angle

Distribution audits are as necessary as financial audits, although they rarely get treated that way. Part of the reason for this is that there is not a well laid down process for auditing the distribution system as there is for checking the financial system. Secondly, the cost of the distribution system, which is always a nagging worry, never gets to the top of the list of management priorities. Everyone connected with distribution has day-to-day crises to cope with, and there is rarely anyone who can put in the necessary time to critically examine the whole system. The job is sometimes given to cost accountants or the company's auditors, but while these specialists do a good accounting job, they cannot be expected to see the problem through the eyes of a marketing/distribution man. The purpose of such an audit is firstly to discover the total cost of the distribution system and, secondly, to see what happens to the total cost as components of the system are manipulated, hoping to achieve lower unit costs or take advantage of more efficient methods and achieve higher levels of service.

The audit should be begun in such a manner that the components of the system are isolated and treated as cost centres. Each business will be slightly different from other businesses, but broadly the usual pattern of systems components will be:

(a) finished inventories;
(b) field warehouses, inventories and establishment costs;
(c) trunk haulage between finished inventories and field warehouses;
(d) radial deliveries out of field warehouses;
(e) order processing at both finished and field warehouse levels; and
(f) information flows.

This can be illustrated as shown in Figure 26.3.

There are many conflicting interests requiring decisions. The finished and field warehouse inventories, for example, can be handled

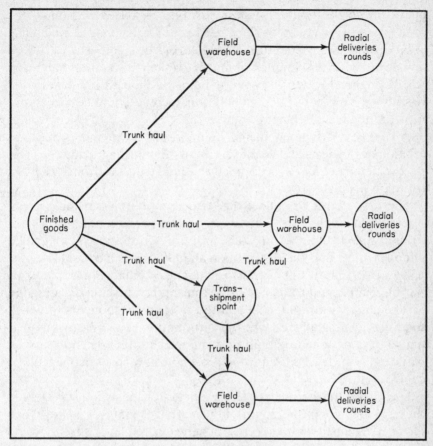

Figure 26.3   The usual pattern of systems components

by the traditional inventory control mechanism which will be mentioned later. The establishment of field warehouses consitutes a separate problem. The fewer field warehouses the lower will be the absolute establishment costs and unit cost of truck haulage; but the radical distribution costs will shoot up. There will be an upper limit to the area that a field warehouse can cope with, so there will be a minimum number of warehouses the network can get away with.

Order processing is both an establishment cost in the total systems cost, and also a factor which can add to the lead time in the replenishment of stock levels. This factor has received a lot of computer specialists' attention, and the higher establishment cost of order processing by computer is often justified by the reduction in the order processing component of the overall systems lead time. The cost of trunk haulage per unit of payload can be significantly affected downwards by transshipment, but there is then the counter balancing cost of higher inventories held at field warehouses because of the resulting longer lead times. In addition, increased handling costs are incurred for transshipment points.

It is this constant balancing of opposing costs and benefits in relation to the desired level of service on the one hand, and the level of investment in inventories on the other, that constitutes the distribution problem.

The first step is to collect the costs and volumes of the present system, allocating costs to the various systems components. This is straight-forward, but at this stage a future information flow must be established, so that the distribution audit becomes a continuing process and is regularly updated with changing cost and volume patterns. It is then important to spend a little time at the outset in deciding the best breakdown of total cost and the systems components to which costs are to be allocated. As the information flow progresses over time a data base will be built up from which forecasts and seasonal patterns can be traced in addition to a whole new series of operational control ratios.

Having established what the present system costs in total are and the cost per component, this information is only of value when matched against two major criteria – the desired level of service and the alternative methods available, i.e. the central core of physical distribution.

Optimum level of service

No physical distribution system can simultaneously maximise customer service and minimise distribution costs. An increase in the level of service will increase the cost of the service, but the total bill is not known because companies typically lack centralised management and accountancy checks on the cost of distribution. As the level of service improves and costs more, the level of inventories should decrease and cost less. Rarely does anyone know this with any degree of accuracy. As inventories are reduced, the chances of being out of stock become more probable, given normal demand, and highly likely if demand shifts upwards.

Service levels are normally computed in days in transit between receipt of replenishment order at the finished goods store, to receipt of merchandise at the field warehouse. Although the problem of setting realistic and economically viable service levels is central to effective physical distribution, not a lot of work has been done in this field, except that with a heavily mathematical and statistical basis. Some simple rules of thumb can be given to help in the decision making, but basically one has to set a service level, see what effect this has on inventory level effect, and so on. So many factors, which cannot be quantified, go into the problem of setting service levels that scientific techniques are often invalidated.

Basically, service levels should correlate closely with customer demand. If an improvement in service level produces an improvement in sales, clearly the level of service improvement is a critical part of the distribution system. It has been suggested, however, that the relationship of service level to customer demand is very much akin to the life cycle of a product. Between a low level and a high level of service, customer response is more than proportional to the betterment of the service level. Beyond a high level and below a low level of service, customer response is less than proportional, as in Figure 26.4.

A high level of service is required if the product is highly priced or of such a nature that the customer will not wait for the product to be ordered. In such a case a sale will be lost and the stock out cost will be high. This brings up again the nature of the product and the product buying patterns. Two other features should be borne in mind when setting service levels. Consistency is required in both the order processing stage and in the actual goods in transit stage. The field warehouse supervisor has got to be able to rely wholly on the predetermined service level being maintained. Sudden flashes of brilliance when impossible service levels are achieved, followed by a run of failures to maintain the level can be disastrous to the system. When this erratic state of affairs develops one finds people along the system starting to build their own safety margins into inventory levels and reordering, with the result that demand gets out of hand.

In a multiproduct company, assessing the effect on customer demand of improved service levels will invariably show that products require different levels of service. This will come as no surprise and is known as the '80:20' rule meaning that 80 per cent of the revenue

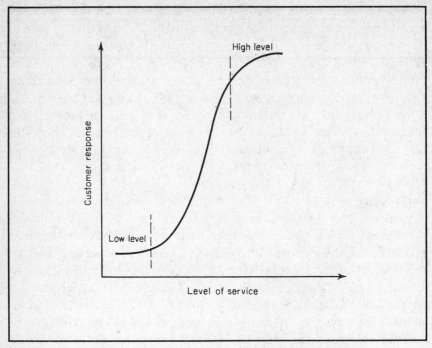

Figure 26.4   Customer response less than proportional

comes from sales of 20 per cent of the product line. The same problem will be found in industries making both original equipment and replacement products. Replacements will require a much tighter level of service than the original equipment. Figure 26.5 sets out the usual optimisation model, well known in inventory control theory, where two conflicting factors lead to an optimum point in the total problem.

Transport cost is shown set against service level, showing that as service levels lengthen cost decreases. But the tighter the service level the lower the stock out cost, and as service levels lengthen the stock out costs grow rapidly. The total cost is shown as a U-shaped curve, from which the level of service giving a minimum total cost can be found. The two main components of this model, the cost of transport and the stock out costs, can be separately analysed to show the options available for different transport modes, different inventory levels and different cost levels. Whatever the standard of service set, consistency of service is utterly critical, so much so that data should be

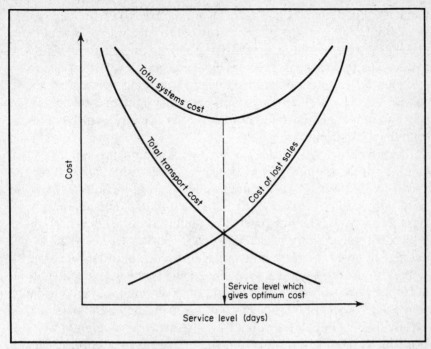

Figure 26.5 Two conflicting factors lead to an optimum point in the total problem

kept of the number, and reasons, for service failures. This information will be invaluable when the time comes to review the distribution system.

Inventory control problems

Inventories are held to level out the peaks and troughs of customer demand. If stocking to peak demand a sale will never be lost, but the investment in inventories will be high. On the other hand, to reduce the stock level means a lower investment in inventories, but a higher probability of lost sales through stock out. Inventory control techniques have been one of the major areas of development in management science over the past 45 years; consequently, there is a vast literature on the subject ranging from the highly mathematical to simple outlines of the problem.

The inventory model can be applied to many other business problems where there is a fluctuating demand for services or productive capacity, and a time lag in producing more services to meet increased demand. In this section the inventory control technique is applied to the warehouse problem of satisfying fluctuating demand with the knowledge that there is a restocking lead time (level of service to be taken into account). From this angle of satisfying customer demand within a level of service constraint, inventory control is being used to satisfy a management objective, i.e. is a service level which conforms to a cost constraint.

The inventory model is concerned with minimising (a) the cost of holding stock, (b) the cost of procuring replenishments and (c) the cost of being out of stock. Stock-holding costs include many fixed costs which do not vary directly with the unit of stock, i.e. rent, heat, light and wages. The only costs that should be considered are those which will be directly affected by the decision to keep stock, i.e. capital involved, interest on capital, insurance and depreciation.

Procurement costs are also part fixed and part variable, and it is the part that varies directly with the unit of stock that is to be considered here. The stock out costs can vary depending upon whether an unsatisfied customer takes his business away permanently or temporarily. If the former, the cost is the lost profit on all future sales; if the latter the profit on the lost sale. Unless the customer and the extent of his business can be identified and quantified one usually assumes the sale is only temporarily lost. Operational research textbooks will show that the inventory problem can be brought down to:

Cost per unit of=cost of buying+cost of holding +Average time
inventory   one unit   one unit in stock   in stock

This model is optimised (by using the calculus) and becomes:

$$\frac{\text{Minimum}}{\text{stock units}} = \sqrt{\frac{2 \times \text{Units per time period} \times \text{Cost of ordering batch}}{\text{Cost of stock holding per unit} \times \text{Time period}}}$$

This is the well-known economic lot size formula attributed to F.W. Harris when he carried out his analysis into inventory holding costs and manufacturing set up costs in 1915.

To interpret the inventory model one can immediately see that if demand doubles it is not necessary to double the stock quantity. The minimum number of stock units increases as the cost of buying increases, i.e. larger units are ordered for fewer orders placed. The minimum number of stock units decreases as the stock holding cost increases.

The problems of inventory levels, reordering quantities and variable service levels can be handled by a knowledge of techniques such as inventory control. It is, however, unwise to treat these models as more than a basis for decisions. They have to be supplemented with experience and judgement. Slavish use of formula can produce answers which are theoretically correct but are, in fact, not always practicable.

Transport options

The physical distributor has a wide range of modes of transport to select from, and the transport industry is constantly producing new services in attempts to provide better services. The primary problem is not so much the selection of the best mode as the mix of modes providing the most effective service at the optimum cost. Many companies stick slavishly to one mode of transport because they have either a large investment in, say, road vehicles and vehicle maintenance facilities, or because they have always traditionally used one mode.

Basically, the manufacturer has the following facilities to draw on:

(a)   his own road vehicles;
(b)   contract hire vehicles;
(c)   parcels and small freight operators;
(d)   road haulage operators;
(e)   railways;
(f)   canals;
(g)   post office deliveries, and
(h)   air freight operators.

Within any of these modes various handling systems can be utilised to speed up handling, maintain security and reduce costs of packaging and labelling. These handling systems are basically pallets or containers ranging from small lockable metal boxes and wire cages to the full-size freightliner container. It was pointed out earlier that the cost of transport curve could be reanalysed in relation to the level of service and the mode adopted. Figure 26.6 shows this cost curve broken down by three modes.

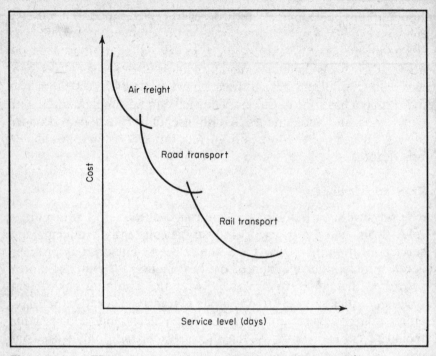

Figure 26.6   The cost curve broken down by three modes

For a very high level of service at high cost, air freight starts the curve; at a lower level of service and cost road transport appears, and at a lower level still of service, and cost rail transport is seen. It must be noted that there is an 'envelope' effect where each mode overlaps, and the balance between the overlapping modes is the correct theoretical method of transport to select. The physical characteristics of the various methods have to be taken into account. Air freight has to be collected and delivered to the air cargo sheds; rail traffic has to be taken to the depot unless a private siding is used. Road traffic starts at the consignor's premises and goes straight through to the consignee, but is subject to traffic congestion. Rail and air transport covers a long distance faster but suffers from the collection and delivery aspects at both ends of the journey. Freightliner containers start and finish at terminals where the heavy handling equipment is situated. It must be added that services exist both to collect and deliver, into and out of rail and freightliner terminals either by the customer himself or the operators of the system.

The prime factor in the selection of transport modes is really the degree of control the consignor has over his shipments especially with regard to loss during transit. Control can either be inherent in the system or an integral part of the system. When one posts a letter there is a fairly high probability that it will be delivered given that it is posted at an official postbox and correctly addressed. Control is inherent in the system. Control is part of the system when one uses one's own motor vehicle. Transport systems outside the consignor's own business adopt various methods of ensuring control; not many, however, are very successful and almost all control mechanisms concentrate on a system of finding the goods once they are lost.

In some systems a receipted dispatch note is returned to the consignor when goods have been delivered. It is hard to see what system of control would work with complete success. It is most probably this dilemma which brought about the phenomenal upsurge in the number of private goods vehicles in operation.

Many parcels and small freight and other road hauliers are offering 'total distribution' services in an effort to integrate their own distribution with the customers' networks. Some of these operators offer warehousing, stock control facilities, stock picking, labelling and packaging services. The total distribution concept works in the following fashion. Bulk loads are picked up at the originating point, be it factory or finished goods warehouse. These bulk loads are trunked to selected distribution points and taken into stock. Deliveries are made to, say, retailers on the orders of the owner of the stocks, the haulier keeping simple in/out stock records and advising the owner of the stock balances. Control is fairly good in this system and provided good communications exist between the producer and the transport operator savings accrue to both parties.

The benefits to an overseas producer who wishes to rapidly set up a distribution in this country are obvious. The benefit of using a transport organisation's distribution system is that the manufacturer retains his own sales force and maintains his marketing effort, ensuring sales volume at a higher level. This can only be alternatively achieved with a company distribution system, where a high level of fixed costs have to be borne. Before the total distribution concept the alternative to the company system was the use of wholesalers. Again, fixed costs were avoided, but a wholesaler's sales never achieved the higher levels, where real profits were made.

In selecting the mode of transport certain decision criteria must be kept in mind. There are 10 critical factors which are speed of transit, reliability of transit, prompt availability of vehicles, security, minimum loss of goods, minimum damage of goods, price per unit of consignment, control over consignments, availability of proof of delivery and geographical limitations on service. Four major factors are uppermost in the transport user's mind when he comes to consider the mode to use – speed of transit, reliability of transit, prompt availability of vehicles and price per unit of consignment.

Consignments overseas require special attention. Shipping either by surface or air has become a complex problem because of the customs regulations and shipping practices built up over the years. The company that has no shipping department with specialised staff is well advised to use one of the many shipping and forwarding agents who will arrange the collection and delivery to the ship or aircraft, including the preparation of necessary documentation. Air cargo agents are again important because of their consolidation arrangements with airline operators. The agent operates a bulk load agreement with a particular airline and can pass on to an individual shipper a rate lower than he would be able to obtain from an airline direct. This consolidation arrangement is similar to a groupage scheme operated for shipping containers by hauliers, especially on short sea routes to Eire and the continent.

The central problem in the choice of transport methods is between operating one's own vehicle fleet, or using an outside haulier. The acid test of a haulier's service is the four factors previously mentioned, speed, availability, reliability and price. Availability not only means prompt collections, it also means collections at the end of the day. In order to complete their collections, hauliers have to call no later than a time which enables them to return to their depot in time for the merchandise to catch the trunk vehicle. An outside haulier therefore has to keep to a 'cut-off' time but the owner of a fleet does not. There is a sales value or prestige to operating one's own vehicles in the company's livery which is missing when one uses an independent haulier, and a certain value must flow from the relationship between a company driver and the customer, again missing when one uses an outside haulier.

In using an independent haulier the risk is run of having one's merchandise mixed with other incompatible products. Drums of oil can leak onto carpets for instance. But these are points the good haulier recognises and tries hard to control. It is usual for independent hauliers to limit their liability for claims for loss and damage. In this respect many claims would never arise if the consignor took a little more care over packaging, labelling and so on. Too much responsibility, in many instances, is thrust on to the haulier for protecting the consignor's goods through faulty packaging.

For all the apparent disadvantages, the manufacturer benefits from the competitive rates, cost savings and capital investment offered by a professional haulier. The fixed or standing costs of a vehicle are considerable. Maintenance costs are also high, both because of the costs of materials and labour, and also because of the increasing standards of maintenance laid down by the law. Qualified heavy goods vehicle drivers are rapidly becoming scarce and, as with every other scarce resource, greater economic utilisation will have to be used. The manufacturer using vehicles which can be operated by drivers without heavy goods vehicle licences probably achieves a great cost saving and an increase in efficiency for low cost per unit movements in the immediate factory locality. The long-distance movements could be contracted out to an independent haulier. This may raise charges, but the total cost of the system is the main concern.

Vehicle and delivery control

The problems of vehicle utilisation and control have been the main concern of transport managers for years, but while techniques have been devised and skills developed, the environment has developed against the transport operator. Towns are nearly at a point of total standstill through congestion; one breakdown on a major motorway sets up a chain reaction out of all proportion to the cause.

Where the transport problem is a straight job of servicing several detail points from a set of stock-keeping points, linear programming and the transportation model have been developed to a high degree of sophistication. One is left with problems of inventory control and vehicle capacities to be solved. Where the problem is one of multi-drops of retailers scattered over a wide area, with the vehicle working out of a fixed depot location, the problem becomes vast and complex. Vehicles are usually allotted 'rounds' and the transport manager is faced with scheduling his vehicles in such a way that there are the right number of rounds to cover the area to a standard of service consistent with the number of vehicles in the fleet. Additionally, he has the constant worry of getting the most work out of his fleet in the face of rising costs.

Vehicle scheduling is another problem that has occupied operational research workers, with little success. Militating against a mechanical or mathematical solution to the scheduling problem is the one-way street system and other traffic control devices. Delivery rounds are also affected by changes in the workload of vehicles, and drivers by the shifts in location of business. Shops open up and close down, industrial estates are set up which means a continual revision of rounds and, therefore, vehicle rescheduling is needed. There is a method of scheduling vehicles which sets a vehicle payload, defines the journey route and sets a driver work performance. This method is called 'Serpent' and can be attributed to the Operations Research Department of the British Railways Board. The journey is circular so that the driver does not cross his path or retrace his previous journey; the system takes account of hazards such as one-way streets, railways, canals or dead ends. The 'Serpent' round-revision technique has to be designed for an individual locality and is, by necessity, manual. In setting workload standards the number of drops to typical consignment sizes have to be taken into account, as well as the average weight of a drop. The mileage to be covered before the first drop is made is important in connection with the total driver's hours worked.

Financial options – buy, hire or lease

There has been a rapid growth in the vehicle hire market and the transport manager must be aware of the financial options this facility opens to him. The use of one mode of transport must always be weighed against the use of another in financial terms and one often hears the term 'trade off' being used. In the case of air freight, for example, while a better level of service for a higher cost over, say, sea freight is found, this extra cost can be traded off against a cost saving. In the case of air freight one might well pay 16 per cent more in actual freight charges over the sea freight charges, but can make an 18 per cent saving in packaging cost. In making the hiring decision one is first of all influenced by the capital saving. Transport becomes a revenue matter, and capital can be released for more profitable projects. An added influence are the fixed cost savings and the maintenance cost savings. Mention has already been made of the difficulty in securing drivers which the contract hire device helps. The traditional break-even chart in Figure 26.7 illustrates the problem.

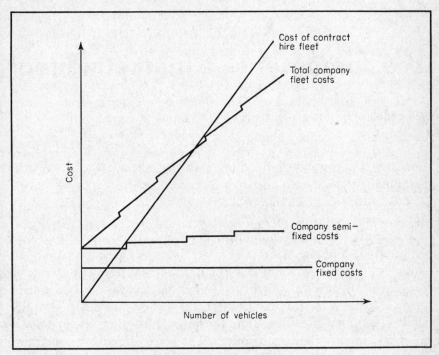

Figure 26.7   The traditional break-even chart

The contract hirer has his capital cost and fixed costs to recoup. It would therefore be naïve to imagine the hired fleet will cost less than one's own fleet; the hirer gets his pay off more in capital terms and convenience. There could well be a stage before the break-even point is reached where absolute savings could be made, and even at the break-even point, where the costs of a hired fleet and an owned fleet are equal, the hirer still has the capital and convenience benefits.

27

The computer as a marketing tool

Alan Melkman, Managing Director, Marketing Dynamics Ltd

Computers are good at handling information. They can store it, manipulate it, analyse it and then regurgitate it in a variety of forms. This is fortunate, since one of the basic tools of marketing and sales management is information.

Unfortunately, many marketing decisions are made on too little information and the data that is available is often not analysed sufficiently well. For example, sales forecasting is frequently a totally judgemental exercise with little substantial analysis carried out to provide a basis for forecasts. Often the reason for this is that the analysis is both difficult and time consuming. Another case in point is when a company changes its prices. The price effect on net margins and profit is rarely worked out because it is necessary to take into account product mix as well as off-invoice discounts enjoyed by customers. This is usually a complex and tedious task.

Until very recently, marketing and sales executives had very little help available to assist in managing their information handling requirements. Many organisations use computers mainly for order processing, accounting, stock control and other administrative functions. The information received by the marketing department is generally a spin off from the main administrative system. Many marketing managers have tried with varying degrees of success to get the computer to produce information more specific to their needs. Generally this is a very lengthy process involving the DP/finance department which controls the computer and it has, according to a recent survey, frustrated many a marketing man.

Fortunately these problems can now be overcome. The developments in computing during the 1970s and the impact of the microchip now mean that both the techniques and equipment are available, at low cost, to enable the marketing man to use the computer as a practical tool in carrying out his job. The main benefit from all these new developments is that the marketing executive, as the user of the required information, can now have direct control over the computer. He can, therefore, very easily determine what information he wants, making sure that he gets what he wants, when he wants it, in a form that means something to him and which he can actually use. The challenge for the marketing man lies in understanding the changes and then using them to advantage.

CHANGES IN COMPUTING

There have been a number of significant developments in computing which mean that computers:

(a) are less costly;
(b) are easier to use; and
(c) can communicate via the telephone network.

Each of these developments has a direct impact on the use of computers in marketing so it is important to understand them, at least in outline.

The cost of computing

The dramatic reduction in cost of the basic computer circuitry means that computer systems are now available for only a few hundred pounds. Unfortunately, such small systems are unlikely, as yet, to meet the needs of the marketing manager. A working system of sufficient power to be of real practical help will cost between £5,000–£8,000 or about half the annual cost of an average salesman. As computer costs continue to fall, and salesmen continue to become more expensive, the relative cost of computers will be even lower.

Computers come in three sizes. Small computers, costing less than about £15,000, are called microcomputers. As they increase in size, power and versatility, they are called minicomputers and range in price from £10,000 to £100,000. The largest computers, generally costing over £100,000, are called mainframe and tend to be located in air-conditioned rooms. The silicon chip is having an impact throughout the range and means greater computer power is available at the same cost, or the same power at lower cost. As a result, whether he has his own microcomputer or merely access to a larger mini or mainframe, the marketing executive now has available the computing power he needs at a price he can afford to pay.

Ease of use

The advent of interactive computing has made the computer much easier to use because it enables the user to communicate directly with the computer via a terminal with either printer or TV screen. The user can carry out a dialogue with the computer receiving back messages which help tell him what he should do. The jargon used by computer experts to describe these systems is 'user friendly'. Generally, the more 'user friendly' the systems are, the easier they are to use, but the more limited in their breadth of application.

At its simplest level, the computer will send prompts or questions to the terminal requesting the user to make certain inputs. For example, when the user switches on his terminal he may get the following response:

System–?

The computer is asking the user to enter the number or name of the system he wishes to use. If a valid response is typed in, the next prompt may be:

Password–?

The user must now type in a password if he is going to be allowed to use the system.

Sometimes the computer will ask specific questions which the user must answer in turn, for example:

Which sales figures do you wish to see?
Enter starting date (cannot be earlier than period 1, 1975).
Enter period (e.g. 1, 2, 3, or 4)?
Enter year (e.g. 1976)?

The degree of user friendliness is dependent on the program designer, who must give very careful consideration to it when designing his program.

Interactive computing can be of considerable help to the programmer since he can enter his program directly, receive immediate feedback from the machine on any errors and hence make corrections quickly. This greatly speeds up the writing and debugging of programs.

For the busy marketing executive, it means that he can now use the computer directly rather than always needing to go through the 'experts'.

Communication

The third significant advance has been the ease with which computers can send information to each other and to users at different geographic locations. Utilising the telephone network a user with a terminal in, say, Birmingham can link with a computer in, say, Bristol. This type of facility is used by computer bureaux, among others, offering time share facilities. In some cases communication takes place via satellite or transatlantic cable to computers in North America and elsewhere.

These networks can consist of a large number of computers and terminals all linked together and each having access to each others' information. They can be of particular value to sales and marketing operations. For example, using small microterminals, salesmen can enter their day's orders via the telephone direct into their company's computer for subsequent order processing. This eliminates the need to write out pieces of paper and send them through the post with the accompanying time delay, error and possibility of loss. Likewise regional sales offices can be linked to head offices.

USING COMPUTERS IN MARKETING

There is virtually no limit to the number of applications to which computers can be put in marketing. The only limit is that imposed by the marketing man's vision or the cost and difficulty of collecting the basic raw data. It is only possible, therefore, in this short chapter to look at a few marketing applications in outline.

Broadly, three types of computer applications are found in market-ing, although there is some overlap between them:

(a) handling and presenting marketing information;
(b) using computers as marketing/sales tools; and
(c) developing models.

Handling and presenting marketing information

Without speedy information on his market and his company's per-formance in it, the marketing manager cannot do his job effectively. Usually either computer, or manually compiled statistical reports arrive on the manager's desk which tell him how much the company sold in the preceding period, the revenue received, discounts given and so on. Information is also received from the sales force on the numbers of calls made, by area and the numbers of orders obtained as well as reports on competitor activity and other market information. In addition, information may be received on the total market from government or trade bodies and from market research.

In total this represents a tremendous volume of information of which only a fraction is generally used. The reason for wasting so much is that the task of analysing, collating and presenting the rest in a meaningful form is generally extremely time consuming. The dull-ness of the task often blunts the keenness of the intellect. Thus, although professional marketing managers would very often like additional information before making decisions, they know that the trouble in obtaining the information would not repay the benefit derived. For example, a decision may need to be taken on eliminating a product from the range. To help him make this decision the man-ager would like the following information:

1 What have been the volume and value sales of the product over the last three years, in total and as a percentage of the product group?
2 What has been the average percentage change in sales per year for the last five years for the product?
3 Who are the five largest customers for the product, how much do they buy and what would be the effect on their turnover?
4 How much profit has the product contributed over the last three years?

All this information is likely to be available somewhere in the company. The difficulty lies in getting it, sorting through it, doing the analysis and calculations and presenting it in a form that is easy to understand. This problem can be solved by setting up a marketing data base on computer. For all but the most complex of marketing information needs, a microcomputer or small minicomputer can be used.

Typically these systems operate as shown in Figure 27.1. The basic information is stored in a number of files on magnetic disc.

The user enters his information requests via a keyboard and the relevant items of information are extracted from the appropriate files, analysed and an output report produced. The way the files are set up is crucial to the success of the system and considerable care must be taken.

The ease of use and flexibility of these types of systems varies. For example, if a product manager wished to obtain a listing of all trade promotions on his product range costing more than £1,000, the date of commencement of each promotion and the additional sales achieved, then the instruction to be entered by his secretary or himself might read:

List proms by buy-in sales cost where cost GT 1000

The product manager would then receive a chronological list of all promotions.

Although the simple instructions are written in English, they obey special syntax rules and a two/three day training programme is needed if the user is to be able to write such programs.

To overcome this possible problem, specific marketing data base packages have been designed which are very simple to use. For example, the promotions information would be requested by answering a series of questions from the computer:

Which products do you want to consider?
What is the earliest buy-in period?
What is the latest buy-in period?
What is the minimum promotion cost?
What is the maximum promotion cost?
Which of the following do you wish printed out (Enter Y/N):
Product code?
Product name?

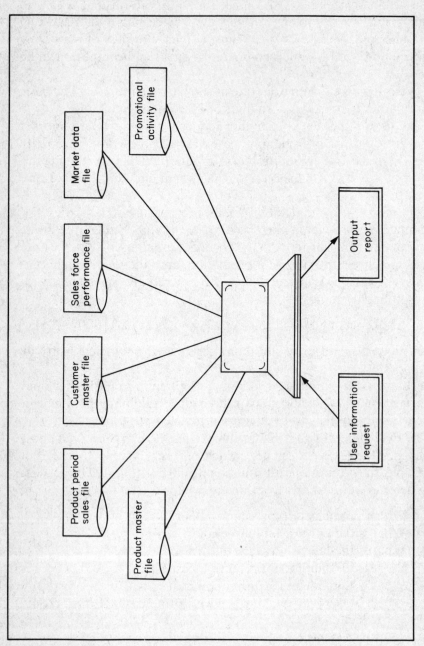

Figure 27.1 Marketing database

Pack size?
Volume sold?
Buy-in date?
End date?
Promotion cost?

Each question would be asked and answered in turn. The computer is, therefore, being used to help the marketing manager utilise the considerable amount of available information and in turn improve the quality of the decisions made. Such systems dramatically reduce the vast amount of paper the manager receives and ensure he gets only what he wants, when he wants it. It is significant that the marketing man needs no knowledge of how computers work or complicated languages to work these systems.

Although some companies will want to develop complete marketing data bases, others may wish to set up one aspect at a time. For example, they may first set up a market information data base, then a sales performance one and so on, gradually linking them together. One particular application which has proved very useful is in market research. By setting the survey results up on a data base, the user can easily obtain whatever additional information he wants after he has received the research report.

Using computers as marketing sales tools

As well as handling and presenting market information the computer can assist in carrying out a large number of day-to-day marketing tasks. In this section we look at nine application areas. This list is very far from being exhaustive but serves to indicate the range and scope of the available tools.

Price list updating. The process of regularly updating their price lists is, for many companies, a long and tedious process. Each new price must be calculated, appropriate discounts considered and the resulting price judged against that of other products in the range to ensure differentials are maintained. During inflationary times the frequency with which price lists must be updated increases and some organisations, like wholesalers and other distributors, often do it monthly.

The computer is used to carry out the necessary calculations and quickly produces the new price list. The logic of a typical system is

339

shown in Figure 27.2, which gives the user the facility to update all, or just part, of his price list, on either an individual, percentage or absolute basis. Having calculated the new prices the user can vet them and change any which are unacceptable before the new price list is printed. The system can be extended to show the effect on sales value at budgeted (or any other) volume of sales, and even the impact on gross and net margins and profit at a variety of different prices.

The computer is, therefore, being used to take the drudgery out of a time-consuming task and greatly speed it up. It can then be extended to give management additional useful information to help decide on the most appropriate price levels.

Direct mail. Whether on a selective product offer, or to announce a general price increase, most companies use direct mail to communicate to the market. By storing names and addresses on computer, the laborious job of typing them out can be eliminated.

In many instances the message that the marketer wishes to communicate will be of interest only to a segment of the total list. For example, a car dealer may want to mail all customers who purchased new cars of less than 1,600 cc. from him three to five years ago with invitations to test drive new 2000 cc. models. Or a manufacturer of agricultural equipment may wish to notify all dairy farmers with a herd of more than 100 cows of a particular new bolt-on attachment to their milking parlours.

The facility to access subsegments of the total list saves both time and money, as well as improving response rates. If the computer also has on it a word processing package then it will also be able to compile personalised letters to each potential customer, as well as type the envelopes.

This type of application is very straightforward and numerous well tried packages are on the market. Generally they can be run on an inexpensive microcomputer, although a good quality printer is needed to produce well typed letters.

Word processing. A word processing machine is merely a dedicated microcomputer, that is a microcomputer which is designed and programmed to do only one thing, namely store, retrieve and manipulate text. This is a very useful facility since it allows documents such as quotations, which are substantially the same for each customer, to be produced quickly with suitable amendments to meet the needs of

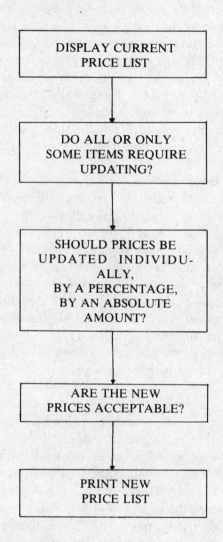

┌─────────────────────┐
│   DISPLAY CURRENT   │
│   PRICE LIST   │
└─────────────────────┘

┌─────────────────────┐
│ DO ALL OR ONLY   │
│ SOME ITEMS REQUIRE │
│   UPDATING?   │
└─────────────────────┘

┌─────────────────────┐
│ SHOULD PRICES BE   │
│ UPDATED INDIVIDU-   │
│   ALLY,   │
│ BY A PERCENTAGE,   │
│ BY AN ABSOLUTE   │
│   AMOUNT?   │
└─────────────────────┘

┌─────────────────────┐
│   ARE THE NEW   │
│ PRICES ACCEPTABLE? │
└─────────────────────┘

┌─────────────────────┐
│   PRINT NEW   │
│   PRICE LIST   │
└─────────────────────┘

Figure 27.2   Updating a price list

each customer. Substantial savings in time and staff in a busy sales office can be made by computerising routine typing functions of this nature.

Many micro and minicomputers have available a word processing package which can be loaded into the machine as and when it is required. This can have a number of advantages over a dedicated word processor in terms of linking in with the rest of the marketing system. For example, if customer records are stored on computer, then the customer's address can automatically be looked up after the name is entered and, therefore, it does not need to be manually typed in. Also the customer record file will automatically be updated to show a quotation has been sent, the value of the quotation and the product quoted.

One standard application for a word processor is that of producing reports. The marketing man can produce as many drafts as he likes since report updating and editing are easy to carry out.

Planning, budgeting and forecasting. Some time before the end of their financial year, most companies go through the process of trying to forecast their sales and costs for the following year and drawing up plans and budgets. The amount of 'number crunching' that must be carried out is enormous and there is rarely the opportunity (or the inclination) to try a number of possible projections to assess the most desirable. The computer can take a lot of the hard work out of budgeting, make them much easier to revise and greatly speed up the process.

The starting point for the budget is the sales forecast which is prepared by using statistical techniques and/or by getting the sales staff and marketing management to guestimate future sales. A number of good forecasting packages exist using statistical methods such as exponential smoothing, classical decomposition, generalised adaptive filtering and Box-Jenkins. One particular program, 'Sibyl Runner', helps the user to choose which of the available statistical forecasting methods are suitable for his data and then runs the appropriate method. This enables the marketing man to run a number of methods and the computer will work out which is the most accurate. He can then choose the most appropriate to use for his forecasts.

The user needs to know very little about the actual statistics and even less about computers. The programs are 'user friendly' and all the user has to do is answer a series of questions. For example:

xxxSIA time sharing servicexxx
xinteractive forecasting packagex
Good morning
Need held – (yes/no/recover/change)
? yes
Help: The interactive forecasting system is divided into two segments. The first segment, referred to as 'Sibyl' analyses data, suggests appropriate forecasting methods. The second, 'Runner' can be used alone or after 'Sibyl'. It runs any forecasting methods, stores the results on a file and compares different methods. However, you can run the programs individually too.
Do you want to use:
(a)   Program data (40 obs)?
(b)   Your own data, in a file?
(c)   Your own data, to be typed in at a terminal?
(d)   Data generated by the program?
?2   What is the name of your data file?
?   Tony

Communicating with the market. Prestel/Viewdata is a British invention that provides a means of bringing the home or business directly into contact with an almost limitless range of information. This public service, operated by the GPO, has information stored in the form of a data base on a network of computers, which can be accessed through an adapted TV set via the telephone network. The user accesses the system by using a keypad rather like an electronic calculator.

A buyer who wants to buy a washing machine, for example, could use Prestel to help him. He would first want to get some impartial advice on the machines available and would, therefore, summon the consumer's advice magazine *Which*. The relevant sections would be displayed on the screen and the buyer would decide which he felt were worth further consideration. The customer would then want to know who stocked the machines and their cost. He would then summon Comet Warehouses, Curry's etc. each of whom would have their latest price lists on display. He could then choose which supplier offered the best deal and even, in some cases, make a purchase by entering his credit card number. The supplier would then check his credit status and arrange delivery.

It is significant that so far the customer need not have left his armchair. Prestel, therefore, provides an additional communication and purchasing channel to the consumer which must be carefully considered by the supplier. It gives the consumer added information and the facility to compare alternative offerings, while giving the supplier the means to get directly to the customer when that customer is actually making up his mind on what he wants to buy.

Communicating with the sales force. Prestel can also be used to send information to the salesmen in their homes. This can be done via a facility called a 'closed user group'. Only users with special adapations on their TV sets and knowledge of special passwords can get into a closed user loop. If, for example, only first line sales managers have this facility then information of, say, their sales teams' performance can be beamed to them at the end of each day in the knowledge that no one else will be able to gain access to it (see figure 27.3).

Typically, the sales manager wants to know how many calls have been made, orders obtained, particular product sales, particular account sales and so on. The information can be analysed and presented by the computer in the form most useful to the managers. The basic information on the salesman's performance is obtained from the salesmen themselves who enter it direct into their company's computer using remote entry microterminals. The keypads are not too dissimilar to the Prestel keypads and link directly into the telephone lines.

The main advantages of the system are that it speeds up the transmission of orders from the customer, hence expediting cash flow and getting information to sales management quickly. This is turn enables managers to take action promptly to overcome problems and redirect sales effort.

Sales force reporting and control. To keep their management informed salesmen usually do a lot of paperwork. Typically this includes daily reports, weekly reports, order forms, customer records and so on. These reports are then analysed to ensure that the salesman is directing his effort appropriately and identifying any significant problems. This analysis can be done using a computer as shown in Figure 27.4.

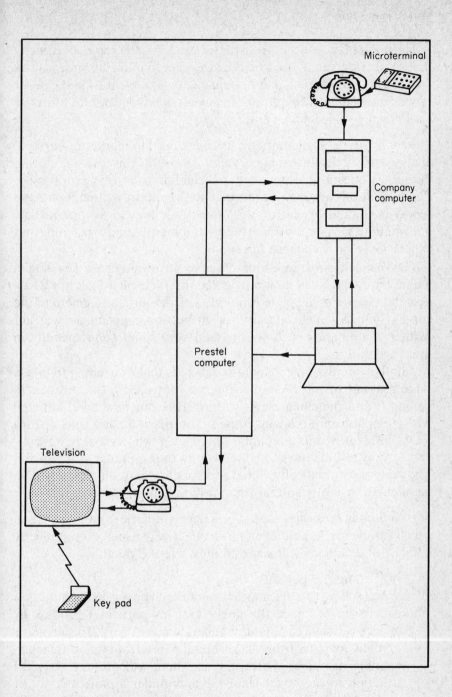

Figure 27.3 A closed user group

The input may be either from the salesman's daily report or directly from a microterminal used by the salesman to enter his orders. The system can, therefore, either be separate or a spin-off from the order processing system. The output can be sent in tabular printout form or via Prestel to sales management.

Market research. The computer has been used in market research to analyse survey results for many years. Typically, this involves getting the survey questionnaires coded, punched onto cards and processed. The tabulations are then produced and the report written. Once the report is studied by the user it often leads him to ask for further information. Using traditional methods it is both time consuming and expensive to answer these questions.

This problem is virtually eliminated by setting up the survey data in a data base which can be interrogated interactively to get out whatever data, in whatever form is required. Thus, any subsegment of the survey sample which, after initial inspection, appears to warrant further examination, can be analysed very simply and speedily in greater detail.

Another problem faced by researchers is that of needing to take a large amount of information from the interview forms, editing it, coding it and punching it onto cards. This can now be eliminated when telephone interviewing is used. The questionnaire is set up on a VDU in front of the telephone interviewer who types the respondent's reply to each question directly into the computer as it is given. The reply is automatically edited and if incorrect or illogical it will be highlighted instantly so that the question can be asked again.

The computer as a sales tool. The salesman carries out many tasks which can be carried out even more effectively using a computer. A number of examples will serve to illustrate the point.

(a) Selling the benefits
When selling to a distributor or industrial buyer, many salesmen will try to convince the buyer that his particular product or service will save costs and/or generate more profit. This happens in many markets from oil to capital plant, from toilet tissues to vending machines. Often the salesman will present a typical situation to the buyer, showing how under a particular set of circumstances the product produces a certain cost saving or level

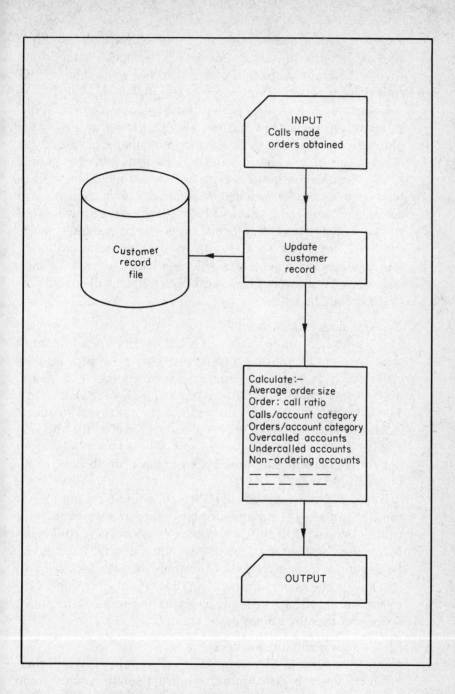

Figure 27.4   Reporting and control system

of profit. Unfortunately, the particular example is usually a generalised one and each customer's particular situation is slightly different. The computer can help the salesman in this case present his arguments even better.

For example, the salesman of filtration equipment for lubricating oils to be used in machine shops will want to justify the purchase of his products by showing how they can extend the useable life of machine oil and thus save money. He merely needs to make a note of the particular customer's method of operation, recording such details as number of machine tools of each type, work load, value of lubricating oil used, type of oil storage facility etc. This information is sent back to head office where the computer works out the most economical solution to the customer's problem. The salesman can then, on his next visit, show the customer how must better off he will be and how much money he will save.

(b) Reducing routine work

Many salesmen, selling through retail outlets, spend much of their time merchandising the shelves. Where the products are bulky, such as toys, soft drinks, paper products and so on, making an attractive display can be extremely time consuming. The salesman must take into account the particular products stocked by the outlet, the particular dimension of the shelving and the actual rate of sale in the store. These factors vary from outlet to outlet and generalised planograms of displays are often of little relevance.

By feeding the appropriate information into the computer, it can design the most suitable display and print a simple plan of which items should be put where and how many there should be. It can also list the cost of the display and the profit it produces. By getting a second computer printout for a display, say, two feet longer, the clever salesman can show the store manager how much extra profit will be made by giving his products more shelf space and thereby obtain more facings.

(c) Customer support packages

Companies such as Ford and General Motors, who sell their products through distributors, support their distributors and help them manage their businesses more efficiently. They often help to install specific management systems and give the distributor regular management information produced on their own computer. In this way the distributor becomes more successful, sells more products, and is a better credit risk for the supplier.

(d) Salesman routing

The majority of salesman's time is spent in his car travelling between calls. This time should be kept to a minimum so that the salesman can spend as much productive time as possible in front of the buyer.

There are a number of routing packages on the market which minimise the time spent travelling. The location of each call is typed in together with the time required in front of the customers. The computer will then work out the order of calling and produce a route plan. This can then be discussed with each salesman and any necessary minor modifications made.

Developing models

Any discussion of computer applications in marketing would be incomplete without referring to market models. These applications have been developed for many years, yet are of only limited use in practice.

A model is the specification of a set of variables and their interrelationships designed to represent some real system or process in whole or in part. Thus, for example, a market model can be developed which assesses the level of sale of a particular product or product group at varying levels of price, advertising support, sales effort, etc. The models can be very complex because they can take into account a large number of variables. They are particularly useful for predicting fairly homogeneous markets such as that for potatoes, eggs or cars.

Ideally, any marketer would like a model of his market so that he can try to assess the effect of a variety of marketing policies before implementing the best. The difficulty in developing a realistic model, however, usually acts as a barrier to one being produced. There are a number of modelling packages available which reduce the development time. In general, they ask the user to suggest the variables which determine, say, the level of sales of a product. Data is entered for each of the variables and the computer works out how well the variables explain variations in the level of sales and also any correlation between the variables. By trying a number of different variables the marketer can develop the model which most accurately suits his market.

CAPITALISING ON COMPUTERS

Spotting the opportunities

This chapter has given some examples of how computers are being used in marketing. Potentially they are one of the most powerful tools available to the marketing manager. However, the applications for which they can be used are not always very obvious. Before embarking, therefore, on any computerisation programme, the marketing executive should carry out an opportunity audit to identify and rank the opportunities. The audit should examine the following:

1 How is the market going to develop over the next ten years and how is the buying process going to change?
2 How is the cost structure going to change over the next ten years?
3 What actions are the competitors likely to take?
4 What elements of the marketing mix are likely to change and in what manner?
5 In the light of the trends, what actual and potential applications are there?

> Where is there a lot of data which is currently not effectively used?
>
> Where is there a lot of paperwork which could be computerised?
>
> What analyses are carried out which require a lot of time to produce?
>
> What information would it be useful to obtain but which does not warrant the additional paperwork that is currently required?
>
> Where would speeding up the flow of information improve the quality of decision making and/or save money?
>
> Where can the offering to customers be tailored to meet

their needs even better and increase the likelihood of getting the sale?

What decisions are taken on a trial and error basis which can be improved by a systematic approach?

Where are customers using computer-based techniques and how should the supplier react?

Having systematically conducted the audit, all the potential applications should be identified and can then be ranked. A strategy for computerisation in the marketing department can then be formulated.

SUMMARY

This chapter has examined the new developments in computing, how they can be used in marketing and how the marketing man should capitalise on the opportunity they represent. Because of their breadth of application, computers are probably one of the most powerful and exciting tools that the marketer has at his disposal.

Those companies that exploit the opportunities, adopting a planned and controlled approach, will reap substantial benefits and thereby achieve an advantage over their less innovative competitors in the market place.

28

Financial control

J.E. Smith, Senior Lecturer, University of Aston in Birmingham

ATTRACTING AND USING FUNDS

Whatever the business, manufacturing or distributing, consumer products or technical products, funds are required to allow launching in the first instance, and then to permit continuity of operations. These funds have to be used effectively if the business is to survive, and so be in a position to generate or attract more funds. Looking at a business from a financial control viewpoint means first of all examining the separate aspects of fund raising and fund using.

Attracting funds to a business is not an easy matter. Capital is never in plentiful supply; it has always to be prised out of a reluctant money market and inevitably costs something to obtain. The sources of capital are many and they can be classified from a duration point of view as short term, medium term and permanent. Short-term capital is that which is attracted from the banks as overdrafts on current account or from creditors, i.e. suppliers prepared to supply materials and services on credit. Such capital is in theory immediately repayable and normally used in the business as working capital. Medium-term capital is debt capital, money borrowed from banks, financial institutions and the public, where the capital is required in the business for a longer period of time, often to purchase assets like land, buildings, plant and equipment. Permanent capital is, in the case of the limited liability company, the share capital provided by the owners which is normally kept in the business and added to by the profits made by the business and retained in it. The responsibility for finding funds for the business is often called a 'treasury' responsibility.

On the other hand, the funds are not normally sought unless someone on the operations side of the business has uses for such funds. The spending of the capital in a business is of two types:

1   Capital expenditure, i.e. spending of large amounts of the funds at particular points in time on fixed asset items such as land, buildings, plant equipment, office fixtures, fittings etc. Quite often, such spending is significant in that it alters the direction of a company's activities for years ahead.

2   Revenue expenditure, i.e. day-to-day spending on the bought-out materials and services of the trade and upon wages, salaries and the other costs associated with making products or providing services for sales.

In practice, it is usual for many managers in the business to have responsibility for the use of funds.

OPERATING STATEMENTS

One of the important financial statements, the balance sheet, depicts this aspect of raising and using funds. Examination of the balance sheet will tell one just how much capital is available in a business, where it is being used and has come from. Most important, it will indicate how much of the capital is invested in fixed assets and how much is being used as working capital. The other financial statement, the profit and loss account, looks at the business from an income point of view. It shows the sales turnover or gross income, the operating costs are deducted from this, leaving the net profit. The balance sheet and profit and loss account are statutory documents of stewardship accounting for limited liability companies, i.e. they must be submitted with an annual return to the Registrar of Companies. They are intended to give an annual account of the directors' stewardship of the shareholders' funds.

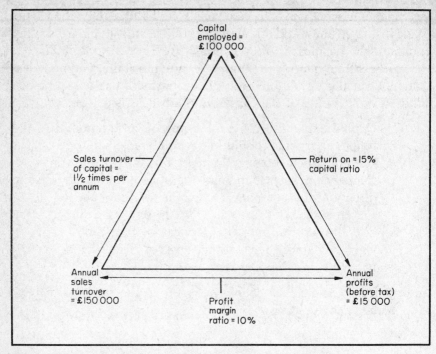

Figure 28.1   A breakdown on the return of capital

ANALYSIS OF BUSINESS PERFORMANCE

To analyse the objectives of a business is a complex matter, since so many of these objectives prove to be unquantifiable, but there is usually common agreement on the fact that some of these objectives are financial in character. The most important financial objectives are:

1   Making an adequate profit return on the resources employed in the business and in particular on the capital employed.
2   Proper balancing of cash flows in and out so that the business never runs short of funds and never has funds lying idle.

It is necessary to measure regularly the achievement of the business in these terms and this is usually done in terms of certain accounting ratios. A periodical critical examination of results by the use of ratios can be a very useful management discipline. The right starting point is an internal comparison with the previous years' results, giving a breakdown of the return on capital employed into its basic constituents, i.e. the profit margin on sales and the sales turnover of capital employed (see Figure 28.1).

Even this simple ratio analysis over a number of years will normally reveal some substantial variations as well as some consistent trends. For the marketing man, such measurements have implications. It can be readily seen that:

$$\text{Percentage return on capital} = \text{Percentage profit margin} \times \text{Sales turnover of capital}$$

with all that this implies in terms of pricing policy, either low prices to encourage volume or high prices to give a good profit margin ratio. This form of ratio analysis can be extended to relate the profit made to the fixed assets, the working capital, and the sales to the same expressions of the capital employed. Then, bearing in mind that the difference between sales turnover and profit is in operating costs, these costs can be analysed by type or function and related either to the sales turnover or to the total of operating costs. It is sound management practice, for example, to know what percentage marketing, selling and distribution costs bear to the grand total, and to keep this under regular observation. Often lines of enquiry are prompted by ratio analysis which can lead to the spotting of corrective action. Two areas of great significance in day-to-day operations of a business are stock holding or inventory levels and the amount of money owed by customers. It is as well to check the relationship of both of these figures to a suitable measurement of output, inventory levels to both production and sales and debtors to sales. This often reveals undesirable trends which have not been planned, and ought to be of interest to the marketing man.

The need might become apparent to discover whether other firms in the same industry or other industries showed different ratios and trends. This implies the possibility of the company joining in some form of interfirm comparison which is carried out by some trade associations or rather more specifically by the Centre for Inter-Firm Comparisons Ltd. The use of such comparisons and ratios is no substitute for management but it can be a very considerable aid to management.

PLANNING THE USE OF FUNDS

Capital expenditure

Capital expenditure on fixed asset items is normally so significant as to demand special planning. Procedures are necessary to attempt to stimulate the innovation which is very often the forerunner to capital expenditure, and then to ensure proper authorisation of the spending after it has been systematically evaluated. Later, control of the spending is required and finally a post-audit of the progress of the project in financial terms.

The word 'project' has been used because a company's capital expenditure budget is normally comprised of many such projects with different characteristics. A look at an annual capital expenditure budget would reveal some projects merely designed to maintain existing business, e.g. machine replacement; some which indicate extensive expansion, e.g. new products for new markets, while others would be made necessary by government legislation. Other items of capital expenditure might be directed specifically at cost saving or productivity improvement, but others might be entirely different, the acquisition of other businesses or other forms of outside investment. Clearly, capital expenditure can affect the amount of capital employed in a business and the effectiveness of it can affect the return made on that capital.

There are various methods of evaluating proposed capital investments, the simplest being the pay-back period method, in which the estimated annual cash flows (or cost savings) which arise from the project are related to the initial cash outlay to finance the project, so that it becomes clear how many years will be required to replace the capital fund. The internal rate of return method requires one to estimate the profits which will be made during the life of the project, convert these to an average annual profit, which is then related to the capital employed, to give an average rate of return. A more sophisticated yet realistic approach is afforded by the use of discounted cash flow techniques which reflect the time value of money in the appraisal.

It is important that the appraisal of capital expenditure should be carried out systematically, and that a financial analysis is made. This means estimating the capital expenditure and the cash flows that will arise from that capital expenditure. This will mean in many projects, forecasting sales and estimating the cost of those sales. This is work to be done partly by the sales organisation and needs to be treated seriously. If the capital expenditure is significant, the whole future of the business could depend upon the accuracy of the assessment of the market and the share of that market which the business can capture.

Working capital

Taking British industry in general, some 40 per cent of the funds employed in it are in use as working capital, i.e. capital basically employed in the form of stock (raw materials, work in progress and finished goods), debtors and cash. The view taken by accountants is that the last two items are liquid – in cash or readily convertible into cash – whereas the stock items have to be sold (in the case of raw materials and work-in-progress, the products still have to be made). It is not overstating the case to say that many quite profitable businesses have been wound up because of a failure to plan and control the liquid resources.

What are required are policies of stock holding, credit control and cash holding, and clearly these are relevant to, and therefore need to be set in conjunction with, the marketing manager. There the problem is not only what can be afforded from the point of view of liquid resources, but what must be aimed at in the way of stocks carried and credit terms to encourage trade and, therefore, profitability. The setting of the policies required in this area is a combined management task, and clearly this is another area in which the marketing manager has a role to play in the effective use of funds.

FINANCIAL PLANNING THROUGH BUDGETARY CONTROL

A technique often used in financial planning is that of budgetary control. This implies expressing the plans of the business in quantitative and monetary terms and then exercising control, i.e. measuring actual performance, costs and cash flows against the budget, and taking corrective action where necessary.

There are two main stages in budgetary control:

1 Deciding upon the budget period, which must be appropriate to the nature of the trade and the time of production, and then forecasting and planning activities for that period. High, yet attainable, standards of performance will be the basis of the budget.

2 Taking action and evaluating performance in the light of the plans and standards developed in the first stage.

Budgetary control is aimed at the planning and control of the overall performance of the business, costs and cash flows. The budgets required can be reviewed under three main headings, operating budgets, financial budgets and the capital expenditure budget. The two main questions which arise when preparing the operating budgets are:

1 What will be sold, in what volume and at what prices?

2 What, therefore, will need to be produced, and what should the costs of production, administration, marketing, selling and distribution be?

The sales budget deals within the first question and is often the starting point and linchpin of budgetary control procedures. This is the area in which the marketing manager will be expected to be thoroughly involved, and so he should be. The effective use of resources in the business cannot be planned without a meaningful sales budget, taking into account not only current market, customer and product aspects but also any limiting factors within the business such as control space, labour skills or bottlenecks in particular plant or equipment. Care needs to be taken in the preparation of this budget because the estimating of cash flows in and out of the business depends upon it. All operating costs in the business have to be budgeted by managers in charge of their respective budget centres, and these have to be translated into cash outflows, whereas the sales budget figures are converted into cash inflows. The accountant is essentially the person responsible for the flow of funds in the business, and he has a major responsibility for making arrangements for the availability of funds at the appropriate times. He inevitably becomes heavily involved in the plans and aspirations of other managers.

The discipline of expressing plans in quantitative and monetary form represents an invaluable exercise because managers are forced to face the future. The budgeting system can act as a coordinating device and as a means of communication. Managers become more aware of their specific roles in the business and, most important, standards of performance and cost have to be developed. The feedback of control information comparing actual performance and costs with the budgets motivates managers, reminds them of their responsibilities and prompts corrective action. If there is a danger in the use of budgetary control, it is that it is a short-period technique concentrated upon providing assistance in the control of day-to-day operations within the framework of an annual budget. Concentration on the annual budget could lead to neglect of the necessary longer-term planning. The marketing function would be largely responsible for ensuring that this did not happen.

Out of the system of budgetary control should come useful information for the marketing function, e.g. comparisons of actual sales achievement compared with budgets, all figures being analysed as appropriate to representatives, areas, customers, product groups and products. There should also be available details of all actual costs in the marketing area compared with budgets. To the extent to which some selling and distribution costs are likely to vary more or less directly with sales, there should be a 'flexible budget' for these costs, in other words, a budget based upon standard costs which can be adjusted up or down in accordance with the sales achievement.

PROFIT CENTRES

The marketing organisation may not be seen by the management accountant as a budget centre. The latter implies that the marketing manager is a budget holder responsible for the performance and costs of a part of the business against an agreed budget. This budget approach is not the only one which is used to try to instil profit orientation in managers throughout the business. A very popular approach in these times when the overall business objective seems to be an adequate return on investment is the investment centre or profit centre approach. The latter phrase will be used to imply both.

The idea of profit centre accounting is that a particular section of the business, function or department is regarded as a separate business from a profit and loss account point of view. In other words, in each trading period the overall business profit and loss account is broken down into these departments, in respect of each of which is known the sales turnover, operating costs, net profit and, in some cases, the capital employed. It is then possible to calculate the return on investment made by each of the profit centres. It is felt that a suitable measure of profit performance is needed wherever management responsibility is divided among subsidiaries, divisions and departments for such purposes as guiding the operating managers in their day-to-day control and decision making and helping top management to appraise their work.

Theoretically, the profit centre is a good idea, but it creates problems. First of all, it is not universally applicable. It is not really possible to talk about the sales income of a department that has output measurable in quantities but not in value. This is particularly true of service departments, e.g. the maintenance department in a manufacturing business. Some businesses have tried to overcome this problem by setting up a system of transfer prices, i.e. artificial selling prices for the transfer of products or services from one department to another. Several organisations treat the production department and the selling function as two separate profit centres, transferring production from the former to the latter at transfer prices. At the best, such prices can only be arbitrary, and the level at which to set them is likely to be a subject for discussion for a long time into the future. In practice, the danger in the profit centre approach is that there will be an over-concentration on the achievement of the wrong objectives. What is required in the end is not the profitability of individual profit centres but of the business as a whole.

COSTING AS AN AID

Management accounting is different from stewardship accounting. Whereas in the latter the emphasis is on year-end financial statements prepared in accordance with the Companies Acts of 1948 and 1967 for the business as a whole, the work of management accounting is directed towards measuring activities within the business and providing financial and cost information which will assist management in its day-to-day work of planning and control as well as in its decision making. Much of the work of management accounting is costing, and the objectives of costing are as follows:

1 A knowledge of what costs are incurred, which are significant, and in what locations of the business they are incurred is a pointer to cost control and a stimulant to cost reduction.
2 Cost data, particularly departmental cost rates, are required to enable cost estimating for price fixing to be accurate. The cost estimating function also requires feed-back information to assess the accuracy of its work.
3 Product cost information is required both for checking upon the adequacy of existing selling prices and also to facilitate the calculation of the relative profitability of product .
4 The planning of future operations and the setting of budgets cannot be done without information on costs in the various functions of the business and the behaviour of such costs. Feedback of actual cost information against the budgets is also needed.
5 There are so many decisions which management has to make which involve financial and cost considerations, and the cost information needs to be available.

The two primary functions in the business, production and marketing, are in need of help from the costing function.

COST ANALYSIS AND THE TECHNIQUES OF COSTING

At the outset, costing is essentially a matter of analysis. Costs have to be analysed:

(a) into materials, labour and overhead costs and into the particular items within each;
(b) by locations within the business;
(c) by product groups, products, contracts or jobs according to the production methods of the business;
(d) by those costs which vary more or less directly with the output of the business and those which remain more or less fixed.

Where one is using cost information which recognises the different proportions of variable and fixed costs, one is using a particular costing technique called marginal costing. Where cost information which is not bringing out this point of cost variability is employed, a technique called the absorption cost or total cost approach is being used.

If the business is to be profitable, the total costs of running it must be recovered (or absorbed) in the long run, but this does not mean that total cost information is the relevant information for every decision, not does it mean that every product can or should have a selling price which is greater than its normal total cost.

To look at it from a marginal cost point of view, one divides the costs between marginal or variable (with output) and fixed (irrespective of output). To do this means observing the behaviour of costs over a long period. It will probably be found that direct material costs, direct labour costs and certain overheads such as power, tools and consumable materials vary directly with output, whereas depreciation, rent and rates, salaries and the like remain relatively constant. The marginal costs are much more directly the costs of products, whereas the fixed costs tend to be period costs or policy costs.

BREAK-EVEN ANALYSIS

When the above breakdown of costs is known, a break-even chart can be prepared (see Figure 28.2).

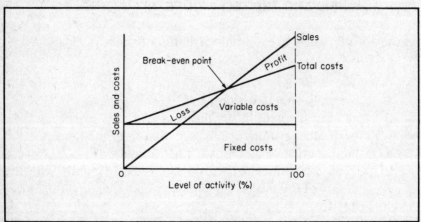

Figure 28.2   A breakdown chart of costs

This is a useful tool for costing. Plotting the levels of fixed and variable costs against sales income discloses the break-even point, the point at which neither profit nor loss is made. Above the break-even point are profits, below are losses. The break-even chart shown in the figure is an over-simplication because the lines of cost and sales are not in practice straight lines. At the very best it provides a rough guide to the profits and losses likely at different levels of activity; it is only a rough guide because it assumes a certain product mix, and this is a dangerous assumption. Consider the same chart drawn in a different way (Figure 28.3). Exactly the same basic figures are used upon which the alternative chart is drawn, but in this case the block of fixed costs has been imposed on top of the variable costs. The advantage which one obtains from this chart is that an additional measurement called 'contribution' can be gleaned from it. This is the margin left after deducting the variable costs from the sales value, and is the 'contribution to fixed costs'. When the fixed costs have been fully absorbed or recovered, then contribution becomes profit.

This is the reality of the business situation. Some of the costs of running the business are not directly related to production or the provision of services: they are the fixed or constant period costs. Profit only arises when the total contributions from the production activity exceed these constant costs, so that to maximise profit in the short term contribution has to be maximised, and this is not the same as maximising turnover.

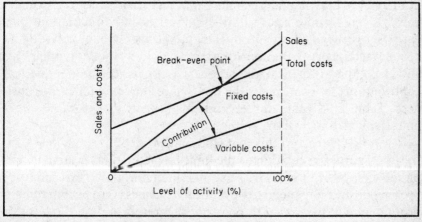

Figure 28.3   A breakdown chart of costs

PRODUCT COSTING AND PRICING

It is important for managers to have a knowledge of what products cost to make, sell and distribute either as an aid to the fixing of selling prices for those products or in order that the relative profitability of different products can be calculated. This is basically marketing information. Once again the approach to calculating product costs can be on a total or marginal cost basis.

The total cost of a product is the sum of materials, labour and overhead costs of that product. It is not usually too difficult to calculate the direct materials and direct labour costs of products: the problem is normally with the indirect materials, indirect labour and expense items which comprise the overhead costs. A common practice is to collect these overhead costs according to function or department in the business and then calculate cost rates by which they can be absorbed into the costs of products. This involves the apportionment of many items of cost, notably the fixed costs on what are at the best, arbitrary bases. It also means that cost rates calculated for individual departments are based upon the costs for a period related to the departmental activity for that period, so that inevitably the 'total cost' of a product only holds good at a certain level of output and contains arbitrary apportionments of certain costs. In this respect, it is no more than a rough guide as a basis for price fixing.

The marginal cost of a product is much easier to compute, comprising only the directly attributable variable costs. In this way apportionments are avoided. The marginal cost of a product normally comprises the prime costs of direct materials and direct labour plus variable overheads. If the product marginal cost is deducted from the product selling price, the contribution the product makes is apparent, and a good way of ranking products is to relate their individual contributions to whatever is the limiting resource factor in the business. Table 28.1 ranks three products made from the same direct material which is in short supply.

It will be clear from this example that product C is the best contribution earner in relation to the limiting factor. This is an oversimplified example but will serve to make the point that assessments of product profitability need to be made if a business is to be and remain profitable, and they need to be made accurately and on the basis of cost information which is relevant.

Table 28.1 Three products made from material in short supply

	Direct material cost	Direct labour cost	Variable overhead cost	Marginal cost	Sales price	Contribution	Contribution as percentage of material cost
Product A (£)	100	50	100	250	300	50	50
Product B (£)	80	50	100	230	290	60	75
Product C (£)	60	50	120	240	300	60	100

This is vital information for the marketing function which must be pursuing policies aimed at maintaining and improving profitability. A knowledge of which products to be pushing is necessary. The other point is that in the long term, prices of products should be reflecting the required contribution from the limited resource.

RELEVANT COST DATA FOR DECISION MAKING

It is also important that reliable cost information is available for other decisions such as make-or-buy, the desirability or otherwise of overtime or second-shift working, which particular production methods to use, and so on. Such cost information will need to take into account the different characteristics of cost and particularly that of variability.

THE MARKETING CONTRIBUTION TO THE EFFECTIVE USE OF FUNDS

It has already been explained that funds are either used to buy fixed assets or to provide working capital. It will be obvious that such spending needs to be planned and controlled, and the marketing function must join in the management exercise to ensure effectiveness of such spending. In practice, the business will almost certainly use budgetary control procedures, so that a sales budget and a sales cost budget will be focal points of financial planning. Upon the accuracy of the sales budget will depend the estimates of resources required and the precision in allocating financial resources. No doubt the marketing manager will have capital expenditure proposals to put which will need to be evaluated. Certainly he will have some say in the matters of inventory levels and credit terms allowed to customers.

The marketing manager must be aware of the effect of volume on costs and profits, and have some knowledge of break-even points at different levels of activity. He must have reliable information on the relative profitability of different activities, product groups and products. Only in this way can his contribution be effective.

Index

Index